Pasold Studies in Textile History 5

The East Anglian Linen Industry

The Pasold Research Fund

The Pasold Research Fund's field of interest covers the study of the history of textiles in all their respects – embracing the economic and social history of textiles, their technological development, design, conservation, the history of dress and other uses of textiles. The Fund was established in 1964 by the late Eric W. Pasold OBE, who had a special interest in the history of knitting, and its work was developed and extended by the late Kenneth G. Ponting as Research Director from 1967 to 1983. Negley Harte, Senior Lecturer in Economic History at University College London, is now the Director.

In addition to providing grants for research, and organising conferences in conjunction with the Economic and Social Research Council, the Fund sponsors the journal *Textile History* which appears twice a year and other publications.

Pasold Studies in Textile History

1 European Textile Printers in the Eighteenth Century: A Study of Peel and Oberkampf
  S.D. Chapman and S. Chassagne

2 Cloth and Clothing in Medieval Europe: Essays in Memory of Professor E.M. Carus-Wilson
  edited by N.B. Harte and K.G. Ponting

3 The British Wool Textile Industry, 1770–1914
  K.G. Ponting and D.J. Jenkins

4 Medieval English Clothmaking: An Economic Survey
  A.R. Bridbury

5 The East Anglian Linen Industry: Rural Industry and Local Economy, 1500–1850
  Nesta Evans

Pasold Studies in Textile History 5

The East Anglian Linen Industry

Rural Industry and Local Economy, 1500–1850

Nesta Evans

Gower
The Pasold Research Fund

Published by
Gower Publishing Company Limited,
Gower House, Croft Road,
Aldershot, Hants GU11 3HR,
England

and

Gower Publishing Company,
Old Post Road, Brookfield,
Vermont 05036,
U.S.A.

British Library Cataloguing in Publication Data

Evans, Nesta
    The East Anglian linen industry.—(Pasold
    studies in textile history; 5)
    1. Linen industry—England—East Anglia
    2. East Anglia (England)—Industries—
    History
    I. Title   II. Series
    338.4′76771164′09426   HD9930.G73E2

    ISBN 0–566–00847–5

Typeset by Inforum Ltd, Portsmouth
Printed and bound in Great Britain by
Biddles Ltd, Guildford and King's Lynn

Contents

Illustrations

Acknowledgements
The author and publisher are grateful to the following for granting permission to reproduce illustrations: the Syndics of Cambridge University Library for Figures 2.2, 2.3, 4.1, 5.1 and 5.2 and the dust cover illustration; The Colman and Rye Library, Norwich for Figure 5.3; and the John Innes Charity for Figure 2.1.

Preface

I am most grateful for the help of Professor D.C. Coleman, who read an earlier draft of this book and made many helpful suggestions for its improvement. He is in no way responsible for its deficiencies.

So many kind friends have assisted me by providing references that I hope none will be offended if they have been omitted here. In particular I should like to thank Susan Amussen, David Dymond, Mr Richard Emms, Alayne Fenner, Jane Fiske, Rachel Garrard, Victor Gray, Roger Greenwood, Mr C.W. Gurteen, Elsie McCutcheon, Alan Metters, Peter Northeast, Ursula Priestley, Margaret Spufford and Peter Warner, to all of whom I owe a great debt. Finally I must express my gratitude to the staffs of the Norfolk County Record Office and of both branches of the Suffolk County Record Office, to James Gilroy of the Computer Centre at the American College in Paris, to Philip Judge who drew the maps, and to my family for their support.

The early stages of research for this book were supported by a grant from the Twenty-One Foundation.

Map 1.
Suffolk places mentioned in text.

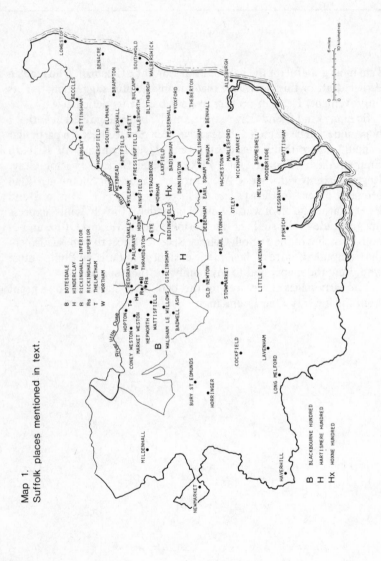

B   BOTESDALE
H   HINDERCLAY
R   RICKINGHALL INFERIOR
Rs   RICKINGHALL SUPERIOR
T   THELNETHAM
W   WORTHAM

B   BLACKBOURNE HUNDRED
H   HARTISMERE HUNDRED
Hx   HOXNE HUNDRED

Map 2.
Norfolk places mentioned in text.

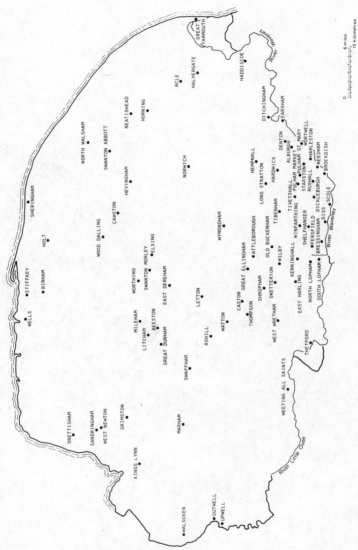

Map 3
Norfolk linen weavers

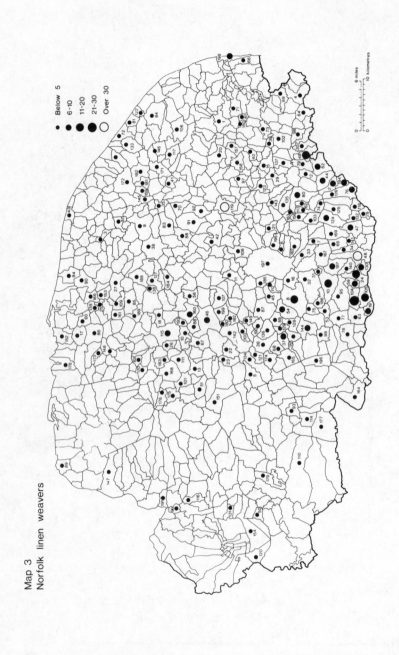

Below 5 •
6-10 •
11-20 •
21-30 ●
Over 30 ○

0 ___ 6 miles
0 ___ 10 kilometres

No.	Parish	Count
1	Acle	2
2	Alburgh	9
3	Aldeborough	1
4	Aldeby	3
5	Ashill	2
6	Ashwellthorpe	1
7	Aslacton	1
8	Attleborough	13
9	Aylsham	2
10	Banham	14
11	Barnham Broom	1
12	Bedingham	2
13	Beeston	
14	Beetley	5
15	Bergh Apton	1
16	Besthorpe	1
17	Binham	1
18	Bintree	1
19	Blo Norton	6
20	Blofield	1
21	Bracon Ash	1
22	Bradenham East	1
23	Bradenham West	1
24	Bressingham	17
25	Brinton	2
26	Brisley	2
27	Briston	2
28	Brockdish	2
29	Brooke	2
30	Broome	3
31	Buckenham New	3
32	Buckenham Old	2
33	Bunwell	1
34	Burston	4
35	Buxton	4
36	Carbrooke	6
37	Caston	4
38	Cawston	1
39	Chedgrave	1
40	Claxton	
41	Coltishall	1
42	Costessey	2
43	Cromer	2
44	Denton	6
45	Deopham	
46	Dereham East	6
47	Dickleburgh	7
48	Diss	32
49	Ditchingham	12
50	Downham Market	2
51	Dunham Great	3
52	Earsham	8
53	Eccles	1
54	Ellingham Great	9
55	Ellingham Little	1
56	Elsing	3
57	Erpingham	
58	Felthorpe	2
59	Fersfield	6
60	Field Dalling	1
61	Freethorpe	
62	Fritton	4
63	Garboldisham	
64	Gillingham	2
65	Gissing	2
66	Gorleston	1
67	Gresseinhall	2
68	Griston	
69	Haddiscoe	5
70	Hainford	
71	Halvergate	1
72	Happisburgh	1
73	Hardley	
74	Hardwick	2
75	Hargham	
76	Harleston	6
77	Harling East	4
78	Harling West	1
79	Hedenham	
80	Hempnall	8
81	Hempstead with Eccles	
82	Hempton	3
83	Hevingham	2
84	Hickling	1
85	Hindolveston	
86	Hindringham	2
87	Hingham	2
88	Hoe by E. Dereham	
89	Holme next the Sea	
90	Holt	
91	Horsford	
92	Horsham St Faith	
93	Ickburgh	
94	Kelling	
95	Kenninghall	5
96	Kings Lynn	4
97	Kirby Bedon	
98	Kirby Cane	
99	Larling	
100	Letton	
101	Litcham	1
102	Loddon	4
103	Long Stratton	22
104	Lopham North	12
105	Lopham South	2
106	Ludham	3
107	Mattishall	
108	Melton Great	4
109	Melton Constable	
110	Methwold	1
111	Mileham	1
112	Morley St Botolph	
113	Morningthorpe	1
114	Mundford	
115	North Elmham	8
116	North Runcton	
117	Neatishead	2
118	Needham	
119	Norwich	56
120	Outwell	1
121	Ovington	
122	Palling	2
123	Poringland	1
124	Pulham Market	10
125	Pulham St Mary	
126	Redenhall	3
127	Reepham	3
128	Rockland All Saints	4
129	Rockland St Peter	2
130	Roydon by Diss	3
131	Runcton Holme	7
132	Rushall	
133	Ruston East	1
134	Saham Toney	1
135	Saxlingham Nethergate	
136	Scoulton	1
137	Seething	2
138	Semerston	
139	Sharington	1
140	Shelfhanger	
141	Shimpling	2
142	Shipdham	
143	Shotesham	3
144	Shropham	
145	Skeyton	8
146	Smallburgh	
147	Snettisham	
148	Snoring Great	
149	Southburgh	
150	Southwood	1
151	Sporle	1
152	Stiffkey	1
153	Stody	1
154	Stow Bardolf	2
155	Stow Bedon	1
156	Stratton St Michael	
157	Strumpshaw	2
158	Surlingham	
159	Swanton Abbotts	3
160	Swanton Morley	6
161	Swanton Novers	2
162	Tacolneston	2
163	Tasburgh	3
164	Thetford	5
165	Thompson	2
166	Thornage	1
167	Tibenham	5
168	Tittleshall	
169	Tivetshall	5
170	Toftrees	
171	Tunstead	1
172	Walsham North	3
173	Walsingham Parva	
174	Watton	2
175	Weasenham All Saints	
176	Weasenham St Peter	
177	Weeting	
178	Wells next the Sea	
179	Wereham	2
180	Westfield	
181	Westwick	2
182	Whinburgh	1
183	Whissonsett	
184	Whitwell	1
185	Wicklewood	
186	Wilby	2
187	Winfarthing	9
188	Wood Dalling	3
189	Wood Norton	1
190	Wood Rising	
191	Wootton South	2
192	Worstead	
193	Worthing	3
194	Wortwell	
195	Wreningham	6
196	Wretham East	1
197	Wymondham	4
198	Yarmouth	6
199	Yaxham	1

NOTE: The figure to the right of each place name is the total number of linen weavers found in that parish.

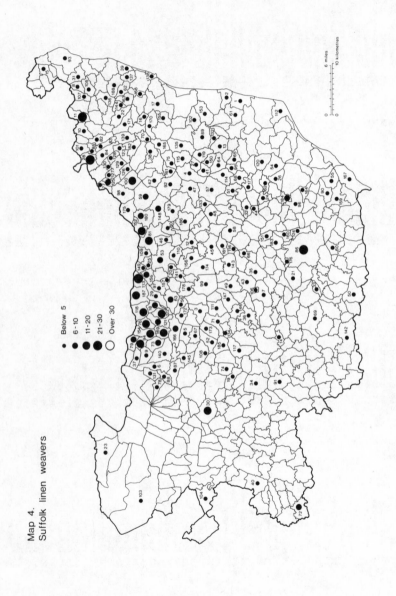

Map 4.
Suffolk linen weavers

- Below 5
- 6 - 10
- 11 - 20
- 21 - 30
○ Over 30

6 miles

10 kilometres

#	Parish	Count
1.	Aldeburgh	1
2.	Aldringham	2
3.	Bacton	2
4.	Badingham	2
5.	Badwell Ash	3
6.	Bardwell	2
7.	Barking	2
8.	Barnby	2
9.	Barningham	5
10.	Barsham	1
11.	Beccles	22
12.	Bedingfield	2
13.	Benhall	3
14.	Bildeston	2
15.	Blundeston	1
16.	Blyford	1
17.	Blythburgh	1
18.	Botesdale	7
19.	Bradfield St George	1
20.	Braiseworth	1
21.	Bramford	2
22.	Brampton	2
23.	Brandon	1
24.	Bredfield	2
25.	Brome	4
26.	Bromeswell	5
27.	Bruisyard	1
28.	Bungay	30
29.	Burgate	4
30.	Bury St Edmunds	15
31.	Carlton Colville	1
32.	Charsfield	2
33.	Chattisham	1
34.	Cockfield	1
35.	Coddenham	2
36.	Combs	2
37.	Coney Weston	3
38.	Cookley	1
39.	Cowehithe	2
40.	Cowlinge	2
41.	Cransford	4
42.	Cratfield	4
43.	Creeting St Mary	1
44.	Debach	1
45.	Debenham	4
46.	Denham	1
47.	Dennington	2
48.	Earl Soham	2
49.	Earl Stonham	1
50.	East Bergholt	1
51.	Easton	1
52.	Elmswell	7
53.	Eye	2
54.	Eyke	1
55.	Falkenham	1
56.	Finningham	3
57.	Framlingham	
58.	Framsden	2
59.	Fressingfield	10
60.	Freston	1
61.	Friston	2
62.	Frostenden	1
63.	Gislingham	7
64.	Great Glemham	1
65.	Little Glemham	1
66.	Gosbeck	
67.	Great Ashfield	3
68.	Hacheston	5
69.	Hadleigh	4
70.	Halesworth	5
71.	Haughley	1
72.	Haverhill	6
73.	Hepworth	9
74.	Hessett	1
75.	Heveningham	15
76.	Hinderclay	1
77.	Homersfield	1
78.	Honington	10
79.	Hopton	5
80.	Horham	20
81.	Hoxne	1
82.	Ilketshall St Andrew	2
83.	Ilketshall St Lawrence	1
84.	Ilketshall St Margaret	3
85.	Ilketshall St John	1
86.	Ipswich	25
87.	Ixworth	3
88.	Ixworth Thorpe	15
89.	Kelsale	4
90.	Kirton	1
91.	Lavenham	1
92.	Laxfield	3
93.	Lowestoft	3
94.	Market Weston	2
95.	Marlesford	2
96.	Martlesham	1
97.	Mellis	2
98.	Mendham	5
99.	Mendlesham	2
100.	Metfield	17
101.	Mettingham	3
102.	Middleton	4
103.	Mildenhall	1
104.	Moulton	1
105.	Mutford	2
106.	Needham Market	10
107.	North Cove	1
108.	Norton	2
109.	Oakley	5
110.	Occold	5
111.	Old Newton	5
112.	Orford	29
113.	Palgrave	3
114.	Parham	3
115.	Peasenhall	1
116.	Pettaugh	1
117.	Rattlesden	13
118.	Redgrave	1
119.	Rendham	1
120.	Rendlesham	1
121.*	Rickinghall Inferior	9
122.	Rickinghall Superior	12
123.	Rumburgh	2
124.	Rushmere	2
125.	S. Elmham St Cross	6
126.	S. Elmham St James	5
127.	S. Elmham St Margaret	1
128.	S. Elmham St Michael	1
129.	S. Elmham St Nicholas	1
130.	S. Elmham St Peter	1
131.	Sapiston	1
132.	Saxmundham	3
133.	Saxtead	1
134.	Shelland	
135.	Sibton	2
136.	Sotterley	1
137.	South Cove	1
138.	Southwold	1
139.	Spexhall	1
140.	Stanton	1
141.	Stoke Ash	1
142.	Stoke by Nayland	1
143.	Stonham Aspal	2
144.	Stoven	1
145.	Stowlangtoft	1
146.	Stowmarket	4
147.	Stowupland	1
148.	Stradbroke	10
149.	Stuston	3
150.	Swefling	2
151.	Swilland	1
152.	Syleham	12
153.	Theberton	1
154.	Thelnetham	20
155.	Thorington	1
156.	Thorndon	2
157.	Thornham Parva	1
158.	Thrandeston	8
159.	Trimley St Martin	1
160.	Tuddenham	1
161.	Ubbeston	1
162.	Ufford	3
163.	Uggeshall	1
164.	Waldringfield	3
165.	Walpole	2
166.	Walsham le Willows	8
167.	Walton	1
168.	Wangford	2
169.	Wattisfield	13
170.	Wenhaston	3
171.	Westhall	4
172.	Westhorpe	1
173.	Wetherden	2
174.	Wetheringsett	4
175.	Weybread	4
176.	Whitton	1
177.	Wickham Market	4
178.	Wickham Skeith	5
179.	Wilby	2
180.	Wingfield	9
181.	Winston	4
182.	Wissett	2
183.	Witnesham	1
184.	Woodbridge	6
185.	Woolpit	2
186.	Worlingworth	1
187.	Wortham	19
188.	Wrentham	2

NOTE: The figure to the right of each place name is the total number of linen weavers found in that parish.

Note on Sources

Most of the original sources used are housed in the county record offices of Norfolk and Suffolk. The principal classes of documents searched were probate records, poor law papers and newspaper files. The documents consulted at the Public Record Office were the Norfolk hearth tax returns, port books, state papers and the national apprenticeship registers. Full references to all documents cited are provided in the footnotes. The following is a list of abbreviations used in the footnotes.

NRO   Norfolk Record Office
NCC   Norwich Consistory Court
PRO   Public Record Office
SP   State Papers
SROB   Suffolk Record Office, Bury St Edmonds branch
SROI   Suffolk Record Office, Ipswich branch

1 Introduction

East Anglia is an area usually associated with wool, but a linen industry also existed there and contributed to the continuing prosperity of the region after the collapse of the manufacture of broadcloth in the later sixteenth century. The Scottish and Irish linen industries have already received the attention of historians,[1] as have those of Lancashire and Yorkshire,[2] but linen manufacture in those regions of England that did not become industrialised has been neglected. Small-scale linen production for home consumption and local markets was almost universal in pre-industrial England, but in some regions it grew into something more important in the seventeenth century. Two of the main centres of production were the area round Yeovil,[3] and East Anglia;[4] and in both these districts it played a major part in the local economy.[5] An indication of historians' ignorance of the East Anglian linen industry is that a recent writer could state that the main centres of the English linen industry in the eighteenth century were south Yorkshire, the Manchester area and Somerset, and make no mention of Norfolk and Suffolk.[6] Concentration on the wool trade, and neglect of other local industries, has tended to distort the economic history of Suffolk and Norfolk, and this study is an attempt to right the balance.

The medieval wealth of East Anglia was not entirely based on its wool trade, which was concentrated in south-west Suffolk and the Norwich district. In other parts of the region fishing and the leather trades made an important contribution to the local economy, and by the sixteenth century East Anglian farms were supplying the London food market, mainly with dairy produce shipped to the capital from the numerous small ports on the Norfolk and Suffolk coasts. Intensive, small-scale

---

[1] Alastair J. Durie, *The Scottish Linen Industry in the Eighteenth Century*, (Edinburgh, 1979), henceforth Durie, and John Horner, *The Linen Trade of Europe*, (Belfast, 1920), henceforth Horner.

[2] Norman Lowe, *The Lancashire Textile Industry in the Sixteenth Century*, (Manchester, 1972), henceforth Lowe, and *A History of Nidderdale*, edited by Bernard Jennings (Huddersfield, 1967), henceforth Jennings.

[3] N.B. Harte, 'The Rise of Protection and the English Linen Trade, 1690-1790', in *Textile History and Economic History*, edited by N. B. Harte and K.G. Ponting (Manchester, 1973), henceforth Harte.

[4] Throughout this book East Anglia means the counties of Norfolk and Suffolk only.

[5] E.W.J. Kerridge, 'The Agrarian Development of Wiltshire 1540–1640' (unpublished Ph.D. thesis, University of London, 1951), p.255, and Joan Thirsk, *Economic Policy and Projects*, (Oxford, 1978), *passim*, henceforth Thirsk 1978.

[6] Durie, p.147

farming in the eastern halves of the two counties in the seventeenth century helped to provide an economic climate suitable for the growth of rural industries, such as linen-weaving, whose diversity gave a sound basis to the local economy.

Norfolk and Suffolk can be divided into two main farming regions: sheep-corn husbandry in the western halves of the two counties; and the wood-pasture district, the home of dairy-farming, in the centre and east.[1] This is an over-simplification, which omits the differing agrarian economies of the marshlands and the coastal sandlings, but nevertheless it gives a reasonable indication of the two most important farming regions. In East Anglia, as elsewhere, it was the pastoral districts which provided the conditions necessary for the growth of rural industry, and linen-weaving and the preparation of its raw material were predominantly rural occupations which were concentrated in the wood-pasture district on the heavy clay lands. Not until the years of its decline did linen-weaving become to a certain extent urban-based.

Maps 3 and 4 show the distribution of linen-weavers in Norfolk and Suffolk, which conforms very cosely to that of the two major farming regions described above. Few linen-weavers are found in the sheep-corn district in the west, or near the coast, and they are concentrated in the wood-pasture area. The chief source in the preparation of these maps was the probate records of the Norwich consistory court and those of the four archdeaconry courts covering the two counties. Other sources used were marriage licence bonds, quarter sessions records, newspapers, national apprenticeship registers and nineteenth-century census returns. Although these sources cannot be regarded as giving a comprehensive coverage of all East Anglian linen-weavers, there seems no reason to doubt that they provide an accurate view of the geographical distribution of those who pursued this craft over a period of three hundred years, 1550–1850. Confidence in these sources is increased by the fact that they all point to the same areas as the centre of East Anglian linen-weaving.

Regional manufactures, such as linen and the leather crafts, probably generated more employment at the local level than did the more prestigious and better-known export-orientated trades, but they are poorly documented and it is impossible to put figures to East Anglian linen output or consumption of hemp and flax. Complaints made over a period of some two hundred years about the quantity of linen imports have further tended to obscure the existence of a flourishing English linen industry. Although never of major consequence as a national

[1] *The Agrarian History of England and Wales, volume IV, 1500–1640*, edited by Joan Thirsk (Cambridge, 1967), pp. 40-49, henceforth Thirsk 1967.

industry, linen was one of several which served the bottom end of the market.

Writing about the difficulties of discovering evidence for 'the ordinary activities of ordinary people in the Middle Ages' Bridbury said: 'They leave no mark because they call for no record.'[1] It is this absence of positive information which makes it so hard to recall the everyday rather than the exceptional events of the past not only in the Middle Ages but also in later centuries. For many families the preparation of linen yarn and its weaving into cloth was a normal activity which called for no comment. From the sixteenth century onwards the survival of local records becomes far greater than for the Middle Ages, and it is these rather than central government archives which are likely to prove the most fruitful source of evidence for the lives and economic activities of ordinary people. This has certainly proved to be true where the East Anglian linen industry is concerned.

Probate records are the major source for this study of East Anglian linen weaving, especially between 1600 and 1730, so it will be as well at this point to proceed to a critical examination of their value. Table 1.1 demonstrates their importance during the two centuries of the linen industry's expansion and success.

Table 1.1   Numbers of linen-weavers by decade

1600–09	24	(20)	1700–09	38	(26)
1610–19	64	(50)	1710–19	60	(28)
1620–29	65	(57)	1720–29	67	(41)
1630–39	81	(71)	1730–39	29	(24)
1640–49	72	(69)	1740–49	25	(20)
1650–59	42	(32)	1750–59	43	(13)
1660–69	115	(106)	1760–69	107	(21)
1670–79	73	(65)	1770–79	59	(12)
1680–89	84	(67)	1780–89	40	(12)
1690–99	52	(42)	1790–99	38	(8)

Sources: as for maps 3 and 4.

After 1700 there are no occupational indexes for any of the four archdeaconry courts in Norfolk and Suffolk, so most of the post-1700 wills used belong to the consistory court. In an attempt to rectify the bias this gives towards Norfolk and to richer weavers, the two Suffolk archdeaconry courts were sampled by looking for linen weavers in the registers for every twentieth year, starting in 1720 for the Sudbury and 1710 for the Suffolk archdeaconry. This sampling uncovered only three linen weavers.

Figures in brackets indicate the number of linen-weavers' wills and inventories for each decade.

[1] A.R. Bridbury, *Medieval English Clothmaking: An Economic Survey* (1982), p.vii

Table 1.1 sets out the numbers of known East Anglian linen weavers in each decade of the seventeenth and eighteenth centuries. The fall in numbers in the 1650s and the marked increase in the following decade can be attributed to the dislocation of the probate courts during the Commonwealth and Protectorate. Nearly all the seventeenth-century linen-weavers were found in probate records, but the sources used for the eighteenth century are more varied. The importance of probate records as a source diminishes considerably after 1750 and is almost negligible by the end of the century. After 1700 there are no occupational indexes for any of the four archdeaconry courts in Norfolk and Suffolk, so most of the wills used belong to the consistory court. In an attempt to rectify the bias this gives towards Norfolk and to richer weavers, the two Suffolk archdeaconry courts have been sampled by looking for linen weavers in the registers for every twentieth year, starting in 1720 for the Sudbury and 1710 for the Suffolk archdeaconry. This sampling uncovered only three linen-weavers. In the seventeenth century, only in the 1650s do non-probate records represent a significant proportion of the total.

Recently several historians have drawn attention to the pitfalls of an uncritical use of probate inventories and wills, but it is perhaps as well briefly to recapitulate these.[1] In the first place there is the unresolved problem of what proportion of the population made wills and what percentage of these have survived. That not all wills drawn up have come down to us is clear from a perusal of court rolls, which, in the course of registering copyhold land transfers, frequently quoted from wills, many of which cannot be found in today's county record offices. Theoretically it was obligatory to make a will, and one of the duties of the parish clergy was to ask dying persons if they had done so. The incidence of nuncupative wills makes it clear that many men left this duty until they were on their death bed and a high proportion of other wills indicate that the testators were ill when they were drawn up. Therefore, some individuals must have failed to make a will because death overtook them, but to many others the task may have seemed superfluous and not only because they had nothing to bequeath. Many potential testators, who lived long enough to see all their children settled in life, had already provided marriage portions for their daughters and set up their younger sons in trade, and in some cases had virtually retired, handing over their land or tools of trade to their eldest son. Richer men had often provided all their sons with land and houses,

---

[1] John Patten, 'Changing Occupational Structures in the East Anglian Countryside, 1500–1700', in *Change in the Countryside: Essays on Rural England, 1500–1900*, edited by H.S.A. Fox and R.A. Butlin, (1979), pp. 103–121, henceforth Patten, 1979; and Ursula Priestley and P.J. Corfield, 'Rooms and Room Use in Norwich Housing, 1580–1730', *Post-Medieval Archaeology*, 16 (1982) pp.93-123 are two examples

so in both these cases there was no real need to make a will. The same is true of those who had an obvious sole heir, usually a son.

It is thus worth studying wills in an attempt to answer the question who made wills and why. In the sixteenth century at least will-making was atypical and 'men who made wills did so primarily because they had dependent children to provide for.[1] Dr Spufford's claim is based on a study of wills made between 1575 and 1600 by inhabitants of the Cambridgeshire fen-edge parish of Willingham. Here 75 per cent of those who made wills in the final quarter of the sixteenth century had to make provision for two or more sons or for under-age children. A study of 282 wills made between 1550 and 1640 by people living in the South Elmham group of nine parishes in north Suffolk shows that here too the same motives applied, although less markedly. In the Suffolk villages just over a quarter of all testators either bequeathed land to two or more adult sons or were leaving under-age children. Another 13 per cent of the wills were made by men who were apparently childless. 'It seems that the absence of an obvious natural heir or heirs was another pressing reason for making a will.'[2].

Yet another group given to will-making was widows. A sample of all wills proved in the Norwich consistory court between 1560 and 1686 showed that during the reign of Elizabeth I 17 per cent, and in the seventeenth century 13 per cent, of testators were widows. Taking the South Elmham wills referred to above, 17.5 per cent were those of widows. Thus in South Elmham well over half the wills (56.5 per cent) can be attributed to the existence of minors, more than one adult son, no obvious heir or the fact that the testator was a widow. An analysis of the wills of 55 South Elmham widows suggested that the main reason why they made wills was to dispose of personal property, usually inherited from their late husbands. In these villages the great majority of male testators whose wives survived them left them either all their moveable goods or the residue. As these bequests of household goods and livestock were usually unconditional they provided a motive for the making of wills by widows, whose bequests were normally concerned only with goods, animals and cash. Just as with male testators, child-lessness or the existence of under-age children were strong motives for drawing up a will.[3]

---

[1] Margaret Spufford, 'Peasant inheritance customs and land distribution in Cambridge-shire from the sixteenth to the eighteenth century', in *Family and Inheritance: Rural Society in Western Europe, 1200–1800*, edited by Jack Goody, Joan Thirsk and E.P. Thompson (1976, p. 176.)

[2] N.R. Evans, 'Testators, Literacy, Education and Religious Belief', *Local Population Studies*, 25 (1980), 43

[3] N.R. Evans, 'Inheritance, Women, Religion and Education in Early Modern Society as revealed by Wills', *Park Place Papers*, forthcoming

The question of what percentage of early modern adults made wills is not the only problem facing the student of probate records. Wills and inventories have been widely used to study the occupational structure of areas ranging in size from parishes to regions. Not all probate records include an occupational description, but those that do must not be accepted uncritically. Comparison of wills and inventories, where both survive for the same individual, shows that a man's own view of his social status did not always coincide with that of his neighbours who appraised his goods. This is perhaps a minor problem compared with that posed by the complexity of many men's activities. Historians are becoming increasingly aware that not merely dual but also multiple occupations were very common in early modern England, and this implies that to take occupational and status labels found in probate records at their face value can be very misleading. Reading wills and inventories often provides a guide to the full economic activities of testators, but to undertake this for all the probate records of a diocese is too daunting a task and explains why reliance has been placed on the descriptions provided by testators and appraisers. Provided that historians and their readers are aware of the limitations and misconstructions to which the latter method is prone, we shall have to be content with what is an inherently unsatisfactory use of probate records.

As an indication of the unreliability of occupational information derived from probate records, and of its loss from the many testamentary documents which give no indication of status or occupation, reference will here be made to a study of the probate records of three Suffolk and one Norfolk parishes. This is based on probate inventories only as to have read all the wills for these four parishes would have been very time consuming; they total 913. The Suffolk parish of Thelnetham lies in the Little Ouse valley and more linen weavers have been found there than almost anywhere else in East Anglia. Of the 20 Thelnetham weavers, 15 are known from their wills, 3 from both inventories and wills, 1 from his probate inventory alone and the last from another source. There is a total of 41 inventories extant for this small village, and when all of them were read another 11 weavers, or at least 11 owners of looms, were discovered. It is not possible in every case to be certain that these loom-owners were all weaving linen, but the probabilities are strongly in favour of such an inference. In addition another 8 inventories indicated involvement in preparing and/or spinning hemp, and 19, less than half the total, showed no connection of any kind with the linen industry. The Thelnetham inventories range in date from 1647 to 1762, with 30 (73 per cent) of them falling within the second half of the seventeenth century; 12 of these were weavers' inventories. The 1674 hearth tax returns show 82 households in this parish,[1] so it is

[1] Sydenham H.A. Hervey, *Suffolk in 1674*, Suffolk Green Books XI (Woodbridge, 1905), henceforth Suffolk in 1674

not unreasonable to suggest that 14.5 per cent of them may have been those of weavers, or, 17.5 per cent, if families headed by a widow are omitted from the total.

A few miles to the east of Thelnetham, and close to the head-waters of the river Waveney, lie the neighbouring villages of Palgrave and Wortham. Palgrave has more linen weavers (29) than any other rural parish. Just across the county boundary from the former stands Diss, a south Norfolk town once well-known as a linen market. Just as at Thelnetham a perusal of all the surviving probate inventories for these two parishes has uncovered linen weavers who would have gone unnoticed if only those inventories that so described the deceased had been used: three each at the two places. At Wortham another nine inventories indicate that the deceased or his family spun linen, usually hempen, yarn, and at Palgrave this was true of seven more households. In addition at both places other inventories show involvement in the growing or preparation of hemp. The earliest Wortham inventory was made in 1584 and the latest in 1702; at Palgrave the relevant dates are 1593 and 1728. In the former place there were 81 households listed in the 1674 hearth tax and 44 of its inventories were drawn up in the latter half of the seventeenth century; of these 6 are those of weavers. For Palgrave the relevant numbers are 77 households in 1674, 26 late seventeeth-century inventories; 6 of which belonged to weavers. Thus at both Wortham and Palgrave approximately 7.5 per cent of households in 1674 could have been those of weavers, and, when those of widows are omitted, the percentages are 8 and 9.

In the Norfolk parish of Great Ellingham, which is centrally placed in the southern half of the county, the picture is rather different. Six linen weavers were known from the probate records and a reading of all the inventories uncovered only one more, but another six indicated that linen yarn was spun in these households and a further seventeen that hemp was being grown or processed. The inventories for this parish range in date from 1589 to 1685, and the 19 drawn up in the second half of the seventeenth century include those of 4 linen-weavers. It is less easy to estimate the percentage of weavers' households at Great Ellingham as many of the Norfolk hearth tax records are damaged, and there is no one year when usable returns of both taxpayers and exempt persons are extant for Great Ellingham. The best year is 1664, ten years earlier than that used for the three Suffolk parishes, but unfortunately this return does not include those exempt from the tax[1]. Out of 62 taxpaying households in 1664, 6.5 per cent may have been those of weavers or 7 per cent if those headed by widows are omitted. In 1672, the nearest year for which extant certificates are available, 59 persons in

---

[1] PRO E179/253/45. There are no surviving hearth tax returns for Norfolk in 1674

Table 1.2   Weaving households in four parishes

	Thelnetham	Palgrave	Wortham	Great Ellingham
Male Taxpayers	41	48	48	57
Resident linen weavers 1660–99	12(29%)	6(12.5%)	6(12.5%)	4(7%)

The number of taxpayers comes from 1674 for the three Suffolk villages and 1664 for the Norfolk parish.

Great Ellingham were certified as too poor to pay,[1] so a more realistic figure for the number of linen weaving households in the village would be 3.5 per cent. Table 1.2 shows the position for all four parishes and is based on taxpayers only.

What this exercise demonstrates very clearly is that any survey of occupational structure and the distribution of trades that is based solely on the descriptions of the deceased appearing in the headings of wills and inventories will provide only a partial picture of the true situation. As Patten has pointed out, testators may have given themselves designations which raised their social status above its true level, and the precise meaning of the occupational and status labels used is not always clear.[2] Yeoman is a particularly vague description and is often used to describe those who have no apparent connection with the land; in some cases these persons are probably retired farmers, but yeoman seems by the seventeenth century to have become much more a status than an accurate occupational description. It is noticeable that the relative frequency with which the terms yeoman and husbandman were used varied from one part of the country to another; for instance in Oxford-shire the latter was far more commonly used than in East Anglia.[3] Some of the weavers found by reading inventories were called yeomen by the men who drew them up. The fact that so many occupations were part-time is an obvious explanation for some of the discrepancies between what we can learn about a man's occupation from his inventory or will and how he was described by the appraisors or himself. One reason for the lack of clarity with which occupational descriptions were used in the sixteenth and seventeenth centries may be that in an age when new industries were appearing and old ones were developing, an accurate vocabulary to describe these new trades did not exist.

Elsewhere in England weavers were given an occupational descrip-tion which can be very misleading to casual observation. In Lancashire weavers, chiefly of fustian or linen, were described as chapmen in their

[1] PRO E179/336/17.
[2] Patten, 1979, p. 105
[3] Household and Farm Inventories in Oxfordshire, 1550–1590, edited by M.A. Havinden (1965)

wills and inventories, the reading of which makes clear that they were engaged in weaving. Many were also farmers, and the richest were far wealthier, owning far larger stocks of yarn and cloth and being owed far more money, than any linen-weavers found in East Anglia. Presumably these men were called chapmen because they sold and distributed the cloth they had made.[1] Tradesmen as well as craftsmen can mislead the unwary: the inventories of grocers and drapers frequently include goods which belong to each other's stock; mercers and chapmen are two other examples of tradesmen whose enterprises could vary enormously.[2]

In spite of all the drawbacks of probate records as a source of occupational and status descriptions, in default of anything else they are the best and the largest that we have. In so using them it must always be borne in mind that only the higher levels of early modern society are represented. Possibly as much as a quarter to a third of the adult population was too poor to make a will. Where this study is concerned this implies that master and self-employed weavers will be heavily over-represented, and that those who worked as journeymen for the men who owned the looms on which they wove cloth will unavoidably fall through the historians' net.

Sources other than probate records also give ample indication that the economic activity of early modern households was far more complex than used to be thought, and that it is an error to try to fit individuals into a classification straitjacket. The estate and household accounts of Nathaniel Bacon of Stiffkey in Norfolk, which date from the final quarter of the sixteenth century, indicate very clearly how men, and their families, could in the course of a year be engaged in a great variety of occupations: small-scale farming, fishing, harvest work and general labouring were frequently all engaged in by a single person, and some undertook other jobs, such as fetching and carrying goods from Norwich or elsewhere, making purchases for Nathaniel Bacon or performing more skilled tasks.

Probate records are not very informative about the type of cloth woven by East Anglian linen-weavers, but from the middle of the eighteenth century advertisements placed in local newspapers suggest that locally produced hempen linen was valued by customers. It seems to have been prized chiefly for its durability and hard-wearing qualities. Another problem on which neither probate records, nor any other

[1] I am grateful to Dr Margaret Spufford for allowing me to see her xerox copies of the inventories of the Lancashire chapmen/weavers

[2] D.G. Vaisey, *Probate Inventories of Lichfield and District, 1568–1680*, Collections for a History of Staffordshire, 4th series, X, Staffordshire Record Society (1969); Barrie Trinder and Jeff Cox, *Yeoman and Colliers in Telford*, (1980), henceforth Trinder and Cox; Margaret Spufford, *The Great Reclothing of Rural England: Petty Chapmen and their Wares in the Seventeenth Century*, (1984), henceforth Spufford, 1984

documents, have shed much light is the source of the weavers' raw materials. Both flax and hemp were used for linen, but the general impression, and it is an impression not a certainty, is that the latter was more commonly used in East Anglia. Given the complete lack of hard evidence, it is even more difficult to determine how far the local linen industry was dependent on raw materials grown elsewhere in Britain or abroad. There is nothing to suggest a great increase in hemp, or flax, cultivation in East Anglia during the period when the numbers of linen weavers are known to have risen steeply. Indeed, the area under these two crops may even have decreased during the seventeenth century. The tithe account books kept in this century by the vicars of Fressing-field, which lies in the hemp-producing area of Suffolk, show a definite decline in the number of tithe-payers growing flax and hemp. In 1634 25 farmers paid tithe on hemp, 18 on flax and 4 on both; by 1674 the figures were 9, 11 and 10, and the total number growing these two crops had declined from 47 to 30.[1] The Fressingfield tithe accounts and the absence of evidence indicating an increase in the cultivation of flax and hemp suggest that during the period when the linen industry flourished much of its raw material was imported, but it must be stressed that this hypothesis is almost entirely based on the absence of evidence to the contrary. Indeed there is also a dearth of information about imports of flax and hemp into East Anglian ports, which points to the possibility that these crops were grown in other parts of England for Norfolk and Suffolk weavers.

The prosperous period of the East Anglian linen industry coincided with the last two centuries during which the region played an important part in the English economy. Chapter 6 shows how two once wealthy counties declined into abysmal poverty, and the history of the decline and disappearance of linen-weaving there provides a case study of the economic and social decay of the region.

Briefly, the most important reason for the transformation of East Anglia from the economically most advanced to one of the most backward areas in England was that the industrial revolution of the late eighteenth and early nineteenth centuries passed it by. With no rivers really suitable for providing water power, and in the absence of coal, it was inevitable that local industries were unable to mechanise their processes and were outstripped by their new rivals in more favoured regions. In East Anglia not only was there no new employment for the rising population of the late eighteenth century, but at the same time the traditional trades were shrinking. Parallel to the loss of industrial employment, changes occurred in agriculture which served to deepen

[1] SROI FC90/C1/3

the poverty of the region. The number of small farms had decreased considerably during the eighteenth century, at the end of which Arthur Young could write that the size of farms in Suffolk 'must, in a general light, be reckoned large.'[1] Farm sizes had always been greater on the light land than on the heavy clays, but even in the latter district many formerly successful smallholdings ceased to be viable in the changed economic circumstances of the eighteenth century. In addition, the replacement of pastoral by arable farming in response to the high prices commanded by grain during the long French wars further diminished opportunities for employment. Dairy-farming is far more labour intensive than is corn-growing, but after the return of peace in 1815 caused grain prices to tumble, East Anglian farmers seemed unwilling to return to the type of agriculture which had served them well for many centuries. Over-specialisation by both farmers and industrial workers limited their opportunities, and their failure to react to changed circumstances led them into a downward economic spiral.

The East Anglian linen trade was engulfed in the general decline of the region, but it is worth stressing the two main reasons for its failure and final disappearance: no attempt was made to industrialise and the competition from cotton became overwhelming. Ultimately the latter is the more important, because, even if the industry had become mechanised, it would still have been destroyed by its cheaper rival, cotton.

Dr Thirsk has drawn our attention to the great diversity of industries that were either entirely new or experiencing an unprecedented growth at the turn of the sixteenth century.[2] Few of these novel or expanding trades have received a thorough investigation and, as Dr Thirsk suggests, they present a field of enquiry which could shed much light on the early modern period. Our understanding of the economy and society of seventeenth-century England, both at the regional and national level, would be greatly enhanced by thorough research into these industries and trades whose importance has only recently been recognised.

The history of linen-weaving in East Anglia spans many centuries. Hemp was grown in the region as early as around AD 500, and the production of linens made from its fibre survived at the two villages of North and South Lopham near Diss in south Norfolk until as recently as 1925. The story of this industry will be told in the following chapters, with particular emphasis on the period from 1600 to 1850.

[1] Arthur Young, *General View of the Agriculture of the County of Suffolk* (1813), p. 13, henceforth Young, 1813
[2] Thirsk 1978, *passim*

2 The Cultivation and Preparation of Hemp[1]

I

The raw material from which linen is made can be either flax or hemp, but all the evidence points to the latter as the fibre more commonly grown in East Anglia and used by the region's linen-weavers. Broadly speaking both fibres are prepared for spinning in the same way, so the account given here of hemp processing applies also to flax. Except perhaps in the Middle Ages, East Anglian hemp and flax production was probably never adequate to supply local weavers, who, like their fellows elsewhere in England, came increasingly to rely on imported materials.

Cannabis sativa (the botanical name for hemp) has acquired an evil reputation in recent years, and, whereas once the English government passed laws to encourage its growth, today possessing or growing the plant is a criminal offence. However, in Europe the plant was one of the main sources of fibre for centuries before its flowers and leaves were valued only as the source of the drug marijuana. The very word canvas is derived from cannabis. Furthermore, the varieties of cannabis that produce the best fibre are the least suitable for drug production. A recent article suggests that, in the days when hemp was widely grown for its fibres, the therapeutic properties of the plant's seeds and leaves were known, and its uses are said to have included soothing fractious babies and pacifying unmanageable horses.[2]

As long ago as the early third millennium BC the anaesthetic and narcotic properties of cannabis were known to the Chinese.[3] The drug's use as a medium of escape from reality and in religious ritual has a continuous history over some 5000 years, although, with the exception

---

[1] This chapter is largely based on material drawn from the following sources, to which reference will only be made when they are quoted: Denis Diderot and Jean le Rond d'Alembert, *Encyclopédie* (Paris, 1751–80), III (1753), article on *chanvre*, henceforth Diderot and d'Alembert; Gervase Markham, *A Way to Get Wealth* (1611), pp. 128–40, henceforth Markham; and Young, 1813, pp. 141–58

[2] John Michell, 'Grow Hemp or else', *The Ecologist*, X, 8/9 (October–November 1980), p.280

[3] Ian Hindmarch, 'A Social History of the Use of Cannabis Sativa', *Contemporary Review* (1972) 252–257

1 *Cannabis mas.*
Male or fteele Hempe.

‡ 2 *Cannabis fœmina.*
Femeline or female Hempe.

Figure 2.1   Male and female hemp plants from Gerard's Herbal (1636)

of Herodotus, classical authors refer only to its medicinal use. Both Greeks and Romans used ropes made of hemp, and Pliny the Elder in his *Natural History* described the cultivation of the plant.[1] Herodotus describes the use of the plant as a drug, but the users were Scythians and not Greeks. The former were said to derive so much enjoyment from the vapour given off by heated hemp seed that they howled with pleasure.[2] Herodotus also tells us that hemp grew wild as well as under cultivation in Scythia, and that the Thracians made clothes from it scarcely distinguishable from linen. He goes on to say that 'anybody who has never seen a piece of cloth made from hemp will suppose it to be of linen.'[3]

In England one of the earliest scientific descriptions of cannabis was

[1] Theodore F. Brunner, 'Marijuana in Ancient Greece and Rome? The Literary Evidence', *Bulletin of the History of Medicine*, 47 (1973) 344–355
[2] Herodotus, *The Histories*, translated by Aubrey de Selincourt (1954), p.266
[3] ibid, p.265

given to the Royal Society in 1689 by Dr Robert Hooke, who thought it might be useful in the treatment of lunacy; in describing Indian hemp he wrote that it, 'seemeth to put a man into a dream'.[1] An early eighteenth-century encyclopaedia gives various medicinal uses for hemp. The seeds were said 'to have the faculty of abating venereal desires', and, when soaked in milk were a cure for jaundice. The leaves soothed burns and their juice was good for deafness, but when powdered and mixed with any 'liquor' they were 'said to turn those who drink therof stupid'.[2] In the nineteenth century both in England and France drug-takers experimented with cannabis, and its effects were well-known to Englishmen in India.[3] It was not until 1920 that it was made illegal to import any extract or tincture of Indian hemp, and another 45 years were to elapse before the 1965 Dangerous Drugs Act made it an offence knowingly to cultivate any plant of the genus cannabis.

Linen cloth has been woven for thousands of years not only in the Near East, but also in England. A Beaker burial of the third millennium BC at Kelleythorpe near Driffield in Yorkshire had 'a mass of cloth, described as linen' under the body.[4] In 1982 the excavation of a Bronze Age settlement site at West Row, Mildenhall, on the edge of the fens uncovered a waterlogged pit containing flax seeds and capsule fragments, and what might be flax fibres. This may have been a flax retting pit dating from c.1200 BC.[5] Flax has been cultivated in England since the Neolothic era, but hemp did not appear in this country until the Anglo-Saxon period.[6]

Hemp is native to India and western Asia; it has been cultivated in the latter area since at least around 900 BC, and is thought to have been used for its fibre in China as long ago as 2800 BC.[7] There is little evidence for its cultivation outside the Mediterranean area before the end of the Roman empire.[8] The earliest known evidence of its presence in East Anglia comes from pollen analysis of a core taken from Old Buckenham mere in south central Norfolk, showing that *cannabis sativa* was being cultivated at this spot circa AD 500. It seems that the appearance of hemp in East Anglia coincided with the arrival there of Anglo-Saxon farmers, and linguistic evidence also suggests that it was Teutonic people who spread the cultivation of hemp across northern

[1] Virginia Berridge and Griffith Edwards, *Opium and the People* (1981), p.210
[2] Ephraim Chambers, *Cyclopedia or Universal Directory of Arts and Science* (1738) sub hemp
[3] Ian Hindmarch, art. cit.
[4] Colin Burgess, *The Age of Stonehenge* (1980), p.180
[5] Personal communication from Mr Peter Murphy of the University of East Anglia
[6] Sir Harry Godwin, *History of the British Flora*, second edition (Cambridge, 1975), p.167
[7] *Encyclopedia Britannica* (1967), article on hemp, henceforth Britannica, 1967
[8] H. Godwin, 'The Ancient Cultivation of Hemp', *Antiquity*, XLI (1967), 42–6

Europe. Archaeological evidence shows that the cultivation of hemp in East Anglia expanded considerably in the period from AD 800 to 1200.[1]

Few people today are familiar with the appearance of a plant which was once such a common crop in English fields. It is curious that a species once so widely grown has not survived as a wild escape in the way of the teazle, another plant connected with the cloth trade. Although not native to East Anglia, the climate and soil clearly suited hemp, probably better than they did flax which prefers a moderately damp and warm climate. East Anglia is one of the dryest parts of the British Isles, and much of the soil in Norfolk and Suffolk is calcareous. Flax grown on land of this type or on stiff clays, which are also common in the two counties, produces poor quality fibre. Furthermore flax, unlike hemp, is not an easy crop to grow, as it needs careful weeding while growing and good judgement is needed to decide when it is ready for harvesting.[2]

Hemp is still widely grown for its fibre in India, Russia and several European countries. That grown today for French paper-makers must resemble that once grown in East Anglia for cloth; both materials use the plant's fibre. The slender, pale green stems bear widely spaced (about nine inches or more apart) opposed pairs of compound leaves, usually three or five on each side of the stalk. They are a slightly darker green than the stems, narrow and pointed in shape, finely ribbed and soft to the touch. The method of cultivation used governs the manner in which hemp grows. When grown to produce fibre the seed is sown thickly, either broadcast or in close set drills, and the plants grow tall, slender, whip-like and free from branches except near the tops. More widely spaced sowing produces plants with much thicker main stems and many coarse branches.[3] This latter method of cultivation is preferred by the producers of drugs as the plants have more leaves and flowers.

The fibre producing part of the hemp plant is the stem, which, like that of flax, consists of a hollow woody core encased in a sheath of fibrous matter held together by a kind of vegetable glue. In other words the fibre is that part of the stem which could be described as bark. There are two kinds of hemp plant, one bearing flowers and the other seed, and they were long incorrectly described as male and female plants; in fact the flower-bearing plants are the female and the fruit is born by the male.[4] The old names for the two plants are fimble and carl, and these were used by the Tudor Suffolk writer on farming, Thomas

[1] Godwin, art. cit. 46–8 and 137–8
[2] Henry Hamilton, *The Industrial Revolution in Scotland*, (1966), p.80
[3] Britannica, 1967
[4] C. Tomlinson, *Cyclopaedia of Useful Arts, Manufactures, Mining and Engineering* (1854), II, pp. 13-15, henceforth Tomlinson; and Britannica, 1967

Tusser, whose homely precepts are expressed in verse:

> Good flax and good hemp, to have of her own,
> In May a good huswife will see it be sown;
> And afterwards trim it, to serve at a need,
> The fimble to spin, and the carl for her seed.[1]

Hemp varies greatly in height from about 5 feet to nearly 20 feet, but the usual height of plants grown for fibre ranges between 5 and 10 feet. Climate, soil and method of cultivation are the deciding factors in the height to which the plants grow.

In East Anglia hemp was generally grown on small plots of land, often of under half an acre, although there were exceptions. Indeed by the nineteenth century the word 'hempland' seems to have become synonomous with a small enclosure of an acre or less. The word is frequently so used on tithe maps drawn up in the 1840s, by which date the growing of hemp in East Anglia had probably almost totally disappeared. The appendix, on agriculture, to the *c*.1816 edition of Kirby's *Suffolk Traveller* states that with hemp 'it is very rare to see more than five or six acres in the occupation of any one man.' In the main this appendix is based on Young's *General View of the Agriculture of Suffolk*.

There are many references to hemplands in wills which make it clear that the crop was grown in small fields. In 1520 John Chapman of Weeting All Saints in Norfolk referred to his hemp growing in the croftyard.[2] Two other Norfolk wills, both dating from 1549, mention small areas of hemp. Thomas Burgh of Snettisham left his brother one acre of hemp,[3] and Thomas Carleton of East Harling bequeathed his wife half a bushel of hempseed 'to be sewen in the yarde at home afore the berne doore'.[4] Growing crops are often listed in inventories, but the area under cultivation is infrequently specified, and rarely so in the case of hemp. In 1776 the court book of the manor of Chippenhall in Fressingfield refers to 'all that peice or parcel of land containing by estimation one rood be the same more or less sometime a Hempland'.[5]

Hemplands were frequently associated with cottages and messuages, which suggests that it was often grown close to dwellings and that it may well have been a garden crop for cottagers. A French writer suggested that hemplands were always near houses because of the necessity for close surveillance during the 7–12 days between sowing and the emergence of the plant above the ground. The seed is extremely attractive to birds, particularly to pigeons, hence the need for constant watchfulness

---

[1] Thomas Tusser, *Five Hundred Points of Good Husbandry*, 1812 edition, p. 153
[2] NRO NCC Coppinger 39–40
[3] NRO NCC Wymer 359
[4] NRO NCC Wymer 355
[5] SROI HB24: 287/15, f.21. Court held 4 November 1776

to prevent their depredations.[1] An admission in the court roll for the Suffolk manor of Blythburgh cum Walberswick mentions 'unam domum cum canabario parcell' unius cottagii unius gardinii'.[2] The churchwardens' accounts for the Suffolk village of Yoxford between 1615 and 1625 include rent of 16s. received for a 'shop and hempland'; by 1627 this had become a 'shop and yard'.[3] Hemplands recorded in surveys and field books are also frequently very small in size. A field book of Stiffkey on the north Norfolk coast drawn up in 1585 mentions several hemplands ranging in size from as little as ten perches to a maximum of a quarter of an acre. All these lay in the river valley and were close to houses.[4] Eighteenth and nineteenth-century estate maps are another source of information about the size and position of hemplands. A map of 1812 of the Cornwallis estates at Oakley in the Waveney valley, one of the main hemp growing areas in East Anglia, shows three hemplands adjoining cottages or tenements,[5] and a map drawn in the 1820s of an estate in nearby Hoxne also shows hemplands attached to cottages.[6] Many other examples could be given. The growing of hemp on small plots of ground was not confined to East Anglia. In the Telford area of Shropshire the evidence from probate inventories is that there too most growers cultivated only small amounts of both hemp and flax.[7] Another area of northern England where both plants were grown in small fields was Nidderdale.[8]

As has already been indicated, hemp was not invariably grown in small fields. The 1812 map of the Cornwallis estates referred to in the preceding paragraph also includes an 8-acre 'flax piece' in the parish of Eye. In 1658 the court book of the manor of Little Blakenham near Ipswich mentioned two pieces of hempland totalling 14 acres.[9] Nevertheless, a survey of the tithe maps of 15 Suffolk parishes in or near the Waveney valley produced 138 fields bearing the name hempland, of which only 30 (22 per cent) were over an acre in size. Seven fields (5 per cent) measured two acres or more, the largest being just over five acres, while 11 (8 per cent) were under a quarter of an acre.[10]

[1] Pierre de Saint Jacob, *Les Paysans de la Bourgogne du Nord au dernier siècle de l'Ancien Régime* (Paris, 1960), p. 261, henceforth Saint Jacob
[2] SROI HA30: 50/22/9.6 (5) membrane 7 verso. Court held 29 April 1612
[3] SROI FC73/A1/1 Yoxford Town Book
[4] NRO RAY 4/12, ff. 25, 28, 29
[5] SROI HA68: 484/702 Reference book pp. 33, 35, 40
[6] SROI HD293/3 Map of estate of John Worth
[7] *Yeomen and Colliers in Telford*, edited by Barrie Trinder and Jeff Cox (1980), p.62, henceforth Trinder and Cox
[8] Jennings, p.170
[9] SROB E7/4/202
[10] I am much indebted to Mr Victor Gray of the Essex Record Office, who kindly allowed me to use the material he had collected

On the whole it must be concluded that most of the fields in which hemp was grown were small in size.

Although it has already been suggested that the word hempland came to be synonomous with a small cultivated area, the question may well be asked why the name hemp became attached to specific pieces of land. The names of other crops occur seldom, if at all, in field names. The explanation lies in the fact that hemp could be, and indeed generally was, grown on the same land for many years. It grew best on ground that was well manured annually, but, unlike most other crops, it did not impoverish the soil if continuously grown on the same land. 'With cottagers, the more common method is, to sow it every year on the same land: there is a piece at Hoxne, which has been under this crop for seventy successive years.'[1]

In France, as well as in England, hemp was frequently grown along streams or rivers, or by water-filled ditches. Hemp grown on a rich damp soil, such as that found in valley bottoms, produces strong but coarse fibre, while that sown on poor soil is slender and fine. Thus it is best grown on heavy, well-manured soil when the fibres are required for cables and heavy materials such as canvas and sacking, but on a poor soil when fine yarn is wanted for weaving cloth.[2] According to Arthur Young, the part of Suffolk in which hemp was chiefly cultivated extended from Eye to Beccles and was about ten miles in breadth.[3] In fact this area extended westwards into the valley of the Little Ouse, which river has its source only a few yards from the spot where the Waveney rises in Lopham Fen near Diss, and encompassed several miles on both the Norfolk and Suffolk sides of the two river valleys.

Both the English agriculturalist, Arthur Young, and the French encyclopaedists are in agreement that land on which hemp was to be sown required three ploughings after manuring in the spring. It was usual to sow the seed in the latter part of April, after wheat sowing was finished. According to the *Encyclopedia Britannica* the modern seeding rate ranges from three to six pecks per acre, but Young, writing in 1813, suggests a rate of eleven pecks to the acre.[4] Once the plants were large enough to be safe from the depredations of birds, the crop required very little attention. It needed no weeding as it smothered other plants; because of this property hemp was occasionally grown to clean the ground for other crops. Gervase Markham wrote that hemp 'is naturally of it self swift of growth, rough, and venemous to any thing that grows under it, and will sooner of its own accord destroy those

[1] Young, 1813, p.141
[2] Tomlinson, pp.13–15
[3] Young, 1813, p.141
[4] ibid

unwholesome weeds, than by your labour.[1] When ready for harvesting, some 13 to 14 weeks after sowing, the crop was not cut but pulled by hand, thus leaving no stubble. One of the most notable characteristics of hemp as a crop is the short time for which it occupies the ground.

The cultivation cycle of hemp fitted in very well with the dairy farming so widely practised in wood-pasture East Anglia from the fifteenth to the late eighteenth century. It was a crop which required little or no attention during the months when a dairy farmer was likely to be busiest with hay making, milking, churning butter and making cheese. These dairy farmers diversified by growing some arable crops, mainly wheat,[2] but not so much that they could not cope with the hemp crop at harvest time. When corn-growing became so profitable at the end of the eighteenth century that most dairy farmers converted their pastures and meadows to arable fields, a crop, which required not only harvesting by hand but other attention as well at what was for the arable farmer the busiest season of the year, was no longer an attractive proposition.

Young said that the 'male' and 'female' plants were pulled at the same time, which was when the tops of the plants began to turn yellow, but other authorities state that the 'male' plant was ready for pulling some three to four weeks before the 'female'.[3] Certainly if seed was required of the latter, the true male plant, it needed the extra time to ripen its fruit, and it may well be that Young only had experience of the use of imported seed, which was certainly widely used. French growers considered that the yarn from the incorrectly termed 'male' plants was finer than that produced by the 'female', and Young allows that in his day the two kinds of hemp were frequently separated on the Cambridgeshire fens. How common this practice was in earlier times it is impossible to say. The seed is oily and will not keep for long, so only the previous year's crop could be used. It is this oiliness which makes the seeds particularly attractive to birds, and until relatively recently it was frequently included in bird seed mixtures sold commercially. In the past the seeds were crushed, and the oil was used for making soft soap, for painting and for burning in lamps;[4] in eighteenth-century France the seed was also fed to poultry.

The great attraction of hemp as a crop for cottagers was its high return. Young estimated the average produce of an acre as 45 stone,

[1] Markham, p.130

[2] N. Evans, 'The Community of South Elham, Suffolk 1550–1640' (unpublished M.Phil. thesis, University of East Anglia, 1978), and 'Farming and Land-holding in wood-pasture East Anglia', forthcoming article in *Proceedings of Suffolk Institute of Archaeology*

[3] Diderot and d'Alembert, and Tomlinson, pp. 13–15

[4] Andrew Ure, *Dictionary of Arts, Manufactures and Mines* (1839), p.649

worth 7s. 6d. a stone. He calculated the cost of tillage and pulling, in addition to rent, tithes and rates, at £5 9s. 4d., thus giving a profit of £11 8s. 2d. an acre for hemp sold before any processing had taken place. A further advantage for hemp cultivators was that turnips could be sown immediately after the ground was cleared, and so the same piece of land could produce two different crops in the space of one year.

Precise information about hemp cultivation is scanty, so the accounts kept by the executor of Nathaniel Briggs, a farmer who died in June 1774, are valuable for the light they throw on this subject. Included in these accounts are the purchase of hemp seed, and payments for pulling and dressing hemp. During the winter of 1774–75 15 stones of hemp were dressed, at 1s 6d a stone, and in the following August a man was paid 6s. for 'pulling the Hemp'. Briggs's probate inventory, which rather strangely was drawn up well over two years after his decease, lists amongst his possessions 20 skeins of 'Pulter yarn' (pultow or inferior hemp yarn) and 123 of 'Tare Ditto' (high quality yarn).[1]

II

Growing and harvesting hemp was probably the simplest part of the lengthy process which lay between sowing the seed and producing finished cloth. After pulling, the hemp was allowed to dry in the sun so that the leaves and flowers could easily be removed; the leaves wither almost at once on a hot day. At this stage, if the seed was required, the seed-bearing plants were thrashed or rippled, that is drawn through a fixed comb with wire teeth which removed the seed capsules. The plants were then tied into loose bundles or baits in readiness for retting, the evil-smelling process which dissolved the vegetable glue holding the fibres together, and which is in fact a partial rotting of the plant, the duration of which must be carefully judged.

There were two methods of retting: water retting and dew retting. The former was generally held to be superior and was considerably quicker than dew retting, which was more difficult to control and thought to produce inferior and coarser yarn. In dew retting the hemp was laid on pasture ground for from three to six weeks, depending on the dampness of the weather, and during this period was turned several times. Water retting could be carried out either in specially dug pits, or in running water; the latter was disliked because it fouled the water and made it unfit for drinking by animals or humans. Markham believed that running water was best, perhaps because it produced a better coloured hemp, but by Young's day the use of pits was preferred. An

---

[1] I am grateful to Dr P.M. Warner for showing me these documents, which come from the Blyford Estate, courtesy of Mr J.E.B. Hill

Act of the reign of Henry VIII declared it unlawful for any person to water 'any manner of hemp or flax in any river, running water, stream, brook or other common pond where beasts used to be watered, but only on the grounds or pits for the same ordained', on pain of a forfeit of 20 shillings.[1] An example of the infraction of this law comes from the leet court of the manor of Earl Soham, Suffolk, held on 15 April 1588, when Thomas Revett was fined because he had persisted in retting his hemp in the common river, contrary to statute, and contrary to the order given to him at the preceding court.[2] Long before the passage of the Henrician Act, local by-laws had prohibited the placing of hemp and flax in water courses, and there are many instances of men being fined for this practice by manorial courts.

In the later sixteenth century manor courts were still making by-laws concerning hemp retting. One instance comes from the manor of Snetterton in south Norfolk: 'no inhabitant within the p[re]cinct of the p[ar]ishe of Snyterton shall at one tyme laye above one loade of hempe in ye com[m]on hempitt in Northorpe upon payne of vis viiid', and 'no Inh[ab]itant shall water eny hempe in any other mans sev[er]all water w[i]thout the licence of the owner upo[n] payne of losse of forty shillings'.[3] By Young's day almost all hemp grown in East Anglia was retted in pits, and the frequency of the occurrence of the names 'retting pit' or 'rotten pit' on tithe maps attests to their widespread use. According to Blomefield, the Norfolk historian, the customs of Diss manor, drawn up in 1636, permitted tenants to make hemp pits on Diss Moor and Cock Street Green.[4] A map, dated 1747, of a farm in Hacheston, Suffolk shows a 'Ratering Pit Meadow' and clearly indicates the site and almost square shape of the pit.[5] Evidence has recently come to light of the use of pits for retting hemp in the late eighteenth or early nineteenth century at Thompson in south-west Norfolk, and at Buggs Hole fen, a kilometre north-west of Thelnetham in the Little Ouse valley.[6]

The bundles of hemp were held under water by stones or large pieces of timber, and a good-sized pit could hold the hemp from an acre of land. Water-retted hemp was generally left in the pits for between four and six days before being removed for drying either by 'grassing', that

[1] 33 Henry VIII cap. 17
[2] SROI V5/18/1-11
[3] Manor of Snytterton Newhall Sarrehall Oldehall. Court held 10 September 1572. Seventeenth-century copy, penes Michael Serpell
[4] F. Blomefield, *An Essay towards a topographical history of the county of Norfolk*, second edition, 11 vols (1805-10), I, 9, henceforth Blomefield
[5] SROI HD54:454 Map of Malthouse Farm, Hacheston, 1747
[6] R.H.W. Bradshaw, P. Coxon, J.R.A. Grieg and A.R. Hall, 'New fossil evidence for the past cultivation and processing of hemp (cannabis sativa L.) in Eastern England', *New Phytologist* 89 (1981), 503-10

is laying out on grass fields, or by artificial drying. Grassing required about five weeks and during this time the hemp had to be turned two or three times a week, depending on how often it rained. Hemp could be dried by artificial heat either in a specially built kiln or drying shed, or in houses, where there was always a risk of fire. Drying in a kiln seems to have been a common practice in eighteenth-century France, and is also mentioned by Gervase Markham: 'if the weather be not seasonable, and your need much to use your Hemp or Flaxe, you shall then spread it upon your kilne, and making a soft fire under it, dry it upon the same'.[1] Markham was aware of the danger of fire, and the method he described for averting this involved the construction of something resembling a simplified version of the *haloir* (kiln) for drying hemp illustrated in the *Encyclopédie*. There is no evidence for which method of drying was most commonly used in East Anglia in the seventeenth and eighteenth centuries.

Once dried, by whatever method this had been achieved, the hemp was ready for breaking. It is possible to separate the fibres from the stalk of the plant by hand, but it is an exceedingly slow process as each stem has to be dealt with individually. This hand method was apparently sometimes practised in eighteenth-century France by children while watching herds or flocks. Separation of the fibres by hand may have been practised in sixteenth-century Suffolk. In the course of a defamation case heard by the Norwich Consistory Court in 1580, a witness deposed that she went out into the yard and started to pull hemp.[2] To pull or pill hemp means to peel off the bark or rind from the stems; pilled and unpilled hemp is frequently listed in probate inventories. By far the more usual method was the use of a brake, which as its name suggests, crushed the stems of the plants to facilitate the separation of fibre from core. This was a tiring task requiring considerable physical effort. One of Young's correspondents informed him 'that there are mills erected for breaking flax; and as the mode of breaking is similar, I imagine they might be applied to hemp', and went on to add that 'as hemp is very bulky before it is broken, and small quantities only are grown in each village, in general, I fear it would not answer the expence to erect many of them'.[3] Before the introduction of the hand-operated brake, hemp and flax were beaten with mallets on a block of wood, a method which probably continued in use amongst those too poor to afford a brake. The flax or hemp brake was invented in the fourteenth century[4] and was certainly in fairly general use by the

[1] Markham, p.133
[2] NRO NCC DEP/17 f. 333
[3] Young, 1813, p.148
[4] Patricia Baines, *Spinning Wheels, Spinners and Spinning* (1977), p.21

end of the sixteenth century, as it is mentioned in Markham's treatise. Once broken the fibres had to be separated from the unwanted part of the stem, and this was achieved by scutching or swingling. The hemp was placed on a board raised about four feet above ground and beaten with a swingle tree or scutcher, a wooden implement, flat and narrow in shape with a sharpened edge. This too was a heavy task, and in eighteenth-century Scotland hand-scutching was gradually superseded by water-powered scutching mills.[1] There is no East Anglian evidence for the existence of scutching mills, and the same is true for the Telford region of Shropshire, another rural area where much hemp was grown.[2]

The refuse or 'offal' left over after the processes of breaking and scutching were complete was bound up and sold as hemp sheaves, which according to Young made good fuel. In eighteenth-century Burgundy hemp scutching was apparently a social activity and an opportunity for some jollification. Here, on September evenings, scutching was carried on in the street outside the houses of the hemp growers and the occasion became '*une petite fête villageoise*' around the fires burning the discarded part of the plants.[3] The English climate is less conducive to such outdoor sessions. There is a public house named the Hempsheaf in Stradbroke.

The next stage in the process of preparing hemp fibre for the spinner was heckling, and this required rather more skill than the earlier stages of preparation described above. Heckling was less likely to be carried out by the grower than were retting, breaking and scutching, and indeed heckling gradually developed as a distinct trade on its own. Nevertheless, as late as the date at which Arthur Young was writing not all heckling was carried out by specialists.

Heckling hemp is the equivalent of combing wool, and it completed the process of separating the fibres, which scutching had started. Before the heckler set to work with his heckles or combs, the hemp had first to be beaten once more. Bundles of hemp fibre were laid in round troughs like large wooden mortars and then beaten with mallets or beetles. Hogarth's Bridewell scene from the *Harlot's Progress* shows the unfortunate heroine of the series engaged in beating hemp, a common occupation in eighteenth-century prisons. This beating process was known as bunching and was sometimes carried out on a bunching block, as depicted by Hogarth. A Stowmarket manufacturer of hempen cloth, who was one of Arthur Young's main informants on the subject of hemp, stated that bunching 'was formerly, and is still, in some places, done by hand; but in Suffolk, is now always done by a mill,

[1] Durie, p.3
[2] Trinder and Cox, p.62
[3] Saint Jacob, p. 282

Figure 2.2   'The dressing of Line' from John Amos Comenius, *Orbis Pictus* (1659)
'Line and Hemp, being rated in water, and dried again, 1. are braked with a wooden Brake, 2. where the Shives 3. fall down, then they are heckled with an Iron Heckle, 4. where the Tow 5. is parted from it. Flax is tied to a Distaff, 6. by the Spinster, 7. which with her right hand pulleth out the Thred, 8. and with her left hand turneth a wheel, 9. or a spindle, 10. upon which is a Wharl, 11. The Spool receiveth the Thred, 13. which is drawn thence upon a Yarn-windle; 14. hence either Clewes, 15. are wound up, or Hanks 16. are made.'
The above comes from John Amos Comenius, *Orbis Pictus* (1659), p.121

which lifts up two, and sometimes three heavy beaters alternately, that play upon the hemp, while it is turned round by a man or boy to receive the beating regularly.[1]

These mills were driven either by horses or by water power, and were said to be similar to those used in paper making. With both horse-powered and water-driven mills it was possible to combine a bunching mill with a corn-grinding mill. A case heard in the Court of Requests in 1600 concerned a double horse mill at Deptford, which was designed both to grind grain and to beat hemp with 'stampers'.[2] Doubtless the hemp prepared here was intended for ropes and canvas for the naval dockyard. Celia Fiennes saw at Canterbury a water-mill which at one and the same time pounded rags for paper-making, beat oatmeal and

[1] Young, 1813, p.148
[2] PRO REQ2 78/25

hemp, and ground flour.[1] It has been suggested that bunching mills existed in Suffolk in the seventeenth century, but the present writer has been unable to find any evidence to support this assertion. However, there is no doubt of their presence in the following century. A sale notice in the *Ipswich Journal* for 29 August 1767 advertised an 'ancient, well-accustom'd water-mill with a bunching-mill for hemp adjoining etc in the parish of Homersfield, Suffolk . . . known by the name of Limborn Mill'. The vendor had inherited this property from his grandfather John Moore, a tow dresser, who, in his will made in 1762, described it as 'a water grist mill & mills & hemp bunching mill (being under one Roof)'.[2] This mill, now vanished, was one of the many that once stood on the banks of the river Waveney; Limborn is a lost medieval vill.

The minute book of the Bulcamp Union workhouse for 1768 recorded a resolution 'that the mill made for raising water be converted to a Bunching Mill and that 20 stone of Hemp be bought to be dressed in the House'. In 1837 the minute book for the same Suffolk workhouse referred to a 'hemp-bunching machine'.[3] At Pettistree, near Wickham Market, the tithe map marks a bunch meadow.[4] In his will, made in 1760, Henry Penn, a Fressingfield linen weaver, bequeathed 'my Bunching-Mill' to his son.[5] This, and the hemp mill valued at £6 in Thomas Winter's inventory,[6] were presumably horse mills.

At the end of the eighteenth century the governor of the Forehoe hundred House of Industry showed Arthur Young 'a very simple machine for bunching; men, by turning a winch, move semi-circular cogg'd wheels of iron, which lift, every moment, one of four perpendicular beaters, and let them fall on the hemp coiled under them to receive the stroke'.[7] Was motive power of this kind used to operate the machine 'for the purpose of spenning Hemp' which Stradbroke vestry ordered to be set up in January 1830?[8] In eighteenth-century Scotland water-powered lint mills for scutching flax became common after 1760, but it is likely that the East Anglian mills were used for bunching only.[9]

[1] *The Journeys of Celia Fiennes*, edited by Christopher Morris (1947), p.124, henceforth Fiennes
[2] NRO NCC Roper 38
[3] SROI FC184/G11/1 and 16. I am grateful to Mr Norman Scarfe for drawing my attention to this reference mentioned in J.B. Clare, *Wenhaston and Bulcamp* (1903), p.72.
[4] SROI FC104/C2/3
[5] SROI ICAA1/185/57
[6] NRO NCC INV83/15. 1748
[7] Arthur Young, *General View of the Agriculture of the County of Norfolk* (1804), p.329, henceforth Young, 1804
[8] SROI FC83/A1/1; Stradbroke Select Vestry Accounts 1825–30
[9] Durie, p.72

The finer the yarn required the more beating the hemp needed. At this stage it resembled the bast formerly used by gardeners to tie up plants. When the bunching was completed, the heckler then proceeded to dress the fibres by drawing them through combs or heckles. This process removed any remaining pieces of stem or dust, and broken or short fibres, and left the long fibres ready for the spinner. The heckle was a kind of comb, a flat piece of wood into which were set several rows of long wooden or metal teeth, through which bundles of hemp were drawn; the technique was similar to the combing of wool. The heckle was not held in the hand, but fixed on a board, thus leaving both of the user's hands free to pull the hemp. The *Encyclopédie* illustrates four different grades of heckles with teeth progressively diminishing in size and width of spacing, but many workers employed only two grades of heckle. Although Markham thought that most housewives heckled their hemp only once, or at most twice, he recommended doing it a third time with a fine-toothed heckle to produce 'teare', the highest grade of hemp from which fine, long-lasting linen could be made. Young's Stowmarket correspondent wrote that 'hemp is dressed finer or coarser, to suit the demands of purchasers'. According to its fineness 'the prices of tow vary, from about 6d to 18d per pound'.[1]

It is clear from Markham's book that in his day heckling was not usually a separate trade, and it was probably the seventeenth-century growth in the linen industry which led to specialisation. The chief skill required of the heckler was the selection of the right grade of heckle. Few hecklers (or hemp and flax dressers as they were sometimes known) seem to have left wills, probably because they were too poor or combined this trade with another occupation. Those wills that exist date from the eighteenth century or the first few years of the nineteenth; the earliest, that of a man who called himself a labourer and hemp dresser, was made in 1729.[2] Markham seems to imply that women heckled hemp, but the encyclopedists describe it as a task for strong men.

During the heckling process the shorter fibres were thrown off, and the best yarn was that prepared from the longest and finest fibres. The very short fibres (and these included some removed at the scutching stage) were known as tow. This often received further combing before being spun and used for coarse cloth. Tow combs are frequently listed in probate inventories from hemp and flax growing districts, but it is not clear whether the implements so described were really tow combs or heckles. To add to the confusion the fibres of hemp and flax when ready for spinning were often called tow; Young uses this word to describe

[1] Young, 1813, p.149
[2] NRO NCC Rudd 740

Figure 2.3   Heckling hemp from Diderot and d'Alembert, *Encyclopedie*

hemp ready for the spinner. The best hemp fibre is long, fine, supple, soft to the touch, inelastic and difficult to break; hemp of this quality was equally suitable for weaving into cloth or for rope making. Flax produces finer linen, but hemp has the advantage of greater tensile strength.

III

The impression may have been given that each of the processes already described (growing, retting, breaking, scutching, bunching and heckling) was carried out by different individuals, but this would be false. Markham clearly thought that hemp was usually taken through all the stages of its manufacture into cloth, except weaving, by the grower, or rather by his wife or at least under her direction. But he was engaged in instructing English housewives in their duties, and it is probable that even in his day not all hemp was processed by its primary producers and their families. Anthony Turner, a yeoman of Great Ellingham in south central Norfolk, provides a good example of domestic linen production being carried through all its stages within one household. His inventory, made in August 1635, shows that he grew hemp, processed it and wove it, although he may have employed a weaver to use his two looms. In addition to these, his possessions included a bunching block, a tow comb, a wheel, a warping stage, slayes and a starching kettle.[1] The

[1] NRO NCC INV/41/94.

slayes were part of the loom and the kettle would have been used to size the warp threads.

Nearly two centuries later, when Young was collecting his data, it is clear that hemp was far more likely to pass through several hands between grower and weaver, although even then it was not unknown for weavers to buy hemp and either carry out all the preparatory stages themselves or put it out to specialists. The Stowmarket manufacturer already quoted pointed out that a weaver who regulated all the processes of manufacture was more likely to have yarn of good quality. 'When the trade is conducted by different persons, their interests often clash: by under-retting the hemp, the grower increases the weight; by slightly beating it, the heckler increases the quantity of tow, but leaves it fuller of bark; . . . by forcing the bleaching, the whitester increases his profit, but diminishes the strength of the yarn.'[1] Excellent though his advice was, only the rich weavers possessed the capital which would enable them to follow it. The great majority of weavers were too poor to be able to hold stocks of hemp at different stages of its processing or to wait such a long time for their profits.

One thing is certain and that is that the development of specialisation is a clear sign that the East Anglian linen industry had changed from a peasant to a commercially orientated manufacture. When Markham wrote at the beginning of the seventeenth century, most English linen was still being produced purely for domestic consumption by the producer and his family, and the only specialist whose expertise was called upon was the weaver. When Young made his investigations nearly two centuries later, the most usual procedure seems to have been for hemp to be taken to the breaking stage by the grower, who then sold it to the heckler, who in turn either sold the heckled fibres to spinners or put it out to spin and then sold the yarn to weavers. It was generally the weavers who saw to the whitening, putting out either their yarn or their cloth to bleachers.

Once heckling had been completed hemp was ready for the spinning wheel. The three final processes in the production of hempen cloth, that is spinning, bleaching and weaving, are rather better known than are the earlier stages of its preparation.

Spinning was almost entirely a female occupation, and was a useful source of income for many cottagers' families as well as for widows and single women. In the early seventeenth century spinster was not synonomous with unmarried woman, for which the usual term was singlewoman. An example is Anne Greene, spinster of South Elmham All Saints, Suffolk, whose will clearly indicates that she was a widow

---

[1] Young, 1813, p.152

with children.[1] Her bequests included 'all my hempe which I have now pelled', and hemp growing on some rented land; her will was drawn up in June 1626. Like many rural craftsmen and women Anne Greene was farming as well as following her trade of spinning. Spinning wheels are very commonly found in the probate inventories of all classes, and must have been used by the female servants in the better-off households. Young refers to dairy-maids earning the full amount of their wages by spinning hemp or wool at times of the year when work in the dairy was slack. Even in Markham's day not every housewife was able to spin her own yarn and his instructions were to 'make choice of the best spinners you can hear of, and to then put forth your teare (best quality fibres) to spin'.[2] Spinning was also an employment for the poor from the earliest days of the Elizabethan Poor Law (1601), and from the middle of the eighteenth century was the chief occupation of the inhabitants of the East Anglian houses of industry, as the union workhouses were called.

Like flax and wool, hemp can be spun either with a distaff and spindle or on a wheel. The former was considered by some to be easier as the fibres of hemp are long, and Markham held that it produced a finer thread. The most important point was that the thread should be even; uneven thread 'will never make a durable cloath'.[3] The advantage of the distaff and spindle was that they could be carried around and used by the spinner whilst engaged in other tasks, such as watching grazing livestock. By the eighteenth century different types of spinning wheels were used for linen and wool; the former kind had a far smaller wheel and to accommodate the long fibres was much higher off the ground; the fibres to be spun were attached to a stave similar to a distaff. Although spinning wheels are so frequently listed in probate inventories, it is only rarely that the type of wheel is specified. A few inventories list both woollen and linen wheels, for example Ann Heccty of Wortham, Suffolk, who died in 1669, owned a linen and a woollen wheel, together worth three shillings;[4] and the inventory (1707) of Edmund Moor, a yeoman of the neighbouring village of Palgrave, included two tow wheels and one wool wheel.[5] However, it is impossible to be certain whether different types of wheels have always been used or whether at one time the same kind was in use for both linen and wool. Certainly the same distaff or spindle could be used to spin any type of yarn, and the development of differing kinds of spinning wheels may have stemmed from their gradual ousting of the use of the distaff

[1] SROI ICAA1/62/64
[2] Markham, p.137
[3] Ibid
[4] SROB IC500/3/14/169
[5] NRO NCC INV/86/191

for some kinds of yarn; worsted yarn continued to be rock-spun.[1]

After spinning the yarn was wound on to a reel (sometimes called blades or yarn wyndles in East Anglia), a wooden implement resembling the spokes of a wheel. In inventories reels are frequently listed with wheels, as in the case of Thomas Houchin of Palgrave, who owned a spinning wheel and three reels when he died in 1676.[2] In eighteenth-century Scotland the reel by law had to be 90 inches in circumference because linen yarn was sold by the spindle, which officially measured 5760 threads, each thread being once round the reel; a spindle was 14,400 yards in length.[3] It seems probable that there must always have been a standard size of reel for yarn that was to be sold, although there were regional variations. In late eighteenth-century Suffolk a clue or ball of hempen yarn measured 4800 yards, less than a third the length of a contemporary Scottish spindle of flaxen yarn, and the local thread also differed from the Scottish, being either two or three yards long (72 or 108 inches). The fineness of the yarn produced varied considerably, depending partly on how finely the hemp had been dressed and partly on the skill of the spinner, and ranged from one to three clues from a pound of dressed hemp. The finest yarn earned its producer almost twice as much as did the coarsest, one shilling as against sixpence halfpenny or sevenpence a clue.[4]

It was usual to bleach both the yarn after spinning and the cloth after it had been woven, although in Scotland the yarn seems only to have been boiled to clean it before weaving and some cloth was sold unbleached.[5] The bleaching process included scouring as well as whitening. Although much yarn and cloth was bleached by non-specialists, the trade of whitester, as bleachers were called, became increasingly common in eighteenth-century East Anglia. Like the development of heckling as a separate trade, this was a result of the growth of the local linen industry.

Markam gives lengthy instructions for the scouring and whiting of both yarn and cloth. According to him it took three weeks to clean and whiten yarn before it was taken to the weaver, and at least as long again to wash and bleach the finished cloth. 'Inferior housewives' used bran as the bleaching agent, but Markham advised fine ashes. After being washed and rinsed every day for four days, the hanks of yarn were placed in a bucking tub in alternate layers with ashes, a bucking cloth and more ashes forming the top layer. Warm water was then poured in

---

[1] D.C. Coleman, 'An Innovation and its Diffusion; the "New Draperies" ', *The Economic History Review*, Second Series, XXII, 3 (1969), 420, 423

[2] SROB IC500/3/17/174

[3] Durie, p.4

[4] Young, 1813, p.149

[5] Durie, pp. 4–5

until the tub was full and it was left overnight. In the morning the spigot of the tub was removed and the lye (water in which ashes have soaked) which ran out was collected, reheated and poured into the tub again. This process was repeated for a period of four hours making the lye progressively hotter until it reached boiling point. The yarn was next placed in another tub and well pounded before being rinsed and hung up on poles. For the next week the yarn was soaked in water every night and hung on poles in the open air each day. At the end of the week the bucking process was repeated to be followed once more by a week of alternate soaking and hanging on poles. When all this had been carried out, the yarn was dried, wound into balls and taken to the weaver. As soon as the web or cloth came home from the weaver the whole process had to be repeated, the only difference being that instead of being hung on poles the cloth was spread on grass and staked down, through loops sewn to the edges, to hold its shape; this was akin to the stretching of woollen cloth on tenters. While spread on the grass the cloth was wetted whenever it was dry, and turned over once a week. Comenius also writes of linen webs being bleached in the sun with water poured over them.[1]

Descriptions of the bleaching processes used in the eighteenth century[2] indicate that the time Markham allowed for the whitening of cloth was rather short; six weeks or more seems to have been usual, but on the other hand there is no mention of bleaching yarn, only of its washing. There seem to be considerable differences of opinion over the time taken to bleach cloth and yarn. In seventeenth-century Nidderdale it was considered that both yarn and cloth had to be bleached to produce high quality linen, although some weavers did use brown or unbleached yarn, and the bleaching of yarn could take up to six months.[3] Late sixteenth-century Lancashire was another region where yarn bleaching took as long as six months. Here flax was the main fibre used, and the best yarn was worth almost three times as much bleached as unbleached. As their turnover was so slow, it was probably essential for the whitesters to combine their trade with farming or some other part-time occupation.[4] Unfortunately East Anglian inventories seldom specify the quantities of yarn appraised, but a linen weaver of Great Dunham, Norfolk, died in 1743 possessed of considerable amounts of both white and grey yarn. The difference in price between the two was small: 1s. 7d. a clue for white and 1s. 4d. for grey.[5] The colour of yarn is mentioned sufficiently often in Suffolk and Norfolk inventories to

---

[1] J.A. Comenius, *Orbis sensualium Pictus*, facsimile of third London edition (Sydney, 1967), p.125

[2] *Encyclopedia Britannica* (1967), article on bleaching, and Durie, pp. 5–6

[3] Jennings, p.176

[4] Lowe, p.45

[5] NRO Archdeaconry of Norwich inventories ANW/23/24/35

make it clear that there the usual practice was to bleach yarn as well as cloth.

The method of bleaching generally used in both England and Scotland in the eighteenth century was based on the Dutch method, and differed from that described by Markham, as in addition to using an alkaline bleaching agent in the form of lye, the material was also soaked either in buttermilk or in water in which bran had been infused in order to apply an acid or 'sour'. Towards the end of the century the lengthy traditional method of bleaching was greatly speeded up by the introduction of the use of chlorine in the 1780s. Further improvements were brought about by the invention of Eau de Javel (a chlorine solution) in 1792 and of powdered chlorine in the early 1800s. These developments not only much shortened the bleaching process, but also improved it.

Bleaching, like hemp growing and retting, left its mark on field names; bleach meadow and bleach ground are names quite commonly found on East Anglian tithe maps in linen-weaving districts. As is the case with hecklers, few whitesters or bleachers have left wills, and those that do exist almost all date from after 1700. Only one of these wills, that of John Sadler of Hoe by East Dereham, Norfolk, dates from the first half of the seventeenth century.[1] The probate inventory of Mathew Thurton, a Bungay whitester who died in 1712, amounted to just under £20. If his poverty is typical of his trade, it is not surprising that there are so few bleachers' wills. Nearly a third of the value of his possessions was accounted for by the tools of his trade: 55 poles, a copper and 5 deal tubs.[2]

In recent years hand-loom weaving has become a relatively popular craft, but the looms used by weavers today are rather more sophisticated than those worked in the past and give the observer a false idea of the complexity of the simple looms employed by plain weavers in the seventeenth and eighteenth centuries. In East Anglia, as in Lancashire, a single loom was often called a pair of looms;[3] this practice seems not to have been universal as the word 'pair' is not used to describe looms in Telford inventories.[4] There were apparently no specialised loom-makers in East Anglia, so it must be assumed that looms were built either by carpenters or by weavers themselves. The will[5] of William Levericke of Hopton, Suffolk, made in 1634 names Luke Tocke as the maker of a new pair of looms. Was Tocke a carpenter or a regular maker of looms? They were frequently passed down from father to son, and so must have been solidly constructed. A loom was a typical item of

[1] NRO NCC 1630 original wills 232
[2] SROI FEI/8/25
[3] Lowe, pp. 101–2
[4] Trinder and Cox, passim
[5] SROB IC500/1/90/183

cottage equipment like many other items employed in rural industries. A weaver's slay or reed (the former term was more commonly used in East Anglia) consisted of two parallel bars of wood about six inches apart holding strips of metal about a sixteenth of an inch wide and the thickness of a pen nib (strictly speaking the slay is the frame and the reed the teeth held by it, but slay seems to have been used for the whole apparatus.) Its purpose was to keep the warp threads straight and in position and to act as a guide for the shuttle. The closeness together of the dents varied according to the fineness of the cloth being woven. The name reed stems from the fact that the teeth were originally made of reed or cane; the latter is still occasionally used by modern weavers. Slay-making, like card-making, was a specialised urban trade. Amongst the city of Norwich inventories there are a handful for makers of slays or reeds, and heavels or heddles. Almost all are post-1600 in date, and in several cases slay and heavel-making appears to have been a subsidary occupation for barbers.[1] The will of a barber-slay maker, who died in 1660, mentions reed, flax, heavels and slays as well as 'all my linen cloths belonging to my trade as a barber'.[2] Many East Anglian linen weavers owned considerable numbers of slays, and these were of sufficient value to be bequeathed in some wills.

Other items of equipment that occur frequently in the probate inventories of East Anglian linen-weavers are shafts, by which was meant heddles, slay shafts, which were the two rods holding the teeth of the reed or slay, and warping bars. These last are sometimes listed together with a travis or travers, a vertical frame, or merely a wooden beam, into which were stuck the pegs which held the bobbins of yarn from which the warp was wound onto the two dimensional warping frame or bars. Filling the bobbins with yarn was a task usually carried out by the wives and children of weavers. A later development was the warping mill, which was three-dimensional, revolved and was turned by an 'engine', as any mechanical device was once known. A warping mill speeded up the tedious process of winding the warp, but was probably beyond the means of many weavers, and so did not supersede the use of warping bars.

Only 33 linen weavers' probate inventories (approximately a quarter of the total) list warping bars, and a warping mill appears in only one of them. As this inventory dates from 1677 and the warping mill together with a loom and slays was valued at only £2, it was probably not a true one. The making of inventories decreased sharply after the first decade of the eighteenth century, and only 40 of those of linen-weavers date

---

[1] I am indebted to Mrs Ursula Priestley of the Norwich Survey for the information about slay-makers in the city
[2] NRO NCC Tennant 189

from after 1700 and a mere six from later than 1740. Therefore, if, as seems likely, warping mills did not become common until the 1700s, it is scarcely surprising that they are not to be found in the inventories. Only capitalist weavers employing several journeymen were likely to have been able to afford a warping mill, and their numbers increased during the eighteenth century. So many inventories list weaving equipment as looms and their appurtenances or looms and other things belonging to the trade, that it is likely that these phrases often include warping bars.

A point about which there is some doubt is whether the same loom could be used for weaving different types of cloth. In principle there seems no reason why a simple loom could not have been used to weave either woollens or linens, although it would probably be neccessary to change the 'gears', that is, the reeds and heddles. It is interesting that a weaver of Wrockwardine, Shropshire, possessed, in addition to three looms, '9 woollen geeres & 23 linnen geeres'.[1] He also owned a warping trough, presumably for sizing the warp. According to Jennings it is possible to weave wollen, linen (that is flax) and harden (hemp) cloth on the same loom by using different gears.[2] In East Anglian inventories it is rare to find the type of loom specified. One exception is that of George Roper of Badwell Ash, Suffolk, who died in 1664; he owned one pair of linen looms.[3] Another is James Beamond of Acle, Norfolk, who died in 1589 leaving three looms for 'woollen' and linen.[4] There is one piece of evidence which suggests that considerable adjustments had to be made before a linen loom could be used to weave wool. In 1681 some French linen-weavers, Huguenot refugees, settled in Ipswich. They appear not to have met with much success in their trade and by 1685 were in difficulties. In the following year, on 16 November, the Ipswich Assembly Book recorded that 'Its Agreed that the French shall have six Loomes used in the Lynnen trade to Convert to the use of the Woollen trade at the Townes pleasure.'[5] These Huguenot weavers may have been using complex looms, but even if looms needed adjustment it was apparently not difficult for their users to change from weaving one fabric to another.[6]

A linen-weaver's capital investment in the tools of his trade was not very great. Most of the looms appraised in inventories were worth about a pound or a little more, but some a much lower figure, and the ancillary

[1] Trinder and Cox, p.402
[2] Jennings, p.164
[3] SROB IC500/3/9/111
[4] NRO NCC INV/6/108
[5] *East Anglian Notes and Queries*, New Series, II (1887–8), p.399, quoting SROI C6/1/7
[6] Duncan Bythell, *The Handloom Weavers, a Study in the English Cotton Industry During the Industrial Revolution* (Cambridge, 1969), p.47, henceforth Bythell

equipment, such as warping bars and slays, was generally valued at a few shillings. Even the equipment of the weaver who owned five looms, the largest number found in any inventory, 'in shop and abroad', was worth no more that £14 10s. 0d.[1] Setting up in trade was far more expensive for a frame knitter than for a weaver, as stocking frames were made of iron and were more complicated than looms. The inventories of Leicestershire stockingers give a median value of £5 for frames, and new ones would have cost considerably more, perhaps as much as £20 by the mid-eighteenth century.[2]

IV

All the processes described above in the preparation of hemp and the making of linen cloth are those of a pre-industrial manufacture. It is possible that East Anglian linen-weavers adopted the flying shuttle invented by John Kay in 1733, but there is no evidence to support or contradict this suggestion. Throughout its existence, even where it survived into the twentieth century, the East Anglian linen industry remained unmechanised and in chapter 1 the hypothesis was put forward that this was one of the main reasons for the collapse of the industry. Lack of capital investment and the initiative to modernise in part explain the failure to industrialise, and this aspect will be dealt with in chapters 5 and 6. Here it is proposed to look solely at the technical reasons behind this failure, and comparisons will be drawn with a rural district, Nidderdale, where the move from a hand to a mechanised industry was made.

A full-time weaver had always required the yarn production of more than one spinner, and after the introduction of Kay's flying shuttle some five or six spinners were needed to produce enough yarn to employ one weaver.[3] Thus by the late eighteenth century the linen industry could expand no more as long as it relied on hand spinning. A major problem was the technical difficulty of developing a spinning frame suitable for flax (by this date in Yorkshire most linens were made from flax not hemp). Cotton, unlike flax, is elastic and the technical problems of spinning the former are much less. Mills in Nidderdale, powered by a swift-flowing river, had long both ground corn and fulled cloth, so it was a natural progression to use their power for spinning. The first cotton spinning mill in the dale was opened at Knaresborough in 1791, but it was several years before mechanised flax-spinning

[1] NRO Norwich Archdeaconry Inventories ANW/23/24/35
[2] Dennis R. Mills, 'Framework Knitters in Leicestershire, 1670–1851', *Textile History*, 13, no 2 (Autumn 1982), 189–190, henceforth Mills
[3] Much of this paragraph and the next is based on Jennings, 1967, pp.181–264

reached Nidderdale. John Marshall of Leeds began the mechanical spinning of flax in 1788 at a mill on the Meanwood Beck, then in the country to the north of the town. The spinning frame was gradually improved to produce lighter and finer yarns, and by 1792 the carding and spinning of tow had also been mechanised. From this time on more and more flax spinning mills were built to meet the demands, for rope tow for the navy and cloth for uniforms, created by the French Revolutionary and Napoleonic Wars.

A hand-spinner produced only one thread at a time, but with mechanisation a girl or woman could tend 20 or 30 spindles and later as many as 120. Thus the problem of spinning had been overcome, and the mechanisation of cotton-weaving was not long to follow. Linen was a different matter, and its weaving remained a hand process long after the introduction of the spinning frame. Just as with spinning, the technical difficulties caused by the inelasticity of linen yarn delayed the development of an efficient power loom for this material until the middle of the nineteenth century. It was not until about 1850 that the power-loom weaving of linen began, and by that time linen had lost much of its market to cotton. Power-loom weaving was best suited to the production of sheeting and shirting, but the finest linens were still better woven by hand, and hand-loom weaving survived in Niddlerdale until the end of the nineteenth century. As the demand for linen cloth and thread continued to fall, some of the Nidderdale mills went over to spinning heavy yarns from hemp and tow from which twine, cords, rope and string were made. Indeed this trade continued in the dale at Glasshouses mill near Pately Bridge until the 1970s.

It is not difficult to see why the East Anglian linen industry failed to follow the path taken by the Yorkshire linen trade. In the first place, in East Anglia the relief is low and it is not an area of high rainfall; thus its rivers are slow-flowing and lack the power needed to drive large numbers of mills. True, there were corn and fulling mills on the rivers of Norfolk and Suffolk, but fewer than in hillier districts. Windmills were much used for corn-grinding as well as for pumping water, and the open expanses of these two counties are admirably suited to the use of wind power. It is said that one of the reasons for the success of the worsted industry in sevententh-century Norfolk was that this cloth, unlike the heavier old draperies, did not require fulling. After the first quarter of the nineteenth century, steam power began to supersede water power, and in industrial districts this led to the concentration of mills in towns where the price of coal was lower because of better transport facilities. East Anglian industry could not take advantage of the development of steam power, as it was far from any coalfield and the high cost of importing fuel would always have enabled producers in the north of England to undercut those in a distant rural area. Sea coal had long been burnt on East Anglian hearths, but to bring in sufficient steam coal to power factories was out of the question without capital investment of a kind which was not forthcoming. As time passed, the combined competition of linen and cotton produced in the industrial north made the decline and collapse of an entirely hand operated industry inevitable. In the early nineteenth century there were small linen-weaving factories in East Anglian towns, but the weaving was carried out on hand-looms and the places in question were small market towns. Industrialisation had nothing to do with this move to urban manufacture, which was connected with the pauperisation of the hand-loom weavers and will be discussed in chapter 6.

VI

At this point something must be said about the types of linen cloth manufactured by the East Anglian linen-weavers. The general impression is that they wove mainly rather coarse cloth, and that the finest linens were imported from abroad. How true this is it is difficult to say, but linen-weaving survived at Lopham in Norfolk until 1925 because it concentrated on high quality cloth. Only very rarely do the inventories of linen-weavers list cloth in any detail. It is more usual to find entries such as six yards of cloth in the looms and a remnant of coarse cloth,[1] or 40 yards coarse linen cloth unwhited,[2] or hempen cloth in the linen shop.[3] Most inventories lack even this degree of precision, and of course many weavers did not own the cloth they wove, so any in their hands when they died would not be valued. Two eighteenth-century inventories give slightly more information: that of James Kent of South Elmham St James in Suffolk refers to cloth, twill and twill sacks;[4] and James Jex of Brampton, also in north Suffolk, owned huckaback, 'teeking checks', woolsey and 'strainers'.[5] Twill and huckaback are both coarse linen cloths, 'teeking checks' was presumably a checked material and 'strainers' was probably a cloth used for sifting flour or straining liquids. The presence of wolsey in James Jex's inventory suggests that he wove woollens as well as linens. Unfortunately the inventory which lists the greatest quantity of linen cloth differentiates it only by price; the price range was not very wide: eightpence to one shilling and threepence.[6]

[1] SROB IC500/3/15/72
[2] NRO NCC INV/24/69
[3] SROB IC500/3/23/93
[4] SROI FEI/27/83
[5] SROI FEI/27/33
[6] NRO Archdeaconry of Norwich Wills ANW/23/24/35

The inventories of linen drapers and of chapmen are much more informative about types of cloth, but unfortunately there is no means of telling what was produced locally and what came from elsewhere. Many cloths, such as hollands, ossenbrigs, hambrow and denim, were named after the place where they were first made, but they were much copied elsewhere and the names often came to mean no more than a particular type or quality of cloth. Did Manchester inkles for instance always originate there? Inkle was a linen tape, varying in width and quality, and much used for girdles, garters, apron strings and the cheaper sort of trimmings. Inkles were woven on a special narrow inkle loom, and were part of the stock in trade of all chapmen. Scotch cloth is another material widely sold by drapers and chapmen, and in the eighteenth century it probably indeed came from Scotland. It is said that originally Scotch cloth was made from nettles, which can be prepared for spinning in exactly the same way as hemp or flax and produce good fibre about a metre in length. It is certain that nettle fibre can be used to make cloth as readers of Hans Anderson's tale, *The Wild Swans* will recall. After the passing of an Act to regulate linen and hempen manufacture in Scotland in 1727, it is unlikely that cloth made from nettles continued to be produced there. Even in the early seventeenth century there was more than one quality of Scotch cloth. The inventory of a Great Yarmouth linen draper made in 1614 includes coarse Scotch cloth valued at 7½d. a yard and some of better quality at 1s. 3d.[1] At the end of the seventeenth century a Suffolk linen-weaver, who also kept a small shop, was selling three varieties of linens: hempen cloth, scotch cloth and blue linen.[2] One point that retailers' inventories make absolutely clear is the enormously wide range of cloths, both linen and woollen, available to customers in pre-industrial England. In 1614 the Great Yarmouth draper referred to above was selling thirty different kinds of cloth, and his inventory lists several varieties or colours of a number of these. Over a century later, in 1729, a grocer at Laxfield, a village in north Suffolk, stocked 21 varieties of materials, some in more than one quality or colour.[3]

This survey of the technical side of the East Anglian linen industry is a necessary introduction to its history, and should aid the reader to understand the background to its growth and subsequent decline. It has indicated the range of employment created by a pre-industrial cloth manufacture, described the methods used in processing hemp and manufacturing linen cloth, and shown some of the reasons for the failure to make the move from a hand-operated to a mechanised

[1] NRO NCC INV/26/252
[2] SROB IC500/3/24/26
[3] NRO NCC INV/78A/118

industry. Subsequent chapters will trace the rise of East Anglian linen weaving from its medieval base, its flourishing in the seventeenth and eighteenth centuries, and finally the economic and social disaster of its decay, which began in the final quarter of the eighteenth century.

3   The Medieval and Tudor East Anglian Linen Industry

I

Before 1600 there is very little precise evidence about linen weavers; only 55 are known before 1600, and of these a mere four are prior to 1550 in date. This paucity of information has three explanations: firstly, it became much more common after 1600 than it had been earlier for the occupations of testators to be given in probate records; in the second place, the annual totals of surviving wills and inventories increased greatly in the seventeenth century; and lastly, linen-weaving was still in what one writer has called its 'peasant' stage.[1] This last implies that most linen-weavers were not following their trade full-time, were meeting a merely local demand and had sufficient time to engage in farming or some other occupation on a part-time basis.

Although little can be deduced for this period about linen weavers from probate records, much more can be said about the growing of hemp and flax. From the middle of the fifteenth century a fairly large number of wills have survived, and they provide evidence for the widespread cultivation of hemp in the late medieval period. Wills proved up to the mid-sixteenth century in the consistory court of the Bishop of Norwich provide many examples, of which only a few can be given here, of the growing of hemp and of the production of hempen cloth. Many wills also mention flax. Robert Barnye, a priest of Ash-wellthorpe near Wymondham, who died in 1553, bequeathed various lengths of hemp cloth including 'two yardes of Newe hempen cloth to be taken at the best ende'.[2] Nearly a century earlier, in 1457, Isabel Beryswelle, a widow of Hacheston in Suffolk, left 20 yards of linen cloth to be divided amongst her married daughters and grandchildren,[3] and seventeen years later we find Isabel's son, Roger Dun, leaving his wife a third part of his flax and 'le hemp'.[4] William Childerhouse of Ashill, Norfolk, made a bequest to his wife in 1546 of three stone of best hemp.[5] An inhabitant of the small Suffolk town of Bungay, who died in

---

[1] Harte, p.96
[2] NRO NCC Wilkins 19
[3] NRO NCC Neve 52
[4] NRO NCC Hubert 40
[5] NRO NCC Daynes 82

1488, bequeathed his messuage and hempland to his wife,[1] and in 1520 John Chapman of Weeting All Saints left half of his hemp 'growing in the croftyerd' to his wife.[2] Other fifteenth and early sixteenth-century wills in which hemp or cloth made from it are mentioned came from places as widely distributed as Snettisham, Harling, West Wretham, South Lopham, Horning and Grimston in Norfolk, and from Benacre, Kesgrave and Palgrave in Suffolk. West and south Suffolk are missing from this list merely because wills from these areas were rarely proved in the Norwich consistory court. Although some of these places, such as South Lopham, Bungay and Palgrave were later to be centres of linen-weaving, others, for instance Weeting and Wretham, were in areas in which no or few linen-weavers were to be found in subsequent centuries. This is another indication that before the middle of the sixteenth century hemp was grown and cloth woven from it almost purely for local consumption; in other words there was as yet no organised, market-orientated linen trade in East Anglia.

Some surnames are derived from hemp cultivation. A number of Hempsteads are to be found in current East Anglian telephone directories, but this must be a locative derivation as there are two places of this name in Norfolk. On means homestead, but Hempstead near Holt is interpreted as a place where hemp grows.[3] In the 1981 Norwich area directory there are 12 persons bearing the surname Hemp.

II

Just before the Black Death there is one excellent source concerning the growing of hemp and flax in Suffolk.[4] Unfortunately the returns for Norfolk have been lost. In 1342 an assessment was made for a royal taxation on the laity of a ninth part of all tithable products; the clergy had just granted the king a tenth of their income for two years. Each parish paid as a whole and one must assume that the parishioners contributed in the same proportion as they paid their tithes. Both the lay and clerical taxation of 1342 were levied to finance Edward III's war with France. For the purposes of this lay tax the value of a ninth was taken as being equal to that of a tenth at the time of the taxation of Pope

---

[1] SROI Vol. 3, f.87
[2] NRO NCC Coppinger 39–40
[3] Eilert Ekwall, *The Concise Oxford Dictionary of English Place Names* (Oxford, 4th edition, 1960)
[4] Much of this and the following paragraphs are based on W.R. Gowers, 'The Cultivation of Flax and Hemp in Suffolk in the 14th Century, as shown in the Inquisitiones Nonarum (1342)', *East Anglian Notes and Queries*, V (1893–4), 180–3 and 200–202; W.A. Wickham, 'Nonarum Inquisitiones for Suffolk', *Proceedings of the Suffolk Institute of Archaeology*, XVII (1921), 97–122; and *Nonarum Inquisitiones in curia scaccarii Temp. Regis Edward III*, (1807), pp. 63–105

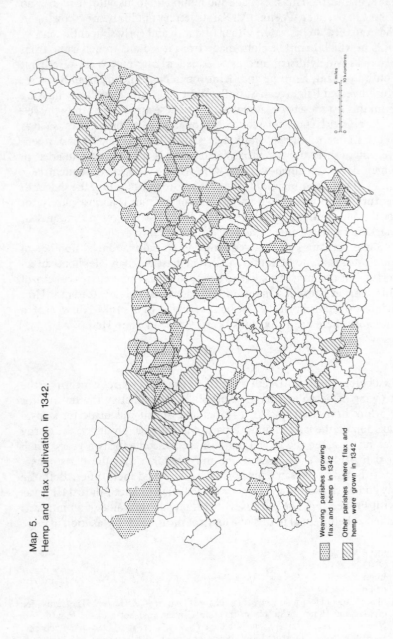

Map 5.
Hemp and flax cultivation in 1342.

Weaving parishes growing
flax and hemp in 1342

Other parishes where flax and
hemp were grown in 1342

0   6 miles
0   10 kilometres

Nicholas in 1292. Hemp and flax always appear together in the text as "decim' lin' & canab' ", so there is no possibility of establishing the relative quantities and values of the two crops.

Map 5 shows the distribution of parishes in which tithes were being paid on hemp and flax in 1342; the parishes in which linen-weavers are known later to have lived are dotted. The two crops are listed amongst the tithes of 140, or slightly over half, of the 274 Suffolk parishes for which the Nonarum Inquisitiones give full details. They were thus fairly important crops and the total annual value of the tithes of flax and hemp for the 140 parishes was £107 19s. 9d. It is impossible to indicate what quantity of hemp and flax this figure represents. However, in the early seventeenth century, when many tithes had already been commuted, the parishioners of Walsham le Willows in west Suffolk were paying sixpence for every peck of hemp.[1] This seems a peculiar way of measuring hemp, but it probably meant hempseed. The other crops individually named as tithed in 1342 were corn and hay, together with the tithes due on wool, lambs, milk and calves; the acreages and the annual values were also given for arable, pasture and meadow. It is impossible to compare the value of the tithes on corn with those on hemp and flax, as the former is valued together with wool and lambs.

Two points stand out: many parishes, which were later the homes of linen-weavers, were apparently not growing hemp and flax; and these crops were being cultivated in a number of places where no linen weavers have been found. To begin with the first point, map 3 shows 193 Suffolk parishes where one or more linen-weavers are known to have lived, but hemp and flax were growing in only 48 (25 per cent) of these in 1342. It is particularly surprising to find so few of the Waveney and Little Ouse valley parishes cultivating these crops, but there is an explanation for this unexpected result. In the two hundreds of Hartismere and Hoxne, which border the river valleys, well over half the parishes are amongst those for which the information about small tithes is general rather then particular. In the former hundred for only 9 (29 per cent) out of 31 parishes are full details given and in the latter this is the case for 10 (40 per cent) out of 25 villages, but 6 of the Hartismere and 8 of the Hoxne hundred parishes with full information were paying tithes on flax and hemp. This suggests that had the small tithes of every parish in these two hundreds been described in detail, a high proportion would have been found to be growing these two crops. However, this variation in the returns made for the Inquisitions of the Ninth means that the distribution pattern they reveal is simply an indication of a minimum.

[1] SROB EL159/3/2.5

Much more interesting is the appearance of hemp and flax on areas of the map that were not later noted for growing these crops, nor as centres of linen weaving. The 1342 tithe values for these two crops in parishes in these areas do not suggest that they were insignificant. The most obvious deduction to make is that hemp and flax were widely grown in Suffolk in the years immediately preceding the Black Death because they were universally used to provide linen for families of their growers, and that in later centuries, when linen production became commercialised, the growing of hemp was concentrated in the districts where most linen weavers worked.

It is especially intriguing to find hemp and flax fairly widely grown in 1342 in west Suffolk, and particularly in the northern half of that area. This was the sheep-corn region, where the soil was predominantly light, and which west Suffolk justices of the peace in 1591 claimed to be unsuitable for the growing of hemp. According to these men 'the holle p[ar]te of the Soyle of the Franchis of Burye is & hath bin in sundrye places tryed to be utterlye unfitt & unapt for the sowing of hempe or flaxe'. They went on to give reasons for this contention: the soil, whether clay or loam, was too cold; the water which ran off clay land was not fit for retting hemp; and in dry summers, such as the two preceding the drawing up of this document, there was insufficient water for retting pits.[1] These objections arose from the enforcement of the Tudor Acts concerned with the growing of hemp, and, as is so often the case with protests, were rather exaggerated. In fact hemp was then being grown successfully in those parts of the Franchise of Bury that lay in or near the Little Ouse valley, and there was nothing intrinsically unsuitable for its growth about the light land. The fact that hemp grown on poor soil produces the finest fibre, which is the best suited to high quality linen was pointed out in chapter 2, so the claim that light soil was unsuitable was clearly invalid. It is possible that hemp growing had declined in the light soil region because the local product was not able to compete with high quality imported hemp and flax, and because corn-growing and sheep-rearing were more profitable. In addition, the labour shortage which followed on the recurring outbreaks of plague in the fourteenth century may have made as labour intensive a crop as hemp seem less desirable. The 1327 tax returns indicate that this area was then, in relation to the rest of the county, more densely populated than it was to be later.[2] Furthermore, it was an area of large farms, and less thickly populated than the wood-pasture district where most hemp

---

[1] British Library, Blakeney Bequest, Blakeney MSS vol. 3, no 38. Letter to Nathaniel Bacon of Stiffkey, Norfolk

[2] Sydenham H.A. Hervey, *Suffolk in 1327*, Suffolk Green Books IX (Woodbridge, 1906), henceforth Suffolk in 1327

was grown in the seventeenth and eighteenth centuries. Hemp was a crop particularly favoured by dairy farmers and cottagers, and both were more numerous in wood-pasture areas. The complaints voiced in the 1590s show the shortness of memory of landowners, who were claiming that an area which had grown not inconsiderable quantities of hemp and flax two and a half centuries before was totally unsuited to these crops. A similar case is that of those Suffolk farmers who, at the time of the great agricultural slump in the late nineteenth and early twentieth centuries, insisted that their land was quite unsuitable for growing grass for cows even though barely a century had elapsed since their farms had flourished as dairies.

The Nonarum Inquisitiones are not the only source for medieval hemp-growing in East Anglia. Manorial court rolls frequently record fines levied on those who fouled running water by using it to ret hemp. Two fifteenth-century examples are given here, the first from Norfolk and the second from Suffolk. In 1421 five inhabitants of Shelfhanger were fined for placing hemp and flax in the common river and in 'le Wateryng',[1] and in 1444 the court leet for Littlehaugh manor in Norton near Bury St Edmunds fined Simon Steff for laying hemp in a common watercourse without licence, so that the tenants' animals were infected by drinking the water.[2] At the end of the fourteenth century (1389–90), the manor court of South Elmham near Bungay fined a man for laying hemp in the Lord's river.[3] In only one of the nine South Elmham parishes was tithe shown as being paid on hemp and flax in 1342.

Extents of manors and tithing customs are other sources of information about medival hemp-growing. A 1369 extent of Lopham in south Norfolk records the paying of hemp silver,[4] and the customs of Diss rectory, as recorded by the Norfolk historian Blomefield, show that the rector received 'Every tenth bate or sheaf of hemp in kind.'[5] When writing about Bressingham near Diss, Blomefield describes an extent or composition roll of the manor, dated 1341, as being 'as perfect an account as I ever saw of any manor'. This roll lists totals of rents in kind and work due from the copyholders; these included '20 days to pull the lord's hemp'.[6] Finally in 1458 the rector of Weeting All Saints, which lies in the Breckland region of south-west Norfolk and well

[1] NRO Warnes 19.12.68 (R192D)
[2] SROB 553/1
[3] SROI HA12 unlisted 13/11
[4] Bodleian Library MSS Top. Norfolk d.l, ff. 612–613. I am indebted to the late Mr Michael Serpell for this reference. Hemp silver was paid in lieu of tithes.
[5] Blomefield, I, p.20
[6] ibid, p.52

outside the main linen weaving district, made a bequest in his will of his tithe hemp, 'canabu' meu' decimabilem'.[1]

III

In the Middle Ages, just as later in its history, linen-weaving in East Anglia was predominantly a rural not an urban craft. The greater restraints imposed on trade and industry in towns may well be one reason why so few linen-weavers were found there. This has certainly long been held as the main reason why the medieval East Anglian wool industry grew up and flourished in villages where it was free from the restrictions and regulations of trade gilds. Maps 3 and 4 indicate that, apart from Norwich, the numbers of weavers found in the main towns of the region are insignificant, and that Bungay, Beccles and Diss are the only small towns in which substantial numbers have been recorded; there were few in the two latter places before 1700. Even the 56 noted in Norwich cannot be regarded as indicating that the city was a centre of linen-weaving; they are far outnumbered by worsted-weavers, for whom there are over 200 surviving inventories,[2] and as a proportion of the population of so large a town can only be regarded as negligible. Ipswich, the county town of Suffolk, 'was essentially a commerical and trading town rather than a manufacturing centre'.[3] Textile manufacturing of various kinds was carried on there in the sixteenth and seventeenth centuries, but nowhere near the scale of Norwich.

In 1477 the Abbot of Bury St Edmunds, together with 29 woollen and linen weavers of the town, compiled a set of ordinances to control weavers and weaving.[4] The preamble to this document asserts that many men, women and children in Bury were engaged in weaving all kinds of woollen and linen cloth, mostly 'plain' weaving, and claims that the present decay of the weaving craft is due to deceitful practices by some persons. The ordinances set out strictly to control and regulate both weavers and weaving, and it was doubtless this kind of regulation which led practitioners of the craft to prefer the countryside to incorporated towns. It is interesting to note that throughout the document no distinction is made between weavers of wool and of linen. They all, including apprentices and journeymen, were to meet annually on the feast of the translation of Edward the Confessor (13 October) to elect four wardens or rulers of the craft of weaving. These wardens, who had

[1] NRO NCC Brosyard 112

[2] Information kindly supplied by Mrs Ursula Priestley of the Norwich Survey. There is a total of c.260 weavers' inventories for Norwich, and the great majority are those of worsted weavers; many more of these left wills but no surviving inventories

[3] Michael Reed, *The Ipswich Probate Inventories 1583–1631*, Suffolk Record Society, XXII (Woodbridge, 1981), p.2, henceforth Reed, 1981

[4] SROB B9/1/2

to be freeholders within the town, were given considerable powers, including the right to enter and search the houses of weavers and to impose fines for a number of offences. No weaver was permitted to own more than four looms, apprentices could not be taken for a term of less than seven years, and no one could set up looms in Bury unless he had been apprenticed to the craft and could show that he possessed 'sufficyent kennyng and understondyng in the same'. Before weavers could be admitted to the craft they were examined by the wardens to ensure that they were 'able men to sette up or to occupie the sayd crafte', and paid over the sum of 13s. 4d. Besides fulfilling the aforesaid conditions, no person from outside the town could set up looms or weave there unless expressly granted permission by the wardens, and every 'foreyn' weaver was to contribute towards the cost of the pageants on Ascension Day and Corpus Christi. Although these ordinances were designed to control the quality of the cloth woven in Bury, and this could only be beneficial, they were also full of restrictive practices typical of medieval trade gilds and were particularly harsh with regard to weavers who were not natives of the town.

A year after receiving its charter in 1606, the borough of Bury St Edmunds drew up 'Constitutions and Statutes . . . for the good Government of the sayd Burghe.'[1] Just as did the ordinances of 1477, the statutes of 1607 set out to regulate the conduct of craftsmen and the quality of their work. 'For the Ordering of Lynnen weavers in theire Trade. Inprimis yt is ordered that none hereafter shall set up the misterie or occupacon of a Lynnen weavor within this Burghe withowt the Licence of thalderman and Burgesses . . . except he hath served an apprentise vii yeares & untill he shalbe of thage of xxiiii yeares'. Again, as in the late fifteenth century, the artisans of Bury were particularly anxious to prevent competition from outside the town. No craftsman was allowed to employ any person who was not an inhabitant of Bury unless none brought up in his trade was available. Furthermore, 'noe In[ab]itant w[it]hin this Burghe shall put any worke belonginge to a lynnen weaver to be wrought in the cuntrie yf they maye have the same conveniently done in this Towne'. The small number of linen-weavers found in Bury suggests that the compilers of the 1607 statutes were fighting a losing battle against rural competition.

Attempts to limit the number of men practising the trade of linen weaving by insisting on a long period of apprenticeship were almost certainly self-deafeating. They can only have encouraged weavers to set up outside large towns; living in the countryside not only freed them from irksome restraints, but also allowed them to farm on a part-time

---

[1] SROB D14/2/1

basis, thus making themselves more economically secure than their urban counterparts.

Bury St Edmunds is not the only Suffolk town whose records mention the linen industry. In the eastern half of the county Beccles, an important market town in the middle ages and later, includes amongst its records sixteenth and seventeenth-century references to hemp preparation. The town's 'taske' or tax book for 1593 contains regulations concerning the mangement of the extensive fens. Two of these refer to hemp; no hemp could be laid to ret in any water or ditches on the fen except in a place called the 'Fleate'; and no one was to dig up the soil of the fen to lay on hemp. In the following century the court leet book of the manors of Beccles and Wade Hall records a number of fines levied on those who retted hemp in the river Waveney, and in one case in 1654 a man named James Carter was fined 3s. 4d. for retting his hemp within 40 feet of the river.[1] This last indicates that seepage of fouled water from pits and ditches must have been a problem.

It is doubtful whether a linen-weaver needed to serve a seven-year term of apprenticeship to learn his trade, and this is probably also true of most of the simpler crafts. In the case of weavers of exceptionally fine linen or of complicated patterns it may have been necessary, but the great majority of East Anglian workers produced plain linens. Amongst the many eighteenth-century apprenticeships of pauper children there are a number of linen-weavers, but the length of the term specified (seven years or until the age of 24) may have been due as much to a desire to ensure that the child was permanently off the parish's hands as to a real need for that length of instruction in the trade. In any case the law laid down that boys should be apprenticed until the age of 24 and girls until they were 21. A seventeenth-century example of an apprenticeship of a pauper child to a linen-weaver comes from the parish of Metfield in Suffolk. In return for a payment of £6 Henry Rackham, linen weaver of the same place, agreed to take Robert Goodwin as his apprentice until the boy reached the age of 24 years, and 'to teach instruct and Informe him in the Craft and misterie which he the said Henry Rackham now useth Commonly Called the weaverscraft'.[2]

Later opinion on the whole supports the view that linen-weaving was not a difficult trade and could be quickly learnt. A recent writer has said that 'Cotton hand-loom weaving, from its earliest days, was an unskilled, casual occupation which provided a domestic by-trade for thousands of women and children, whose earnings were normally quite

---

[1] Beccles Town Hall. Taske Book for 1593, and A28/1, Court Books for manors of Beccles and Wade Hall 1635–1711, *passim*.
[2] SROI FC91/G2/4. Apprenticeship indenture dated 20 May 1657

low.'[1] There seems no reason to doubt that exactly the same was true of linen hand-loom weaving, and the same author suggests that plain weaving on hand-looms could be quickly learnt, in as little a time as three weeks, and that only fancy weaving required greater experience and dexterity.[2]

In the case of a craft which can have changed little over two centuries, evidence given in the 1830s concerning learning its skills can be applied to an earlier period. Opinions expressed, on the subject of training of linen-weavers, by witnesses quoted in the report of the Parliamentary Commission on Hand-Loom Weavers (1840) vary. One said that the weaving of sacking could be learnt quickly and easily, but that of hemp and flax was a difficult trade to master.[3] In south Norfolk John of Smith of Wymondham, the son and grandson of linen weavers, 'took to weaving in 1803 at the age of 12', and in twelve months was 'master of his business'.[4] At North Lopham the assistant commissioner was informed that 'The race of weavers is kept up by the fathers teaching their sons.' Boys accustomed to the trade from early youth 'readily learn weaving, but a man from field labour would be difficult to teach'.[5] The witnesses also disagreed over whether linen-weaving could be carried out by women and children. In one case it was stated that the weaving of hemp and flax required the 'exertion of considerable strength' and was too heavy and fatiguing for women and children, yet at Haverhill in south-west Suffolk the commissioner reported that out of 450 looms making drabbetts, a coarse fabric with hemp warp and cotton weft, 300 were worked by women and children. Claims that hand-loom linen weaving was difficult to learn may well have been an attempt by the linen-weavers to limit the numbers entering their trade. Their evidence was inevitably biased; indeed in times of high demand Irish labourers were employed temporarily to weave linen, and this depressed the wages and status of the regular weavers. Finally the fact that linen-weaving was often an occupation for paupers suggests that it was not a particularly hard skill to acquire.

Linen-weavers like other rural craftsmen, turned to urban markets as soon as they produced more than could be sold in their own villages. In the early fifteenth century Newmarket was one such urban linen market, and its court rolls provide evidence of the existence of 'le Draprerowe' in which John Prydynton 'lyndraper' purchased two stalls in 1408. There are a number of other references to stalls in 'le lyn-

[1] Bythell, p.270
[2] ibid, p. 43
[3] *Parliamentary Papers 1840*, XXIII, p.350
[4] Eric Pursehouse, *Waveney Valley Studies* (Diss, 1965), p.180, henceforth Pursehouse, and *Parliamentary Papers 1840*, XXIII, p.328
[5] Parliamentary Papers *1840*, XXIII, p.354

draperye' or 'le Draperye', two alternative names for Drapers row.[1] In the following century the court records for the manor of Harleston mention various rows of stalls, including a drapers rows.[2] The Norfolk market town of Harleston stands in the Waveney valley roughly half way between Diss and Bungay, and it was here that a local gentleman purchased 26 yards of 'hempynge cloth' at the midsummer fair of 1598.[3]

IV

In the sixteenth century the government first began to take an interest in hemp and its products. An Act of Parliament of 1532/3 compelled farmers to grow a quarter of an acre of hemp or flax for every 60 acres 'apt for tillage'.[4] After being twice renewed this Act lapsed at the end of Henry VIII's reign, only to be revived in 1563 when the area to be sown with hemp or flax was raised from a quarter to one acre and the fine for failure to comply was raised from 3s. 4d. to £5, a substantial sum for that date. The preamble to the relevant section of the statute stated that it was made, like its predecessor, 'for the better provision of nets, for help and furtherance of fishing, and for eschewing of idleness.[5] These Acts were not popular, and the latter was repealed in 1593.

There is good reason to doubt their effectiveness in East Anglia, whatever they may have achieved elsewhere. The areas in which hemp was chiefly grown were dairy-farming districts, where there was little arable land, and the fens. A great increase in the quantity cultivated around Upwell and Outwell, immediately after the district had been drained in the seventeenth century, has been deduced from the evidence of probate inventories.[6] In the sixteenth century hemp-growing was a speciality of the Lincolnshire fens, and the working of hemp and flax was a common by-industry there.[7] Farms with 60 or more acres of arable were most likely to be found in the sheep-corn regions of Suffolk and Norfolk, where the light, sandy soil was then considered unsuitable for the cultivation of hemp and flax. Thus the Acts could do nothing to increase the quantities sown of these two crops in areas where they were already widely grown, and only caused them to be disliked and evaded in districts where arable farming predominated. Even greater resent-

---

[1] *Court Rolls of Newmarket in Suffolk 1408-10*, edited by Peter May (Newmarket, 1973)
[2] Harleston Hundred Court Book 1564-71, court held for manor of Harleston 27 September 1571. In private ownership.
[3] SROI HA12/B1/2/107
[4] 24 Henry VIII cap. 4
[5] 5 Elizabeth I cap. 5, section XXVIII
[6] Personal communication from Dr Mark Overton
[7] Joan Thirsk, *English Peasant Farming* (1957), p.41

ment was caused in 1583 when the Queen granted to Robert Kirk a patent allowing him to collect the fines paid in Norfolk and Suffolk for failure to sow hemp and flax, and to use the money so raised to pay for the building of Sheringham pier on the north Norfolk coast. Corn-farmers in these two counties saw no reason why they should contribute to the cost of improvements to a harbour from which most of them were unlikely to derive any benefit. Amongst the papers of Nathaniel Bacon of Stiffkey there are many letters of protest against Kirk's patent, and other documents concerned with the collection of fines, which were considerable. In 1592 the total sum collected in this way in Norfolk was £1115 6s. 4d.; the largest amount was paid by Launditch hundred in central Norfolk and the smallest by Earsham half hundred in the Waveney valley. It is intriguing to find that in hemp-growing districts, such as the latter hundred, it was still possible to levy fines for failing to comply with the Statute.

Henry VIII's chief stated motive in enforcing the growing of hemp and flax was the need to supply the navy with ropes and sails. The Elizabethan Act of 1563 added the giving of occupation to the idle poor to the encouragement of the making of English cordage. Immediately after the repeal of the latter Act in 1593, the inhabitants of Beeston and Sheringham, who saw their hopes of a new pier receding, protested against its repeal.[1] An Act of Edward VI (1551), which confined the manufacture of felt hats, coverlets, dornicks and diaper linen to Norwich and all other corporate or market towns in Norfolk,[2] was different in intention from the Henrician law; its aim was to protect urban industries from rural competition. Blomefield mentions that the south Norfolk village of Pulham was specifically excepted from this Act 'as those trades had there been followed for some time past. . . .', and the materials 'were made in great quantities here'.[3]

Both before and after the repeal of the Act of 1563, other attempts were made to encourage the cultivation of hemp and flax. In 1576 the House of Commons addressed to the Queen a request for regulations for their cultivation and use and also asked that their export should be prohibited.[4] In the same year a petition to the House of Lords requested that it should read a bill for the better cultivation of flax, hemp and rape seed.[5] In November 1601 a bill to enforce the sowing of hemp at the rate of a quarter of an acre for every 20 acres of tillage land was read twice, but proceeded no further.[6] The stated aim of this bill

[1] SP 12 244/112
[2] 5 and 6 Edward VI, cap. 24
[3] Blomefield, V, p.393
[4] SP 12 107/53
[5] SP 12 107/74
[6] SP 12 282/42

was to supply yarn for cordage and the making of linen, while that of
another bill, read once only in the same year, was to furnish the navy
with good and sufficient cordage and to set poor people to work.[1]
An undated document, but probably of Elizabeth I's reign, contains
proposals for making fustian with imported cotton, and linen with flax
grown in England and Ireland. The writer added that growing flax and
making fustian and linen would employ the poor.[2]

Here we already have two of the three main reasons put forward time
and again over a period of three centuries for the encouragement of the
cultivation of hemp and flax. These were to supply the navy with
essential materials, and to provide employment for the poor; the third
motive was a desire to decrease imports both of yarn and of materials
made from hemp and flax. It is only necessary to look at the London
import figures for 1559 and 1565 to see why 'All politicians and writers
agreed monotonously on the necessity to grow these crops at home.[3] In
the latter year linen cloth was not only the most valuable import but also
worth almost double wine, the runner-up. The total value of all
imported items made from hemp and flax was £144,863 in 1559 and
£161,288 in 1565; wine imports were worth £68,454 in the former and
£48,634 in the latter year. Although flax and linens made from it were
more valuable than imports of hemp and its products, the latter were
still considerable; for example canvas, which was always made from
hemp, was worth £39,072 in 1559 and £32,124 in 1565. London was not
the only English port, so total imports must have been greater than the
figures given here.

The patchy survival of port books for London and other places
makes it impossible to study imports of flax and hemp over a period of
years. Rather more are extant for the seventeenth than for the preceding century, so the main discussion of this aspect of the linen trade will
be found in chapter 4. Nevertheless, it is worthy of notice here that
although hemp was a far less significant import in the sixteenth than it
was to become in the following century, the quantity imported from the
Baltic region rose from 12 lasts in 1568 to over 134 in 1588; during the
same 20 years flax imports increased more slowly, from 206 to 279
lasts.[4] Last originally meant a load, and is a variable measure depending
on the commodity and locality. A last of flax or hemp is generally taken
to equal two tons of 4000 lbs each. The demands of the navy may

[1] SP 12 282/63
[2] BL Lansdowne 110, no 50
[3] Thirsk, 1978, p.73 and appendix I for import figures, which are taken from PRO SP
12/8, no 31 and BL Lansdowne MS 8/17
[4] Henryk Zins, *England and the Baltic in the Elizabethan era*, (Manchester, 1972), pp.
219–20

account for hemp imports rising faster than flax, particularly as 1588 was the year of the Armada.

A debt case brought by a King's Lynn merchant and heard in the Court of Requests in 1586 was probably concerned with imported hemp. The quantity of hemp involved was 100 hundredweights. This may have been grown locally, but it seems more likley that it had been imported.[1]

There are many other documents concerned with the import of linen, hemp and flax from a number of countries. In July 1571 John Grey, an English draper, wrote from Hamburg to Lord Burghley about the fall in the price of English wool and cloth exported to the Low Countries, and the rise in the cost of goods imported thence; these included linen. Grey proposed that imports from the Low Countries should be banned and that this would result in their prices falling, and would be damaging to the Spanish Governor, the Duke of Alva, who would lose the support of the inhabitants of the country.[2] In 1591 the governor of the Russia Company wrote to its agent, Christopher Holme, to inform him that hemp was scarce that year,[3] and in the same year of shortage the Hanse towns were ordered not to supply Spain or Portugal with certain goods, including flax, tow, hemp and canvas for sailcloth.[4] The Baltic and the Low Countries were respectively England's main suppliers of hemp and flax, and of linen, but some came from closer to home: in 1599 Richard Carmarden received a licence, valid for seven years, to import linen yarn from Ireland.[5]

Two of the many men, who put forward proposals for increasing the growing of hemp and the manufacture of cordage and cloth, were Thomas Trolloppe and Lawrence Cockson. In 1561 the former wrote to Cecil to give him details of his plans for erecting hemp-beating mills and for the manufacture of canvas and linen cloth in England.[6] Amongst the state papers is a printed tract, also dated 1561, and written by Trolloppe to describe the contents of his book about hemp mills and canvas making.[7] He had devised a mill and a 'kyll' to beat and dry hemp as fine as flax; each mill would cost to build the then very considerable sum of £100. His three main reasons for advocating the growing of hemp and flax were first, their high yield, £10 per acre as opposed to £2 an acre for land used to graze sheep; second 100,000 girls and women, starting at the age of 7, could spin sufficient yarn to employ

[1] PRO REQ2 269/27
[2] *Calendar SP Dom.* 1566–79, Addenda pp. 356–7
[3] SP 12 238/163
[4] SP 12 241/18
[5] SP 12 272/23
[6] SP 12 17/48
[7] SP 12 17/49

60,000 weavers and boys; the latter being engaged in winding yarn; third, he believed that there were 1,800,000 women living in the country, and that if 600,000 of their number spun two ounces of flax or hemp every day they would earn £1,200,000 a year. Not everyone was as enthusiastic about Thomas Trolloppe's project as he was himself. He approached the aldermen of Stamford, who wrote to Cecil in July 1561 about Trolloppe's proposal to make canvas in the town.[1] They explained that they could not afford to purchase £1333 worth of hemp to set to work 300 or 400 people. Their own modest proposal was to buy a mere 20 or 40 stones of hemp and to start a manufacture of canvas with 'suche skilfull p[er]sons as we can gett'. If this succeeded they would then consider proceeding with building the mill and with Trolloppe's much larger enterprise.

Lawrence Cockson's proposals, made to Burghley in 1576, concerned the sowing of flax and hemp, from which linen cloth, cables, nets and poldavis could be made, and of rape to be crushed for its oil.[2] The oil from the seeds of all three plants could be used to make soap, and train oil, which was used in curing leather. Like Trolloppe, he pointed out that hemp, rape and flax were more profitable than any other crop as is 'well known to them that soweth yt in Lincolneshere Norfolke and elsewhere'. His main reasons for putting forward his proposals were that they would employ the poor and idle, at the same time as they decreased imports. In his own words, his proposals were 'for settinge on worke of a multytude for the avoydinge of the great abhomynable vice of Idlenes', and would provide employment for over 100,000 'idle, Rogishe, younge, olde ympotent and lame people' aged from 6 to 60 years. He envisaged this multitude engaged in pulling the crops, and taking then through all the stages of their preparation including spinning, weaving and dyeing. He enumerates a list of goods which were then imported but could be made in England, and which included nets, cables, fishing lines, girths, thread, sack cloth, linen cloth, inckles, dornix and poldavis.

Not only inertia and timidity can be blamed for the failure to adopt grandiose schemes such as those of Thomas Trolloppe; fear of competition from immigrants may also have played its part. Horner believed that Edward III introduced into England linen-weavers as well as other Flemish textile workers in the second quarter of the fourteenth century, at which date Flanders was as much ahead in linen manufacture as it was to be two centuries later. Furthermore, he thought that if English laws preventing foreigners from setting up as master workmen in any trade already known in England had not existed, the linen-weavers of

[1] SP 12 18/22
[2] SP 12 107/51

Antwerp would have moved there rather than to Holland after the sack of their town by the Duke of Parma in 1585: 'England lost a chance, which Holland gained, of establishing a flourishing linen industry.'[1] Horner is not entirely right about the English linen industry, with which only 52 pages of his 576 pages long work are concerned, but where high quality linens are concerned he is largely correct.

Excellent in theory though the ideas of men such as Cockson and Trolloppe may have been, they were not very practical. The constant exhortations of government and private individuals throughout the seventeenth century suggest that much of the advice and recommendations fell on stony ground. Nevertheless, the English linen industry as a whole, and that of East Anglia in particular, did grow considerably in the seventeenth century and the origins of this growth are to be found in the preceding century.

V

As explained earlier, there is a marked shortage of evidence on linen weavers in Norfolk and Suffolk before 1600 (see p. 40). Comparison with Jenning's work on Nidderdale and with Lowe's study of Lancashire textile manufacturing in the sixteenth century reveals that anyone working on industry in East Anglia in the same period is also seriously hampered by the small numbers of probate inventories surviving for the Tudor age. The former was able to draw upon 207 inventories dating from 1551 to 1610 for the Forest of Knaresborough, while 130 sixteenth-century inventories form a major source for Lowe's book. From Norfolk and Suffolk we have 10 linen weavers' inventories prior to 1600 in date. The probate inventories of the Norwich consistory court start in 1553 (but only 23 date from before 1584), and those from the Archdeaconry of Sudbury in 1573, but there is a gap from 1577 to 1647 and they are not numerous before 1660. The case of the Archdeaconry of Suffolk is even worse: its total number of surviving inventories is low, and apart from 1582-4 and 1590, none date from earlier than 1685. Very few inventories are extant for the two Norfolk archdeaconries. Inevitably probate records, and in particular inventories, are a major source for any study of rural industry before 1700 and remain valuable in the eighteenth century.

Although there are only ten pre-1600 East Anglian linen weavers' inventories they cover a fairly wide range and in this respect set the pattern for the following century. In value they range from £3 10s. 6d. to £66 10s. 3d., with a mean of £21 8s. 9d. With so small a sample averages have little value, and it is more useful to know that four

[1] Horner, pp. 218-219

inventories had a total value of under £10, three were worth between £32 and £37 and the richest, that of a twill-weaver, was valued at just over £66. Only the two richest weavers could be described as farming, but five others had a very minor involvement in agriculture. Of these five, one owned harvested crops worth just over £2 in addition to a cow and two fowls, another possessed a yearling bullock, the third a few geese, the fourth a horse and two cows with a little hay, and the last a cow and two young pigs. It is clear that the two wealthiest weavers were in quite a different class: the twill-weaver's livestock and crops totalled £11 4s. 0d., while in the case of the only other man to have left goods worth over £50, his crops, growing on nine acres, were worth over £8, while his livestock was valued at more than £24 and included six cows with four heifers and calves, and eight horses of various ages in addition to pigs and poultry. The presence of far more horses than this man can have needed for his farm suggests either that he was horse-breeding of that he used them to carry his linen cloth to market.

Two of the men possessed no furniture, and the poorest only a few items in addition to his clothes, which rather surprisingly included a silk girdle with a silver pendant. The household goods of all but one other could have fitted into one room, which may indicate that they were lodgers. It is not the richest man who lived in either of the only two dwellings whose rooms were enumerated; but his wealth was concentrated in his farming and weaving activities.

Turning to the information about these men's craft, William Rowse of Worthing in Norfolk was an apprentice when he died in 1598, and his inventory tells us that it was for this reason that his apparel was not appraised.[1] It is curious to note that although his master owned his clothes, he possessed his own loom, and 163 yards of the cloth he had woven was also valued as part of his goods. The only two weavers of these ten not to own at least one loom were Henry Howghton of Ludham, whom we must assume to have been a journeyman or apprentice as reference is made in his inventory to a bond in his master's hands;[2] and Alexander Lybeons of Parham, Suffolk the twill-weaver and the man with the richest inventory.[3] It is odd that neither his inventory nor will mentions a loom. Well over half his wealth was tied up in yarn and 60 pieces of twill or sack cloth; twill was a coarse linen cloth. Even the poorest weaver, John Koke of Wingfield, one of the only two to live in Suffolk, owned a pair of linen looms and six yards of linen cloth when he died in 1584.[4] The other two weavers whose inventories totalled less than £10 owned respectively one and two

[1] NRO NCC INV/15/55A
[2] NRO NCC INV/10/99
[3] SROI FE1/2/126
[4] SROI FE1/1/70

looms. James Beamond of Acle[1] and Edmund Barit of Hevingham,[2] the second richest weaver, both possessed three looms with slays and other 'things belonging', while John Holbroke of Earsham in addition to his two looms owned 'other furniture to them belonging' and this included warping bars and 'travises'.[3] Both the men who owned three looms must be assumed to have been master weavers employing one or more workmen, and it is possible that the two possessors of two looms apiece were also employers. Robert Valye of Bungay, whose inventory made in 1590 totalled just under £20,[4] mentioned two servants in his will.[5] These two men must have been apprentices or journeymen. One, Lionel Browne, was left his master's best loom standing in the 'foreshoppe' together with two pairs of slays, temples and a shuttle; this loom was valued at 10s. in the inventory. To the other, Edward Smythe, Robert Valye bequeathed two more slays. Slays, wheels, pulleys and yarn were also mentioned in the wills in which looms were bequeathed.

Although these ten men do not include in their number any of the really rich linen weavers who were not uncommon in the seventeenth century, they give a fair indication of the range of wealth and activity of members of the trade, including as they do self-employed weavers with one loom, master weavers and one who did not own his loom and worked for another man. They also indicate that it was common for weavers to have some small involvement in husbandry, and not unusual to find those whose farming activities were the major source of their wealth.

Moving to sixteenth-century linen weavers' wills they are rather more numerous, totalling 39 and including those of four men whose inventories have already been analysed. It is impossible to quantify the evidence of wills, and their value as a source of information is extremely variable. Nevertheless, they sometimes mention looms and often indicate ownership of land, crops and livestock. Of the 39 considered here, 18 (46 per cent) include bequests of land and 11 of these also mention houses. One testator, living in Bungay, apparently owned a house, but no land. Two of these wills which do not refer to land include bequests of corn and cattle. Only nine of the testators made bequests of looms, but six of these men owned more than one. The most interesting of these weavers is John Banok alias Barber of the large north Suffolk village of Stradbroke, who died in 1542.[6] He described

[1] NRO NCC INV/6/108
[2] NRO NCC INV/12/106
[3] NRO NCC INV/15/66
[4] SROI FE1/2/47
[5] SROI ICAA2/33/158
[6] SROI ICAA1/12/251

himself as the minstrel of Stradbroke and as a weaver, and his will makes it evident that he also farmed and was thus a man of three occupations. He asked other weavers to divide his looms and other utensils and gear of 'wever crafte' between his two sons. Three of the twill-weavers used the now obsolete word studdles when bequeathing looms. The dictionary defintion of studdles is 'weaver's implements', but one of these wills makes it clear that the term was intended to mean looms: 'all my weavinge lomes or studdles'.[1]

The 39 sixteenth-century weavers whose wills have survived include one dornick weaver and 17 twill weavers. Dornick was a cloth, often of linen, which was originally made at Doornick (Tournai) in Flanders. The twill-weavers form an interesting sub-group. Altogether only 29 are known, nearly 60 per cent of whom died before 1600 and only four later than 1640. The majority are clustered in the area of east Suffolk just north of Woodbridge, not a district in which many other linen weavers are known to have lived. Two conclusions may tentatively be put forward about this sub-group: the first is that after the middle of the seventeenth century twill-weaving ceased to be regarded as a separate trade; and the second is that the twill-weavers may have been involved in the same decline as the Ipswich sail-cloth weavers, whose industry, after a period of success in the second half of the sixteenth century, declined in the following century.[2]

Taken as a group, the 45 sixteenth-century linen-weavers whose wills or inventories have survived must be regarded as the élite members of their craft, whose social and economic circumstances differed little from those of husbandmen or small yeoman farmers. Almost certainly many others were too poor to make wills, and yet more who were part-time weavers must be concealed under some other occupational description.

VI

Nidderdale, Lancashire and the wood-pasture region of East Anglia all shared one important characteristic in the sixteenth and seventeenth centuries: they were areas of pastoral farming. Geographically and scenically the uplands of a Yorkshire dale and of its western neighbour seem today to have little in common with the low relief of Norfolk and Suffolk. But in the early modern period the wood-pasture districts of the two latter counties specialised in dairy-farming and displayed all the characteristics of a pastoral region: scattered villages and outlying farms linked by meandering lanes, small early-enclosed fields, large

[1] SROI ICAA2/25/74, Will of Richard Awger of Eyke
[2] *Victoria County History of Suffolk*, edited by W. Page, 2 vols, II, (1907), pp. 171–3

numbers of smallholders and flourishing by-industries. In sixteenth-century Nidderdale, just as in East Anglia, most weavers were also farmers and the scale of their farming was similar to that of non-weaving farmers; many of them made cloth for their own use only. At the same time there also existed in that area a class of 'customer weavers', mainly cottagers dependent on weaving for their living and who wove other men's yarn into cloth. In the period 1551–1610 only two of the Forest of Knaresborough weavers owned more than one loom. The range of wealth of Nidderdale weavers was small, whereas in both East Anglia and Lancashire it was wide. Although at this date wool was the main fibre worked in the dale, hemp and flax were both grown there and 86 out of 207 inventories listed textile equipment, yarn or fibres.[1]

In the sixteenth century linen-weaving in rural Nidderdale more closely resembled the state of the East Anglian industry than did the 'highly developed industry' in the area round Manchester and else-where in Lancashire described by Lowe.[2] Flax, much of it imported from Ireland, rather than hemp was the chief fibre used by the Lanca-shire weavers, most of whom were independent and bought their yarn from dealers. These middlemen, some of whom also engaged in bleach-ing, were extremely important to the Lancashire linen industry and the long lists of debts included in the inventories of some of them show that they dealt with large numbers of spinners and weavers. A few of these middlemen also bought and sold cloth, and can truly be described as linen manufacturers; they were the equivalent of the wealthy clothiers found in the cloth areas of late medieval Suffolk. Some of these men were called linen drapers and sold the cloth they had purchased not only locally, but as far afield as London and Stourbridge Fair.

The case of Robert Marler, a Lancashire chapman whose will and inventory were proved in the Norwich Consistory Court, shows how far afield some dealers in linens travelled in the late sixteenth century. Most of his few possessions were in his home town of Falsworth, but he had left some sacking and bed hangings in the cloth hall at Norwich, and £52 in cash in the hands of a grocer living in the parish of St Peter Mancroft in the same city. Several Norfolk men owed him money for sacking, including some sold by him at Lynn Mart, and he himself was indebted to a Norwich lace weaver for 20s. Amongst his cash legacies were several small sums to residents of Norwich, including a servant at the White Lion, The evidence of Marler's probate documents shows a dealer in sacking, almost certainly Lancashire made, who travelled across England with his three horses as far as Norwich, where he lodged

[1] Jennings, pp. 163–4
[2] Lowe, pp. 43–55

at the White Lion. The complexity of trading in late Elizabethan England is illustrated by the affairs of this man who was owed money by persons living in places as far apart as Manchester, Newark on Trent and East Dereham.[1]

By the end of the sixteenth century in Lancashire 'the transition from an industry consisting of small but completely independent weavers and spinners, to one in which they were completely dependent for yarn and marketing of cloth, on the capitalist draper or clothier, had begun.[2] Although the East Anglian evidence at this date is very sparse, it seems safe to say that no such development had yet occurred there.

Regrettably the picture of the medieval and Tudor origins from which the East Anglian industry was to spring in the seventeenth century has had to be general rather than particular. The sixteenth century sources will not allow an in-depth study to match those made elsewhere. Until 1600 linen-weaving and its ancillary employments in Norfolk and Suffolk were in the main still in their peasant stage and were widely diffused, particularly in the Middle Ages. In the sixteenth century inventories from many counties, such as Oxfordshire, Lincolnshire, Shropshire and Wiltshire, mention hemp, yarn, linen wheels and other tools used in the production of hempen cloth. In this respect East Anglia did not differ from these widely dispersed areas, but chapter 4 will show that it was one amongst several regions where in the following century linen production grew into something much more highly developed and important than a localised, peasant and predominantly part-time occupation.

---

[1] NRO NCC Home 243, will made 9 May 1588 and NRO INV4/36, inventory made 31 May 1588. I should like to thank Dr Margaret Spufford for drawing my attention to Robert Marler and for allowing me to refer to him.
[2] Lowe, p. 55

4 Growth of the Linen Industry, 1600–1730

'In the days when spinning-wheels hummed busily in the farmhouses'
George Eliot, *Silas Marner*

I

The handful of late Elizabethan linen-weavers' inventories and wills indicates that by the last two decades of the sixteenth century the East Anglian linen industry was already changing from one composed almost entirely of independent single-loom weavers towards a more sophisticated and organised trade in which poor, part-time weavers existed alongside masters employing one or more journeymen. An essential pre-condition for a development of this nature was a social and economic climate in which rural industry could flourish. Before turning to a survey of a century which was that of the industry's greatest growth, and which also saw the largest number of prosperous linen-weavers, we need to look closely at the economic and social conditions which favoured the expansion of the linen industry in Norfolk and Suffolk. What were the social and economic conditions necessary for the development of the linen industry, and were they present in East Anglia? The majority of these conditions were not peculiar to the success of linen production, but were equally necessary for the development of any rural industry.

Anyone writing about rural industries in early modern England owes a great debt to Dr Thirsk, and particularly to her *Economic Policy and Projects* (1978), which has drawn the attention of historians to an extraordinary variety of new industries and crops whose introduction and development wrought a revolution in the country's economy.[1] More than geographic reasons are required to explain the growth of industries in the countryside; social circumstances are also relevant. In some cases the presence of the raw material may well have been the deciding factor as it was for example in the development of metal-working around Sheffield,[2] but other rural industries imported most of

[1] Much of this paragraph and the next is based on Joan Thirsk, 'Industries in the Countryside', in *Essays in the Economic and Social History of Tudor and Stuart England*, edited by F.J. Fisher (Cambridge, 1961), henceforth Thirsk, 1961
[2] David Hey, 'The Rural Metalworkers of the Sheffield Region', *Department of English Local History Occasional Papers*, 2nd series, no 5 (Leicester, 1972)

their raw material. This is true both of the medieval Suffolk clothiers, much of whose wool came from the Midlands, and of the later East Anglian linen-weavers whose demand for flax and hemp could not be satisfied by the locally grown product, although hemp was widely cultivated in the area with the greatest concentration of linen-weavers. Nor was it essential for water transport to be easily available; in the sixteenth century West Country cloth merchants carried their merchandise to London by road. East Anglian linen-weaving was mainly concentrated in the valleys of the rivers Waveney and Little Ouse, both of which were navigable far higher than they are today. These two rivers, and the region's numerous ports, were also used for shipping the cheese and butter produced in the same areas of Norfolk and Suffolk as linen cloth.

Dr Thirsk considered six areas, ranging from Westmoreland to Kent, in which industries with a national market were combined with farming, and found that they had the following factors in common: 'a populous community of small farmers, often mainly freeholders or customary tenants with a tenure almost as good as freehold, pursuing a pastoral economy'.[1] Small freeholds were common, the most usual form of customary tenure was copyhold of inheritance, which offered almost as much security as freehold, and many farmers held by both forms of tenure in wood-pasture East Anglia, which was devoted to pastoral farming.

Another essential pre-condition for the emergence of rural industry is a growing population for which agriculture does not offer sufficient employment. Less labour was required by dairy than by arable farms, and the failure of farming to absorb the growing workforce led to much under-employment in an area where family-run farms were the rule. The late sixteenth and early seventeenth centuries were a period of demographic growth, and certain areas attracted immigrants as well as absorbing their own increased populations. In wood-pasture Norfolk and Suffolk manorial organisation was weak, manors were rarely co-terminous with villages and several small manors within each parish were common. This was an important factor in permitting the rapid growth of population through both natural increase, and immigration from areas unable to absorb a larger workforce. At a later date many linen-weaving parishes were 'open' villages.

It has been suggested that inheritance customs influenced the size of local populations, but this argument is difficult either to substantiate or to refute. A complication is that two manors within one parish may follow different customs. A survey of Suffolk manors that practised Borough English, and based on three sources, was not very conclusive,

---

[1] Thirsk, 1961, p. 86

largely because for many places no information was available.[1] There are two clusters of parishes where Borough English was said to be the custom in at least one manor. The first coincides reasonably well with the main linen-weaving area, but does not extend further down the Waveney valley than Harleston, while the second lies north and north-west of Ipswich. This latter district is not one much associated with linen-weavers, but it is possible that it supported some other rural industry. Gavelkind is rare in East Anglia, and generally speaking partible inheritance was less common than primogeniture. It is possible that Borough English did not resemble primogeniture in keeping only one son on the family holding and forcing the others to move away, but that the youngest son inherited merely the residue of his father's property from which provision had already been made for the elder sons. If this theory – that Borough English achieved the same result as partible inheritance – is correct, it may have had some effect in increasing the numbers of small holdings in the main linen-weaving area of Suffolk.

Having established that weak manorial organisation, partible inheritance, and numerous smallholdings, all factors which encouraged the growth of population and in particular of large numbers of under-employed people, existed in wood-pasture East Anglia, it is clear that by the end of the sixteenth century it was a region ripe for industrial growth. Rural industry influenced local demography in two ways: the existence of a large rural population attracted industry, but at the same time the industry drew in people from areas where similar opportunities were lacking.

The appearance of a new industry or the growth of an old one can often be associated, as in the Forest of Arden,[2] with an agricultural crisis as much as with a surge in population, but in East Anglia it seems that the latter rather than the former must be the main factor behind the region's industrial growth in the seventeenth century. This century was a difficult one for producers of grain and wool, both commodities whose prices fell and remained low for many years. Dr Thirsk concluded that the decline of the small landowner in the seventeenth century was not ubiquitous, but occurred only in arable or newly enclosed pasture regions. Small farmers lacked the capital to improve production and were unable to pay the high costs of the labour required

[1] 'The Custom of Borough English', *Proceedings of the Suffolk Institute of Archaeology*, II (1854–9), 236–241; *The Chorography of Suffolk*, edited by D.D. MacCullough, Suffolk Record Society, 19 (Ipswich, 1976); and W.A. Copinger, *The Manors of Suffolk*, 7 volumes (1905–11). I am grateful to Mr Norman Scarfe for the loan of his map of the county based on the first of these three sources
[2] Victor Skipp, *Crisis and Development* (Cambridge, 1978), henceforth Skipp

on arable farms.[1] Although East Anglian dairy farmers suffered from temporary difficulties, for instance during the Thirty Years War when the activities of privateers interfered with the coastal trade to London, on the whole the demand for dairy produce was consistent and prices remained reasonably stable throughout the century.[2]

Wood-pasture East Anglia was not only eminently suitable for the development of rural industry, but it also resembled other areas that combined cloth-making with dairy-farming. It was a farming region similar to those parts of Wiltshire and Somerset, centred on Mere and Yeovil, where linen-weaving was an important industry.[3] Other areas supported different types of by-employment: fishing, wild-fowling and basket making in the fens, wood-turning and coopering in forest regions and lace-making in Bedfordshire and Hertfordshire are three examples of this diversity.

Economic as well as social conditions in wood-pasture East Anglia favoured industrial development. An inevitable result of an increase in population is a growth in the demand for consumer goods; this creates employment and in turn generates more wealth leading to a further rise in the size of the market for the products of domestic industries. At the same time the increase in wealth and standard of living of those who had benefited from the inflation of the Tudor period (chiefly farmers profiting from the steep rise in agricultural prices) also increased employment by injecting more cash into the economy. By-employments had long been a feature of East Anglia, as they had of other pastoral regions, but in the seventeenth century they increased on a scale never seen before.

Linen was not the only industry to be part of this expansion; the leather-manufacturing trades shared in this growth as did stocking knitting.[4] Dr Thirsk has given us the truly astonishing figures for the employment created nationally by the demand for stockings.[5] The knitting of stockings was a common by-employment in the Waveney valley, and not only in the families of fishermen. The East Anglian diarist, Philip Skipton, when travelling from Diss to Beccles in September 1667 noticed that 'spinning of wool with a rock and spindle, and knitting of stocking employes great numbers of poore in most of the county (Norfolk). The women walk up and downe as they spin and

[1] Joan Thirsk, 'Seventeenth-century agriculture and social change', in *Land, Church and People*, edited by Joan Thirsk, *Agricultural History Review*, 18, Supplement (1970) 157, henceforth Thirsk, 1970
[2] ibid., p. 150
[3] Thirsk, 1967 map on p. 4
[4] Patten, 1979, p.117
[5] Thirsk, 1978, pp. 167–8

knitt, they can knitt a stockin in a day.'[1] Thirty years after Skipton, Celia Fiennes made a journey through East Anglia and she too commented on the knitters: 'the ordinary people both in Suffolk and Norfolk knitt much and spin' and later, when on the road from Attleborough to Thetford, she added: 'still finding the country full of spinners and knitters'.[2] As most knitters were women and the wool they used and the stockings they made were the property of their employers, this industry has left little evidence in probate inventories. Two inventories from this area may be of men who were putters-out in the stocking trade. John Holmes of Palgrave, who died in 1677, was described as a yeoman, but the value of his livestock and crops was not much more than of the 'wooling yarne stockings' in his shop; in inventories this word almost always means workshop and not a retail shop.[3] In 1712 a maltster living in the same village had stored in his shop at the time of his death 200 combs of malt, and a 'parcel' of hose yarn stockings, wool and other materials 'about the yarne trade' valued at £40.[4]

The similarity between net-making and knitting naturally led to an association of the latter with fishing. Production of worsted stockings expanded at much the same time as the growth of the New Draperies, and its main East Anglian centre was along the Norfolk and Suffolk coasts, where the Customer of Yarmouth considered it to be the only employment of many of the poor. Knitting could easily be combined with watching grazing animals, or any other task that left the hands free. In the 1620s about 70,000 pairs of stockings a year were exported through Yarmouth, mainly to Rotterdam, by Norwich and Yarmouth hosiers. Their value equalled that of exports of New Draperies from the same port in this decade, but, even so, they can have represented only a fraction of the total production of stockings, which was mostly for the home market.[5] The existence of other by-employments diminished the workforce available for hemp preparation and spinning and so may have retarded the linen industry's development; yet, at the same time, a diversity of occupations was to the advantage of the local economy and helped to cushion it against changes in demand.

The seventeenth century also saw an expansion in cheese production. East Anglian cheese and butter supplied the London food market, and

[1] Christobel M. Hood, 'An East Anglian Contemporary of Pepys. Philip Skipton of Foulsham, 1641–1692', *Norfolk Archaeology*, XXII (1924) 161

[2] Fiennes, ⌐⌐. 146, 150

[3] NRO N(⌐ ⌐V60/139

[4] SROB IC500/3/38/34

[5] A.R. Michell, 'The port and town of Great Yarmouth and its economic and social relationships with its neighbours on both sides of the seas 1550–1714; an essay in the history of the North Sea economy', (unpublished University of Cambridge Ph.D. thesis, 1978), pp. 165–8, henceforth Mitchell

in time of war was used to victual the army and navy. 'Dairying maintained, and in some areas increased, the number of smallhold-ings.'[1] Thus the economic prosperity of wood-pasture farming helped to support both a part-time workforce for the linen industry and a market for its products. Hemp, like saffron, woad and madder, was a profitable crop to grow and did not require a large acreage. A combina-tion of farming and by-industry was ideally suited to the family wage-earning group, and in the seventeenth century these peasant workers may well have 'comprised somewhere near half the farming population of the kingdom'.[2] A recent article by Professor Alan Rogers indicates that not all villages that became industrialised conformed to the pattern described by Dr Thirsk, and in particular that dual occupations were rare in south Nottinghamshire and that framework knitting was not a part-time craft. He also found that it was not the poorest villages which attracted industrial growth, but those that were economically and socially homogeneous.[3] This dual economy of the pastoral farming regions was the main reason why their economic prosperity was greater than that of arable districts until its very success caused its destruction. Eventually peasant producers could no longer satisfy the demand for their goods unless they gave up part-time farming and became full-time industrial workers. But this development did not occur until the eighteenth century, and even then many rural workers continued to divide their time between two occupations.

II

Skipp, in a thought-provoking book (1978), based on a very detailed study of five parishes in the northern Forest of Arden, underlines the importance of rural industry as a factor in the success of the second attempt to break through the four to five million population barrier.[4] The first had been checked by the famine of the early fourteenth century, followed by the Black Death. No one has undertaken for any East Anglian villages the kind of detailed analysis needed to uncover a demographic crisis similar to that suffered by the Arden parishes in 1613–19. Even if no Malthusian check in the form of an 'imbalance between population and resources' occurred in rural Norfolk and Suffolk, it is clear that here, as in Warwickshire, the response to population growth was positive in that the food supply was increased through improvements in agriculture,[5] and new employment openings

[1] Thirsk, 1970, p.172
[2] ibid
[3] Alan Rogers, 'Rural Industries and Social Structure: the Framework Knitting Industry of South Nottinghamshire, 1670–1840', *Textile History*, 12 (1981) 7–36
[4] Skipp
[5] E. Kerridge, *The Agricultural Revolution* (1967), *passim*

were provided by the growth of rural manufactures.

As Skipp points out, landless cottagers needed not only a supply of food but the money with which to buy it. Farming alone could not provide sufficient extra work; the main source of new employment was the growth of long-established crafts and the introduction of new industries. In Arden the former were tanning, weaving and woodland crafts, and the new were the metal trades which spread from the Black Country. The old-established East Anglian trades such as leather, linen and some types of woollens expanded during the seventeenth century while the new worsted industry showed a remarkable growth in the areas where it took root. Both linen and leather manufacturing became more widely diffused in Norfolk and Suffolk, but it was the former which showed 'the most remarkable growth'.[1] The great virtue of all these industries was that they were labour and not capital-intensive, and in Schumacher's words were 'adding an industrial dimension' to rural communities.[2]

The changes in farming and manufacture which occurred as 'positive responses' to the crisis caused by a rising population involved social costs. Skipp shows that these could take two forms: villages became polarised either because 'the middle was removed from the local community' by squeezing out the small farmers, or, as in Arden, by establishing additional households, which could barely be supported. This latter form of polarisation produced an enlarged community with a wide impoverished base.[3] In Skipp's four Arden parishes 40% of households were exempt from paying hearth tax in the 1670s, and in the two Suffolk hundreds, Blackbourne and Hartismere, where the largest concentrations of rural linen weavers were to be found, 39 per cent of households fell into the same category in 1674. Probably many of the parishes that responded to demographic pressure in the seventeenth century by creating employment and increasing food resources later became 'open' villages, and those that responded negatively by actively encouraging emigration and discouraging immigration in due course became 'close' villages. Certainly the large Blackbourne and Hartismere hundred villages, in all of which from 39 to 55 per cent of households were exempt from hearth tax, could be described as 'open' in the nineteenth century.

The Suffolk subsidy returns for 1327 and 1524, and the 1674 hearth tax return have been used to compare linen-weaving villages with others, and this has been done for the three north Suffolk hundreds of

---

[1] Patten, 1979, pp. 115–6
[2] E.F. Schumacher, 'Industrialization through "Intermediate Technology" ', in *Developing the Third World: the Experience of the Nineteen Sixties*, quoted in Skipp, p.64
[3] Skipp, pp. 78–9

Blackbourne, Hartismere and Hoxne.[1] With a few exceptions, parishes with fewer than 20 taxpayers in 1327 did not subsequently become linen-weaving centres. By 1524 the connection between large parishes and linen-weaving is even clearer. Unfortunately the 1524 roll for Blackbourne is defective, but in the other two hundreds the only small villages in which many linen-weavers were to be found during the following three centuries lie in the Waveney valley. The 1524 subsidy is as much a guide to wealth as to population. In Hoxne hundred the average percentage of taxpayers assessed on land was only 10, and with only two exceptions it was in the parishes with small populations that this percentage was exceeded. The populous parishes had few wealthy landowners, but large numbers of men taxed on goods or wages. Hoxne, which was the largest parish in 1524 and was the home of more linen-weavers in the seventeenth century than any other parish in the hundred, produced the highest percentage of men taxed on wages (55); only 6 per cent of its inhabitants were assessed on land.

In 1674 the relationship between densely populated parishes, with a higher than average number of householders too poor to be taxed, and linen-weaving is obvious. In the majority (82 per cent) of these industrialised villages, that is those with five or more linen-weavers on map 4, a third or more of the households were exempt from the hearth tax. Only one parish stands out as an exception; this was Syleham which, with only 14 per cent of its households exempt, lies on the banks of the Waveney and is one of the few places where linen cloth continued to be produced until the present century. In Hartismere hundred over a third of the householders were exempt from hearth tax in all eight of its industrial parishes, two of which were later to be the site of Union workhouses. It was in this hundred too that two of the most poverty stricken parishes in the three hundreds were to be found. These were Botesdale, which had suffered a fire early in 1674, and Rickinghall Superior; these neighbouring villages were both linen-weaving centres. The industrialised villages were also those where linen weavers owning three or more looms, or whose inventory values were over £100 were most likely to be found. Thus were found living in close proximity capitalist weavers and large numbers of poor to provide a labour force.

Dr Mill's work on the Leicestershire framework knitters, while not completely refuting Rogers's thesis, that the middling rich village was best suited to industrial development, shows a very strong positive correlation between parishes with a high proportion of exempt and

[1] Sydenham H.A. Hervey, *Suffolk in 1327, being a Subsidy Return*, Suffolk Green Books IX (Woodbridge, 1906); Sydenham H.A. Hervey, *Suffolk in 1524, being a Subsidy Return*, Suffolk Green Books XII (Woodbridge, 1910); and Sydenham H.A. Hervey, *Suffolk in 1674, being the Hearth Tax Returns*, Suffolk Green Books XI (Woodbridge, 1905)

one-hearth households in 1670 and those which were heavily dependent on framework knitting in 1844. The industrial villages of Leicestershire and Suffolk, with their high population densities and widely distributed land ownership, resemble each other, and in both counties the continuity of these features over a long period of time is significant.[1]

A detailed inventory-based study has been made of four weaving villages, Great Ellingham in central Norfolk, Palgrave and Wortham in Hartismere and Thelnetham in Blackborne hundred; all three Suffolk parishes lie in the river valleys separating the two counties. The existence of extensive fens and heaths, many of which still survive, on both sides of the headwaters of the Little Ouse and Waveney rivers helped to provide the right conditions for the development of rural industry.

Wortham was the home of fewer linen-weavers than the other two Suffolk parishes and seems too to have been wealthier. In 1674 nearly twice as many Wortham households were taxed on three or more hearths as in Thelnetham, 17 per cent more than in Palgrave, and 14 per cent more than in Great Ellingham in 1664. Looking at the number of families living in detached houses, the relationship between the three Suffolk villages is similar, and taking the percentage of households excused from payment through poverty it is again Thelnetham which is the poorest village, but the fewest exempt persons were found in Palgrave not Wortham.[2]

Thelnetham is one of seven Suffolk Little Ouse valley parishes, all the home of many linen-weavers in the seventeenth and eighteenth centuries. A will-based survey of the distribution of yeomen in Suffolk between 1550 and 1650 does not suggest any social difference between the eastern half of Blackbourne hundred, in which these seven parishes lie, and the hundreds of Hartismere, Hoxne and Wangford to the east. Yet the general impression of these villages today is that there are fewer large or isolated farmhouses and more cottages than are found further east. In common with most settlements in pastoral regions, these villages tend to have more than one centre, each of which is fairly well nucleated.

Wortham is a fairly large parish (2762 acres) by Suffolk standards and is scattered around very extensive commons, most of which have remained unenclosed; Palgrave is small in area (1474 acres), but a neighbour of the prosperous market town of Diss; while Thelnetham is more remote than the other two and never had such large areas of greens and fens as are found in Wortham. These geographical differences

---

[1] Mills, pp. 183–203
[2] It is not possible to tell from the Great Ellingham hearth tax return for 1664 (PRO E179/253/45) whether houses were detached or not, and there are no figures for exempt persons in that year

between the three villages may go some way towards explaining the variations in their economic standing. Between 1698 and 1706 the Palgrave parish register gives the occupations of adult males. During this period six linen-weavers, four stuff-weavers and two hair-weavers were listed in addition to four glovers, three tailors, four woolcombers, two carpenters, two farriers, three shoemakers, three butchers, two maltsters and one each of the following: sawyer, miller, blacksmith, milliner, wheelwright and scrivener. Even using inventories, whose coverage is far less comprehensive, there were six kinds of craftsmen other than weavers in Palgrave, but a mere two, wheelwright and tailor, in Thelnetham. This diversification of employment may have helped to make Palgrave more prosperous than Thelnetham although its small size reduced the opportunities for farming. These three parishes differed little in size in 1674 with populations of 366 at Palgrave, 385 at Wortham and 389 at Thelnetham.[1] Yet only 44 inventories exist for the largest of the three, while there are 70 for Palgrave and 76 for Wortham. Confirmation is given by these figures to the suggestion that Thelnetham was a poorer parish than the other two.

All the evidence points to Thelnetham as a parish which concentrated on weaving to the exclusion of other crafts. It was amongst its inventories that 10 were found listing looms although their late owners were not described as weavers – in percentage terms more than five times higher than at Palgrave or Wortham. Curiously enough while nearly three-quarters of the Palgrave inventories show some involvement with growing or processing hemp, only 57 per cent do so in Thelnetham

At Great Ellingham, the Norfolk parish whose inventories have been analysed in the same way as those of the three Suffolk parishes already discussed, only just over half list hemp, tools for its preparation or looms. It was here too that was found the smallest number of loom-owners who were not named as weavers; only one compared with the ten at Thelnetham.

This village, like Palgrave, lies adjacent to a market town – in this case Attleborough – and its inventories indicate that a variety of occupations were pursued here. In addition to gentlemen, yeomen and husbandmen, there were a comber, a glover, a tanner, a wool chapman, a tailor and a carpenter. The inventory of the wool chapman suggests that he dealt mainly in stockings. In addition to four pairs of wool cards and considerable quantities of combed and uncombed wool, his possessions included stockings and hose yarn, as well as wool yarn and stockings

---

[1] There is no hearth tax return for Great Ellingham which includes both taxpayers and exempt persons, so its population cannot be estimated accurately

'abroad'.[1] It was on the road from Attleborough to Thetford that Celia Fiennes commented that the countryside was 'full of spinners and knitters'.[2] Another Great Ellingham inventory suggests the involvement in linen weaving of a man who was given no occupational description by the appraisers. James Rayner's inventory was made in 1618 and totals £1221, nearly twice as much as any other in the four parishes considered here.[3] He was owed nearly £800 and there was over £200 in cash in his well-furnished house. Amongst his possessions were linen yarn, new linen cloth including one bolt 53 yards long, and yarn at the weavers. There is no other indication of the source of his wealth, and he was farming on only a moderate scale. Was he a capitalist linen-weaver putting out work to journeymen? Rayner's will throws no light on the sources of his income, but shows that compared with other linen-weavers or yeomen farmers he was indeed rich and also charitable to the poor.[4]

Great Ellingham is a parish of medium size (2350 acres) and was described in 1845 as a dispersed village with three manors.[5] It lies in a slightly different farming region from the three Suffolk parishes discussed above. Although dairy-farming was still important, sheep were more frequently found in the Norfolk parish and the flocks were larger. Only at Wortham did as many farmers (nearly 60 per cent) own sheep and in view of the extensive commons there, this is not surprising; at Thelnetham less than 10 per cent of farmers possessed any sheep. The higher relative value of crops and the wider variety grown combined with the greater importance of sheep suggest that Great Ellingham lay in an area of mixed rather than pastoral farming.

The poor condition of Norfolk hearth tax returns make them less useful for analysing the social composition of this village. The only full legible assessment for Great Ellingham is that made in 1664, and the exemption certificate nearest in time dates from 1672.[6] Taking these two documents together, nearly half the households were too poor to pay hearth tax. A rough estimate of this village's population using the same sources is 560, which makes it considerably larger than the three Suffolk parishes; there are 53 inventories for Great Ellingham. However, inventories can be used to estimate the wealth of the community. There are nearly twice as many under £10 inventories as in Thelnetham, the poorest of the three Suffolk parishes, and more really

[1] NRO NCC INV57B/40 (made 21 October 1672)
[2] Fiennes, p.150
[3] NRO NCC INV29/277B
[4] NRO NCC Barber 370
[5] William White, *History, Gazetteer and Directory of Norfolk* (Sheffield, 1845), p.416, henceforth White's Norfolk
[6] PRO E179/253/45 and E179/336/17

rich ones than in any of them. Thus there seems to have been greater polarisation in Great Ellingham than in the other villages.

Table 4.1   Wealth from inventories

	Palgrave	Thelnetham	Wortham	Great Ellingham
Total number of inventories	70	44	76	53
Under £10	3%	9%	10.5%	13%
£10–99	76%	77%	54%	58.5%
£100–199	14%	7%	27.5%	9.5%
£200 and over	7%	7%	8%	19%
Mean value	£87	£90.5	£84	£128
Median value	£56	£50	£65	£50

The median values for all four parishes are very close, and the same is true of the mean values for the three Suffolk villages. The much higher average and the large gap between mean and median at Great Ellingham are due to there being well over twice as many inventories worth over £200 in this parish as in the other three. An indication of the relative poverty of Thelnetham is that the interval between mean and median is much wider there than at Palgrave or Wortham.

This detailed analysis of the social and economic conditions in four linen-weaving parishes, based mainly on material dating from the second half of the seventeenth century, shows that they were not dissimilar from Skipp's Arden parishes which adopted 'positive responses' to the problems created by rising population. They all, both in East Anglia and Warwickshire, display characteristics typical of 'open' villages, and those in Norfolk and Suffolk certainly deserved that description two hundred years later. It is probable that the majority, if not all, nineteenth-century 'open' parishes were industrial villages in an earlier period.

In the Lincolnshire fens village of Wrangle hemp was grown to supply the Boston ropemakers, and was probably the only cash crop for the poor.[1] What was true for this area in the seventeenth century was almost certainly equally valid for cottagers wherever hemp could be grown, and in East Anglia they were certain of a ready market for this crop. In this way the existence of a large population of cottagers helped by providing some of the raw material for a growing industry at the

[1] F. West, 'The Social and Economic History of the Fen Village of Wrangle, 1603–1837' (unpublished University of Leicester Ph.D. thesis, 1966), p.95

same time as this industry gave them employment opportunities which they would not so easily have found in open-field arable districts. One study of occupations in Tudor and Stuart East Anglia suggests that 'the most marked rise in craft manufacturing was that of linen'.[1] Both social and economic conditions in Elizabethan and Stuart Suffolk and Norfolk were right for the growth of rural industry, and the rest of this chapter will trace the development of the region's linen manufacture during the seventeenth century.

In view of the undoubted local importance of the English linen industry in such widely separated regions as Lancashire, Somerset and East Anglia, it is strange that it has been so neglected by both national and local historians. Most English linen was produced for the home rather than the export market, so the suggestion that this is the cause of its neglect is probably correct. Furthermore English linen-weavers concentrated on making coarse linen, much of what they produced continued even in the eighteenth century to be sold locally rather than nationally, and linen imports remained at a high level. Yet an industry which was so important to the economy of several regions, of which East Anglia was only one, deserves greater attention than, for instance, it received in the two standard works on the linen trade in the British Isles.[2]

III

For the period 1600–1729 a total of 842 East Anglian linen-weavers are known from a variety of sources, by far the most important of which is probate records.[3] There exist in a usable state 599 wills and 190 inventories for these 130 years; 106 of the inventories are accompanied by wills, and only 84 have survived on their own.[4] Of the remaining 159 weavers, 49 appeared in the National Apprenticeship Registers, 28 were mentioned in the wills of fellow craftsmen, thus leaving only 82 found in other sources, such as parish registers, listings and court records.

[1] J.H.C. Patten, 'The Urban Structure of East Anglia in the sixteenth and seventeenth centuries' (unpublished University of Cambridge Ph.D. thesis, 1972), p.261

[2] Horner, and A.J. Warden, *The Linen Trade, ancient and modern* (Dundee, 1864), henceforth Warden

[3] The probate records of the Norwich Consistory Court and the two archdeaconry courts covering Suffolk are fully indexed up to 1700, but the Norwich archdeaconry court wills are only indexed from 1604 to 1660 and the index for those of the archdeaconry of Norfolk ends in 1603. There are few inventories for either of these last two courts, but they are all indexed. As the majority of the probate records used for Norfolk linen-weavers are drawn from the higher court, it is inevitable that the existing bias towards richer testators has been increased.

[4] Nine of the inventories date from after 1729 (all but two from before 1750), but they have been added to the rest as nine is far too small a sample for separate analysis.

The linen-weavers, whose wills and inventories have survived, give only a minimum figure for the number of men following this trade. There is no way of estimating what proportion either of all males, or of linen-weavers made wills. All that can be said with certainty is that probate records are likely to represent only a small fraction of their total numbers. Far fewer wills date from the sixteenth than from the seventeenth century, and the increasing prosperity of craftsmen, including linen-weavers, is a reason for the rise in the latter century. The converse applied in the eighteenth century when their prosperity declined. Thus both the growth and later decrease in the figures for craftsmen's wills may be exaggerated. (Table 1.1).

Whatever the real number of linen-weavers working in East Anglia between 1600 and 1730, there is no doubt that their numbers were considerable enough to make this one of the major industries in the region. The number of linen and worsted-weavers' wills proved in the Norwich Consistory Court between 1604 and 1686 indicates that linen-weaving played at least as important a part in the local economy as did the worsted industry.[1]

The 190 linen-weavers' inventories are a sufficiently large sample for analysis, and cover a wide spectrum of wealth, but, like all probate records, are biased towards the better-off. Table 4.2 sets out in seven groups the distribution of wealth in the inventories.

Table 4.2   Wealth in 190 inventories

	1600–49		1650–99		1700–65		1600–1765
	(no.)	(%)	(no.)	(%)	(no.)	(%)	(%)
Under £5	3	6	1	1	2	6	3
£5–10	4	8	8	7.5	0		6.5
£11–20	11	22	14	13	9	27.25	18
£21–50	10	20	36	33.5	6	18.25	27.5
£51–100	13	26	19	17.5	5	15.25	19.5
£101–200	6	12	18	17.5	7	21.25	16
Over £200	3	6	11	10	4	12	9.5
Total	50	100	107	100	33	100	100

1765 is the date of the latest inventory; only two are post-1749.

The outside limits of the range of wealth are £2 13s. 0d. and £550, and there is a fairly wide gap between the mean value of £78 and the median of £45. The positive skew of the average value is due to the influence of

[1] There were 105 linen-weavers, 98 worsted-weavers and 108 weavers undifferentiated by their thread.

the 49 inventories with total values of over £100. The mode, or most commonly found value, is the group of inventories worth between £20 and £50, within which the median also falls. In Cambridgeshire in the 1660s the median wealth of craftsmen was £40, and in nine wood-pasture parishes the median value of all inventories made between 1600 and 1640 was £85, and that of yeomen was £183.[1] The only South Elmham craftsman inventory was valued at £37, so here as in Cambridgeshire the median value of yeomen's moveable possessions was roughly four and a half times that of craftsmen. Thus the median of £45 for linen-weavers' inventories shows no divergence from the usual East Anglian figure for this class.

The divison of the inventories in Table 4.2 into three periods shows a rise in the proportion of weavers with inventory values of over £100 and a decline in that of weavers of moderate wealth, those whose inventories totalled between £21 and £100. This fall is most marked after 1700 and probably marks the beginning of a trend which would continue throughout the eighteenth century. Another indication of this trend is that the gap between the mean and median of eighteenth-century inventories is £12 larger than the seventeenth-century figure. This polarisation within the linen weaving trade between a small group of rich master weavers and the great majority who were too poor even to make a will is reflected in late seventeenth-century rural society as a whole and has already been discussed in this chapter.

Apart from their wealth, much can be learnt about linen-weavers from their inventories. Particularly striking is the high proportion, three-quarters, involved in agriculture either as farmers (78) or small-holders (66). Most linen-weavers needed a horse to carry their cloth to customers or to market, and to bring home the yarn they required. Eleven of the apparently landless men owned a horse and fodder. When wills and inventories were compared, it was found that nineteen of the men whose inventories showed no involvement with farming bequeathed land, and that another six, all town-dwellers, owned houses. Clearly an analysis of inventories on their own can be mis-leading, as they showed that 54 (28.5 per cent) belonged to men with no connection with agriculture, whereas the true figure is 35 (18 per cent). Both wills and inventories have survived for fourteen of these men, who can truly be described as having no involvement in farming.

Of the 19 who bequeathed land, but whose inventories gave no indication that they were working it, three were elderly and had perhaps retired from farming (one had let his land); another seven might have handed over the running of their property to adult children.

[1] Margaret Spufford, *Contrasting Communities* (Cambridge, 1974), p.39, henceforth Spufford, 1974, and N. Evans, 'The Community of South Elmham, Suffolk 1550–1640' (unpublished University of East Anglia M.Phil. thesis, 1978) pp. 185, 217

It is more difficult to account for the absence of crops and livestock from the inventories of the remaining nine. Willaim Barefoot of Redgrave owned only 2½ acres; Nicholas Vincent, who lived at Great Ellingham, possessed nothing but hemplands, and hemp is listed in his inventory; William Flegg of Eye was a town-dweller with a piece of meadow in nearby Cranley; and Robert Garnon of Old Newton had let his land. Of the last five, John Wood of Hoxne's inventory lists dairy vessels, but the others seem totally unconnected with farming.

Table 4.3   Linen-weavers and farming

Farmers	Smallholders	Horse and fodder only	Landless	Total
78 (41%)	66 (35%)	11 (6%)	35 (18%)	190 (100%)

It is more significant that 83 per cent of the men with inventory values of £10 or less, and 38 per cent of those whose possessions were worth between £1 and £20, owned neither crops nor livestock when they died. They belonged to the landless proletariat, apparently wholly dependent on their earnings from their trade. That so few linen-weavers (a total of 28) known from inventories fall into this class is an indication of the importance of dual occupations.

Some of the smallholding weavers had little or nothing in the way of crops, and their livestock was often hardly more than a cow, a pig or two and some poultry. Other smallholdings must have made an important contribution to their owners' incomes. Such a man was Thomas Adkins of Coney Weston in Suffolk, whose three cows, three pigs, poultry and crops were worth £13, more than a quarter of the total value of his inventory.[1] His will shows that his land was freeehold.[2] Other examples are John Ringbell of Thelnetham, who owned four milk neats, two bullocks, a calf, a colt, one hog and poultry as well as cheese and butter worth £2 12s. 0d. and whose only crops were growing grass and hemp; and John Greenn of Runcton Holme near King's Lynn, who possessed no crops but had a small flock of sheep in addition to two cows, two mares and a foal.[3]

The inventories of farmer-weavers resemble those of husbandmen or yeomen of equal wealth. Amongst the poorest of these men was Robert Kempe, who ran a mixed farm at Elsing in central Norfolk. His

---

[1] SROB IC500/3/12/176, made 3 January, 1668
[2] SROB IC500/1/119/159
[3] SROB IC500/3/2/82, made 11 July, 1645, and NRO NCC INV62A/7, made 27 April 1681

inventory was drawn up just before harvest, in August 1682, and shows that he had 17 acres growing barley, rye, peas and grass, valued at £13, and owned three cows, four calves, three horses, five pigs and some hens worth a total of £12 10s. 0d.[1] Had his neighbours who appraised his goods not called Robert Kempe a linen-weaver, he would have appeared to be a husbandman. There is no indication of his trade amongst his possessions: he lived in a four-roomed, one-hearth house and in addition to his crops and livestock owned 70 cheeses valued at £10; indeed over 80 per cent of his wealth can be attributed to his farming activities.

Nicholas Rope of Hardwick in south Norfolk was farming on the scale of a minor yeoman when he died in March 1618. Together his crops and livestock were worth £45 18s. 8d., just under half the total value of his inventory.[2] He grew wheat, barley, maslin, hay and hemp, and owned a dairy herd of five cows and four calves and a small flock of sheep. His twelve ewes had already lambed and there were seven other sheep. A pig and some poultry were in his farmyard, but curiously he seemed to own no horses with which to cultivate his fields. The two looms, slays and other weaving tools listed in the inventory were bequeathed to his son, John. The presence of linen yarn and new cloth in his house indicates that he was an active weaver at the time of his death. He also owned a testament and a gun, described as 'his Artyl-lerye'. His will shows that he owned a messuage and land in Hardwick, and more land in the neighbouring parish of Shelton.[3] For seven years this property was to be his wife's to enable her to educate and bring up their three children; after this term was over it all passed to their only son. Portions of £25 were provided for their two daughters, who were to receive them at the age of 21. Nicholas Rope cannot have been an old man as he left annuities, totalling £7 10s. 0d., to both his mother and mother-in-law.

Amongst the linen-weavers with goods worth over £100 are men whose involvement in agriculture ranks with that of rich yeomen, even though in some cases a large proportion of their wealth was tied up in yarn, cloth, and weaving equipment. When the wealthiest of them all, Jonathan Eastaugh of Horham, Suffolk, died early in 1687 his estate was valued at £550 9s. 10d.[4] Cash, plate, bills, bonds, debts and mortgages amounted to £325; his linen cloth was worth just over £50 and his looms and so forth £12. As his goods included three bucking tubs and two coppers he was probably bleaching his own yarn and

[1] NRO ANW/23/1/76
[2] NRO NCC INV29/122
[3] NRO NCC Barber 243
[4] NRO NCC INV64/112

cloth. His house, whose comfortable furnishings included several books and a clock, contained at least five rooms, and the shop, dairy and bakehouse, all of which had chambers over them, may have been free-standing or attached to the main building. Fire irons are listed only in the hall and the bakehouse, but in 1674 he had paid tax on three hearths; one of these may have heated the coppers. Not surprisingly in a March inventory no cheese, butter or calves were listed, but Eastaugh possessed a sizeable dairy herd of eighteen cows as well as a young bull, five steers and four horses. His main crop was hay, valued at £22, but he also has seven combs of wheat in store and £10's worth growing in his fields. The will that accompanies this inventory contains further evidence of this man's wealth.[1] He was able to leave a house and land to three of his five surviving sons, and substantial legacies to the other two: £80 to one and £150 to the other; in addition £60 was to go to his married daughter and £110 to his single daughter, as well as £100 to an orphaned grandson. All these cash legacies were to be paid within six months of Eastaugh's death, and the property left to two of his sons had been recently purchased. His cash legacies total £586, that is £261 more than the value of his bills, bonds, mortgages and so on. One legacy of £80 was to be raised out of his 'weaving Stocke', but it is not clear where the other £181 was to come from. The combined profits of linen-weaving and farming had placed Jonathan Eastaugh in a position which enabled him to launch seven children into the world in comfort.

Finally John Tooke of Wilby, Norfolk, died possessed of goods valued at £437 19s. 6d. on 11 October 1670.[2] His good debts totalled £94 and the bad £33, and there was £13 in ready money in his six-roomed house. In his case trading activities were less important than for Eastaugh, as his cloth and yarn were worth only £14 and his looms and weaving tools nearly £16. He too was a dairy farmer with 18 cows, and also owned a bull, 10 heifers and 2 calves. As this inventory was drawn up in early autumn it is not surprising to find listed 15 firkins of butter and 12 weys of cheese. His farming was more varied as his livestock also included 3 horses, 10 lambs and 8 swine, and his crops, all of which were harvested, were wheat, barley, hemp, flax and hay. The most valuable crop was the 58 loads of hay, worth £29, which Tooke must have hoped would be sufficient to feed his livestock through the coming winter. His hemp and flax were valued at £9 10s. 0d., an unusually high figure for these two crops in an inventory, and he also owned some flax seed. Together his crops, livestock and dairy produce were worth £224 or rather more than half the total value of his inventory. In comparison Eastaugh's crops and livestock totalled £107, or not quite 20 per cent of his total wealth.

[1] NRO NCC Calthorpe 572
[2] NRO NCC INV61C/16

IV

Inventories are not a good guide to land ownership, although some list acreages of growing crops; wills, on the other hand, are much more informative. A very high proportion of the 599 usable linen-weavers' wills mention land and houses.

Unfortunately testators were seldom specific about the areas of land they bequeathed, and the stock phrase 'all my land and houses' could cover anything from a cottage and pightle to a substantial farm. Nevertheless, it is significant that only 30 per cent of the wills do not mention land and that a rather lower percentage of the inventories show no involvement in farming. The majority of linen-weavers found in probate records were obviously not solely dependent on their trade for a living, a further indication that this source is heavily biased towards the better-off craftsmen.

A number of linen-weavers were clearly substantial landowners. These were the men in a position to leave land and houses to more than one person, usually their own sons, although twenty-five of the childless testators bequeathed real estate to two or more legatees. In 46 wills it is specifically stated that land, and quite often a house as well, had been recently purchased, usually to provide for a younger son. From sixteen wills an idea can be gained of the minimum quantity of land owned, and this ranged from the 6½ acres which George Pecke of Caston in Norfolk bequeathed to his two children, to the 44 acres and more, together with four messuages, left to two nephews and a kinsman by the childless Richard Fowlsham of Letton, who had himself purchased three houses and at least 44 acres of land; the area of land attached to two of the messuages is not specified.[1] This latter man's cash bequests totalled £268, although not all were to be paid immediately after his decease. Another 10 wills mention areas of land greater than 10 acres, and a second in which four houses, each with land, were bequeathed is that of Thomas Harvy of Swanton Morley, who was in a position to leave a dwelling and land to four of his five sons.[2] It is not unusual to find linen-weavers owning property in more than one parish. William Tallbott of Earl Stonham died in 1615 leaving his two sons property in Otley which he had inherited from his own father, as well as a house and land in his own village and a messuage with yards in St Peter's parish, Ipswich.[3] A house and hempland in Bungay, and a mill at Halvergate 'as it is now furnished' and standing on half an acre of land were left to his daughter and only child by Lionie Donne in 1638; he described

[1] NRO Norwich Archdeaconry Bankes 76 and NRO NCC O.W. 1661/58
[2] NRO Norwich Archdeaconry Disney 306
[3] NRO NCC Angell 197

Table 4.4   Real estate in willsa

Land/house	Land/house left to more than one legatee	Land/house left to more than one child	Testator had bought some land
419	102	75	47
70%	17%	12.5%	8%

a Many testators appear in more than one column. Percentages are of all 599 wills.

himself as of Halvergate.[1] William Bott of Norwich owned houses and land in Neatishead, while William Brett of Gislingham left a house with land at Walton and Marham in Norfolk as well as property in his own Suffolk parish.[2] Finally a weaver, with the unusual Christian name Bezaleel and with a brother named Epaphroditus (or Theophrastus – both spellings appear in this will) Theobald, owned two freehold houses in St Peter's parish, Ipswich and in Woodbridge four copyhold dwellings in Pound Street, in addition to the freehold house in which he lived.[3]

Approximately a quarter (153) of the will-making weavers died childless and this was a strong inducement to make a will. Another 101 left at least some under-age children, and to see them provided for and to make arrangements for their upbringing was the main motive for these men drawing up a will.

Both wills and probate inventories are a valuable source for loom ownership, which was spread over all seven income groups of weavers. Only at the two lowest income levels did the possession of looms fall to half or less; in all the other groups it was nearly 70 per cent or more with the highest level reached in the £100 to £200 range where over 80 per cent of inventories list looms. Stephen Fuller of Wortwell was one wealthy weaver whose possessions seemed not to include looms, although he bequeathed an old one in his will.[4] His goods were worth well over £200, and his cloth, yarn and slays totalled nearly £100. Were his looms omitted from his inventory because they were not in his house but in those of his workmen? There are two simple explanations for the absence of looms from linen-weavers' possessions: either the man had retired from his trade, or he was employed by a master weaver who owned the loom on which he worked. Furthermore, inventories are not an infallible guide to the ownership of looms, or for that matter of any other material possession. Where it has been possible to compare wills

[1] NRO Norwich Archdeaconry Spore 207
[2] NRO Norwich Archdeaconry 1654/69 and NRO NCC Jones 180
[3] SROI ICAA1/112/7
[4] NRO INV74A/137 made 7 Nov. 1720, and NRO NCC Blomfeild 221

and inventories discrepancies have been found. John Willson of Badingham, Suffolk made his will in December 1660 leaving his second son, William, a lately purchased messuage and land, some furniture and his looms, but his inventory, drawn up two months later, lists no looms.[1] Another testator, William Cleveland a fustian weaver of Ipswich, bequeathed five looms, but only two appear in his inventory.[2] Three were left to an adult son, Timothy, and another two together with two pairs of slays and two wheels were to be inherited by the youngest son, Simon, when he reached the age of 25. Simon's looms and accompanying equipment are listed in his father's inventory, but those left to Timothy are not. Clearly the latter had removed his legacy which included warping equipment, also unlisted, before the inventory was drawn up. Presumably William Willson had acted in the same way. If it was not uncommon for legatees to remove items specifically bequeathed to them before the testator's goods were appraised, the inventories used here may well underestimate both the total of loom-owning weavers and the number belonging to individuals.

The value of looms varied from 1s. for a little, old loom to £1 13s. 4d. Some may have been worth more, but they were frequently valued together with the rest of the weaver's tools. The average valuation put upon looms was between 15s. and £1, and £15 10s. 0d. is the highest sum found for a weaver's equipment. This consisted of four looms, warping bars, three wheels, two pairs of blades, a shuttle and 43 slays, and was the property of one of the wealthiest weavers, John Tooke of Wilby, Norfolk, whose economic circumstances have already been described. His tools of trade represented only 3.5 per cent of the total value of his inventory, but for many poor weavers they formed a very high proportion of their wordly wealth. Thomas Bucknam of Wortham's loom was valued at £1, 18 per cent of the valuation of his goods.[3] The capital cost of a linen-weaver's equipment was never great, but for a poor man it represented a major investment.

Approximately a quarter of the wills mention looms, and quite often other weaving equipment such as slays and warping bars were bequeathed. Descriptions of looms in wills are frequently more detailed than those in inventories. Thomas Bennet of Debenham in 1675 left his son his 'draufte lomes' standing in the 'drauft' loom chamber.[4] Draft, spelt in various ways, was a type of cloth. A Shottisham, Suffolk, sackcloth weaver who made his will in 1659 bequeathed a great loom and a little loom.[5] The former had an iron reed and slay. A Jacobean Act

[1] NRO NCC INV49D/10 and 1660 O.W. 90
[2] NRO NCC INV21/39 and O.W. 1605 100
[3] SROB IC500/3/576
[4] SROI ICAA1/105/8
[5] SROI ICAA1/93/29; will of Thomas Jessop

Table 4.5   Loom ownership from inventories

Total value of inventory	Weavers owning looms[a]		Range of looms owned
	(no.)	(%)	
Under £5	2	33	one each
£5–10	6	50	1–2
£11–20	25	73.5	1–5
£21–50	36	69	1–7
£51–100	28	75.5	1–10
£101–200	25	80.5	1–5
Over £200	14	78	1–10

[a] Percentage of all weavers in each income group.

of Parliament had stipulated that 'mildernix and powle davies' (poldavis), both used for sail cloth, should be 'well driven with a brazen or iron shuttle'.[1] In 1671 Thomas Smyth, a Badingham linen-weaver, left his grandson and namesake 'my lomme in the backhowse as it now standeth with one brasen reed'. A metal reed was obviously more expensive to make, but presumably more long-lasting. Simon Howse of Cawston died in 1607 leaving to his man, Samuel Edwardes, the looms 'wherin he hath usallie wrought in' and four pairs of slays.[2] The description of the slays in this will suggests that they were intended for cloths of different fineness. The precise position of the loom left to William Hayns of Swanton Abbott is described in his father's will made in 1658.[3] It stood on the west side of the shop towards the brewing shop, and was the loom usually worked on by William.

An unusual feature of the will, made in 1610, of Thomas Hawkins, an Ipswich poldavis weaver, is that he left a loom to each of his three daughters.[4] His inventory lists seven looms, but only four are mentioned in his will.[5] Women certainly operated looms in the nineteenth century, but there are no East Anglian records of their doing so as early as 1610, although George Pecke of Caston in 1635 left his wife a pair of looms and slays.[6] Stephen Boldero of Hopton, Suffolk, in 1696 made a bequest to his wife of 'one halfe of the Linnen we have made since we came together', but her part may have been confined to hemp preparation and spinning.[7] In far off Yorkshire Oliver Heywood's brother-in-

[1] 1 James I cap. XXIV
[2] NRO NCC Rowland 263
[3] NRO NCC Tennant 211
[4] NRO NCC Turner 28
[5] NRO NCC INV23/77
[6] NRO Norwich archdeaconry Bankes 76
[7] SROB IC500/1/150/82

law was 'brought up in Halifax with Elizabeth Roberts, a linen weaver', but as Alice Clark points out spinning was by far the commonest employment for women[1] Female members of weavers' families assisted them in other ways, usually the preparation of flax and hemp and its spinning. In 1665 the wife of John Clerke of Bedingfield, Suffolk, was left 'the flaxen Napkins she spun' and 'the new Coverlett I made'.[2] Robert Amyson of Hoxne died in 1644 leaving his wife four rooms in one of the two houses he owned, much furniture, all his hemp yarn, a tow comb and a pashel, which would have enabled her to continue to prepare hemp.[3]

V

Some 20 dornix or darnick weavers have been included in this study of linen-weaving because the cloth they produced, much used for hangings and curtains, was often made of linen or at least was a linen mixture, although in eighteenth-century Norwich it was more commonly made with silk and wool. Most of the seventeenth-century dornix weavers lived in towns, and were relatively wealthy. The largest number, 10, were found in Norwich, but four were living in the same street, Southgate Street, in Bury St Edmunds in 1614.[4] The only rural dornix weavers were a father and son who lived at Westwick, a village a few miles south of North Walsham. Probate inventories are available for three of the Norwich weavers of dornix. With moveables valued at £64 and £76 two were not outstandingly rich, but their inventories are interesting because of the equipment, cloth and yarn that they list. John Hayward, who died in 1626, was like most of the dornix weavers a property-owner.[5] In his 'workin shopp' were three looms, a draft loom and a warping stage, and in his hall was a quantity of dornix yarn, some green, some plain and the rest 'gresy' (greasy). In the same room were 11 yards of dornix and well over 100 yards of woolsey cloth; like so many Norwich weavers he clearly produced more than one kind of cloth. Finally he had some woolsey and some blue dornix yarn at the dyers.

Thomas Chambers, whose goods were valued at £76, would appear to have been better off, but an account of money paid out by his widow totals 2s. more than the value of his inventory.[6] He owed £65 10s. 0d. on

[1] Alice Clark, *Working Life of Women in the Seventeenth Century* (1919), p.129, henceforth Clark. Reference is being made here to the first volume of Oliver Heywood's Autobiography.
[2] NRO NCC Stockdell 153
[3] NRO NCC Amyson 1
[4] SROB D8/2/1 List of deasners of St Mary's parish. The deasners were males over 16.
[5] NRO NCC INV47/B50
[6] NRO NCC INV46/81

bond, £7 in rent, £14 to 'Goodman Jacques dyer', and John Rosse was paid 4s. for writing the inventory. Yet Thomas Chambers owned 10 looms and their equipment, and a considerable quantity of cloth including a piece 'now making 24 yards in length'. He was carrying on his trade in six different rooms or workhouses, including an attic ('falce roof') and a drying chamber. His ownership of a copper, bucking tubs, yarn poles, posts and 'beakons' in the yards and drying chamber indicates that he was certainly scouring his yarn if not bleaching it.

Thomas Barker, the third of these Norwich dornix weavers, lived in the parish of St Mary Coslany and died in 1674 a far richer man than either John Hayward or Thomas Chambers; his goods were valued at £525, including £175 in debts owed to him.[1] There were at least eight rooms, five of which were heated, in his house as well as attics and various workhouses. His books were valued at £4 and he owned 'a thing to set a booke one'. There was such a quantity and variety of cloth in his parlour chamber that it would appear that he bought and sold cloth as well as making it. The materials listed in this room include dornix, draft, rug, ticken, blanket and woolsey. Like Thomas Chambers he had white, dyed and greasy yarn, and poles on which to hang yarn in his yard; in addition he possessed some 'stufe at the spinning'.

Thomas Chambers was not the only man whose debts were greater than the value of his inventory. John Beets of Beccles died in late 1682 asking his executor to sell his let messuage in Bungay and all his moveable goods and to use the money so raised for the best advantage of his children, the two youngest of whom were to be apprenticed to 'such Trades as they shall best like'.[2] The value of his inventory was only £11 8s. 10d., and the executor's account of charges and debts totalled £26 15s. 4d., so Beets must have expected his Bungay house to sell for a good price.[3] John Beets owed money to eight people and rent to a ninth, and his funeral cost £3 5s. 6d. Other expenses were £1 12s. 5d. towards binding out a child, and £1 6s. 6d. for keeping one child, 'being a cripple', and for his apparel. If we had more executors' accounts the true financial position of testators would more often be known.

The eighteenth-century inventories are more informative about cloth and yarn than are those of earlier date, but it is only the richer weavers who possessed significant quantities. The value of yarn and cloth owned by these men ranged from 20 to 42 per cent of the total of their moveable possessions. Yarn was usually described as white or grey, but it is not possible to deduce whether these weavers were bleaching their yarn or putting it out to whitesters. The largest quantities were owned

[1] NRO NCC INV58/B33
[2] NRO NCC O.W. 1682/39
[3] NRO NCC INV62B/46

by Thomas Winter of South Elmham St James,[1] and William Swatman of Great Ellingham,[2] both of whose stock of yarn was worth over £78 and considerably more than their cloth. A mere three inventories describe the cloth they value: William Jex of Brampton owned teeking checks, woolsey, strainers and huckaback,[3] and James Kent of South Elmham St James had woven some twill.[4] The third man was John Nickhols of Great Dunham in central Norfolk. His inventory, like that of William Swatman, was appraised by two linen-weavers, although in the former case the specialists only valued the items connected with Nickhols's occupation.[5]

John Nickhols was the wealthiest of the eighteenth-century linen weavers not only in respect of his trade goods, but also as a farmer; only four of these men were farming on a considerable scale. Nearly a third of the value of this inventory consisted of ready money in Nickhols's purse and pockets, the price set on his cloth and yarn formed a fifth and his crops and livestock 38 per cent of the total. His cloth is described disappointingly only by length and width. Four of his six looms were in his house, but of the other two one was at Mileham and the second at Litcham. Both these places are not far from Great Dunham and presumably the two looms were in the homes of men who worked for Nickhols. As a farmer this man ranks with wealthy yeomen, for his dairy herd numbered 21 cows with a bull and six followers. His six horses tilled the fields in which he grew barley, wheat, oats and peas; the barley was by far the most valuable of these crops and, naturally enough with so much livestock, hay occupied second place.

A few wills throw light on how weavers marketed their goods. A late sixteenth-century testator, Robert Lovicke of North Lopham, left one son a 'skore of ell wide linen cloth at Thornes of Dysse markyt'.[6] Thomas Butcher, who made his will in 1638 owned a shop in Fish Hill, Holt,[7] and in the same year Robert Ware of Mettinghan near Bungay bequeathed to his three sons 'all my loomes, cloathe, yarne, debtes owinge me for cloathe' and his shop with the chamber over it 'for there tradinge'.[8] This shop may well have been a workshop, but the mention of trading suggests that it may also have been used to sell cloth. The description of the testator's house shows that it stood on the north side of the Bungay to Beccles road with a meadow behind it running down

[1] NRO NCC INV83/15
[2] NRO NCC INV81B/11
[3] SROI FE1/27/33
[4] SROI FE1/27/83
[5] NRO Norwich archdeaconry ANW/23/24/35
[6] NRO Norfolk archdeaconry Carter 99
[7] NRO Norwich archdeaconry Spore 7
[8] SROI ICAA1/75/1/158

to the river Waveney. Even if the shop was not used for retailing, Ware and his sons lived close to two important market towns. Robert Hall, a dornix weaver living in the small towm of Reepham, left his eldest son some looms, pack cloths and saddles, and 'my Tylte'.[1] This last item was presumably used to shelter a stall at the markets to which the pack saddles had carried cloth.

VI

Many linen-weavers were sufficiently wealthy to set up more than one son with a house and land, and this was more common than leaving substantial cash legacies. Over a hundred men were in a position to bequeath land to more than one legatee, while only 15 could be said to have made large cash bequests, totalling over £100 each. The childless Henry Austin of Stadbroke died early in 1662 leaving cash legacies of well over £500.[2] He also made a charitable bequest of a perpetual rent charge of 20s. to be paid annually on 25 December to the overseers of the poor of his parish. Thomas Pett of Wattisfield bequeathed his landed property to his son, and £400 each to his three daughters as they reached the age of 21. These considerable sums were to be raised from his stock, mortages and book debts and, if necessary, by the sale of wood and timber from his esate.[3] Another childless testator, Richard Fowlsham of Letton, who died in 1661 left cash bequests to various kinsfolk totalling £268, but unlike Henry Austin's legacies, they were not all to be paid at once.[4] On the whole it was more usual for bequests of money, whether large or small, to be paid over a period of time.

The size of cash portions in wills varied considerably, but before 1730 around £20 to £40 seems to have been the most usual sum bestowed on their sons and daughters by linen-weavers. Richard Atkinson's bequest of £100 to a daughter was exceptionally high; he lived in Bungay, the home of other rich weavers.[5] More usual was the £40 apiece left to his two daughters in 1615 by William Tallbott of Earl Stonham,[6] or the £20 that Elias Morphew of Hoxne bequeathed to each of his two nieces in 1684.[7] William Brett owned land in Norfolk as well as in his home parish of Gislingham, and was sufficiently wealthy to leave £60 to each of his three daughter,[8] but Thomas Harvy of

[1] NRO Norwich archdeaconry Rownce 96
[2] NRO NCC Tennant 295
[3] NRO NCC Palmer 84, made 1717 and proved 1726
[4] NRO NCC Tennant 433
[5] SROI ICAA1/11/8 (1670)
[6] NRO NCC Angell 197
[7] NRO NCC Calthorpe 386
[8] NRO NCC Jones 180 (1696)

Swanton Morley was only able to make bequests of £10 apiece to his four daughters and £20 to the only one of his five sons not to receive a house and land.[1] Smaller still were the legacies Thomas Irons of Acle made in 1649: £6 each to two daughters and £8 to his younger son.[2] Cash legacies tended to be larger in the eighteenth century, perhaps because fewer poor weavers bothered to make wills. Thomas Pett was not the only eighteenth-century linen-weaver whose business activities had prospered sufficiently to provide him with large sums in cash or easily realisable assests. A Ditchingham man, Edmund Mingay, who died in 1725 left £150 in cash to his only son and another £100 to be invested for his wife's benefit.[3]

Portions for landless sons and for daughters were intended to launch the former on a career and to provide dowries for girls. What kind of figure was adequate for these purposes? In the seventeenth and eighteenth centuries less than £10 was enough to apprentice a boy to many trades, and double that sum was probably an acceptable dowry in the economic class to which most weavers belonged. A chapbook in Pepys's collection, 'A Pleasant Dialogue between Honest John and Loving Kate', suggests that for in-servants a portion of £10 apiece was sufficient for a couple to marry on and set up an alehouse.[4]

Some linen-weavers who were not part-time farmers owned considerable urban property like the bachelor Bezaleel Theobald of Woodbridge referred to earlier. John Smith, who made his will in 1661, possessed three houses in Lowestoft, and lived in one of the two standing in Bell Lane.[5] Two testators were connected with the fish trade. Thomas Bettes of Lowestoft died in 1619 leaving his wife the house he lived in 'booth above the Clyffe & beneath the Clyffe' together with the vats and herring spits belonging to his fish houses.[6] In the same year was proved the will of William Coe of Theberton, whose tenement with a piece of land in Southwold was to be divided between his three children; this property too included a fish house.[7] The religious preamble to this man's will is poetic and biblical: 'For as much as the lyfe of man fleeth as it were a shaddowe not permarnent in one estate neyther hathe yt any certeyntye of contynuance but comethe up & ys cutt downe as a flower.'

---

[1] NRO Norwich archdeaconry Disney 306
[2] NRO Norwich archdeaconry Moore 188
[3] NRO NCC Gregson 451
[4] Margaret Spufford, *Small Books and Pleasant Histories* (1981), p.165, henceforth Spufford, 1981
[5] SROI ICAA1/91/141
[6] SROI ICAA1/55/1
[7] SROI ICAA1/55/94

VII

Only six linen weavers asked that a son should be apprenticed to their own trade, but looms were left to so many others that it is clear that many sons were expected to follow their father's trade. Bequests phrased like John Hasted of Hepworth's 'a payer of Lombes which they worke in' to each of his three sons are common.[1] However, not all linen-weavers' sons followed in their fathers' footsteps. Such a man was Roger, one of the five sons of Gideon Morfewe of Hoxne and described in his father's will of 1633 as a glover.[2] Six wills referred to apprentices, usually as legatees. John Clerke of Bedingfield left 5s., his little boots and best spurs, and some items of clothing to one of his two apprentices and £2 to the other 'towards the up learning of his trade'.[3] In 1602 Richard Huntinge of Great Ellingham bequeathed 2s. 6d. each to three named apprentices.[4] Robert Jarvis of Wood Dalling clearly felt responsible for his apprentice, William Westmor, as he asked his executors to keep and maintain him as well as his nephew and heir until both boys were 21.[5] In his will of 1622 William Chace of King's Lynn expressed his trust in his apprentice when referring to money owed to him 'by my debt booke which my Prentice John Chace (was he a relation?) doth knowe and witnes unto'.[6] Henry Canham was left £150 by his master John Searles in 1680, and a further £20 in return for his taking care for nine months of the sale of Searles's stock and moveable goods, and collecting the money owed to him. During this nine months Canham, who was sole executor of the will, was to be allowed board, lodging and the use of a horse. Searles's two sons were less than 14 years old and their mother was dead.[7] Finally one testator was himself an apprentice or journeyman.

A few wills make provision for the education of sons, such as that of Thomas Wilson of Redgrave, who in 1670 requested his wife and sole executrix to see that their two sons were educated, brought up in the fear of God, taught to read and write well and trained to get an honest living.[8] At the nearby village of Palgrave, William Holmes, who died childless in 1617, left £2 a year for 40 years to teach four of the poorest children in the parish to read at school.[9]

[1]   SROB IC500/1/85/3
[2]   NRO NCC Tuck 221
[3]   NRO NCC Stockdell 153
[4]   NRO Norfolk archdeaconry Offwood 88
[5]   NRO NCC Sone 26
[6]   NRO Norwich archdeaconry Hill 63
[7]   SROB IC500/1/133/202
[8]   SROB IC500/1/122/28
[9]   SROB IC500/1/74/9

Signatures or marks on wills are one of the main sources for the study of literacy. Leaving aside the 34 nuncupative wills and the 152 seen only in register copies, 369 of those dating from the seventeenth century bear marks or signatures; 35 per cent were signed and 65 per cent were those of testators who could only make a mark.[1] When ranking trades by illiteracy in the period 1580–1700 Cressy placed weavers twenty-fourth out of fifty-five, and wrote: 'In the diocese of Norwich, for example, dornix weavers and worsted weavers were generally more literate than linen weavers and weavers unindentified by their thread.'[2] It was more usual for both dornix and worsted weavers to be urban dwellers, and literacy rates were higher in towns than in the country-side. Several testators made bequests of Bibles, and Elias Morphew of Hoxne left his Book of Martyrs to a collar maker's daughter, and one of his great Bibles to a great niece; both Elias and his father, Gideon, were literate.

Generally speaking inventories are a better guide to book ownership than are wills, although as Dr Spufford has pointed out books were frequently not considered worth listing, and chapbooks were practic-ally never included in inventories.[3] Books appear in 48 (30.5 per cent) of the seventeenth-century linen-weavers' probate inventories. Seventeen testators owned only a Bible, or more rarely two or three, but another 20 possessed unspecified books and 11 both Bibles and other books. Not surprisingly book ownership rises with wealth. None appear in the under £5 inventories, while they are mentioned in half of those of the richest group. Books other than Bibles are commonest in the £21–50 bracket, and can perhaps be associated with the weavers' reputation for religious and political radicalism. Seven book owners made marks on their wills, thus confirming that the possession of reading matter is not a sure guide to literacy or rather to the ability to write, although some testators may have been too weak to sign. The percentage of book-owning linen-weavers differs little from that (32 per cent) for the inventories belonging to a group of north Suffolk parishes and drawn up between 1550 and 1640.[4] Cressy has shown that East Anglia was an unusually literate region, and book ownership amongst linen weavers bears this out.[5]

---

[1] Wills made between 1700 and 1729 have been omitted from this survey of literacy because most of them were only available in registers, and only original wills can be safely used as a guide to the ability to sign.

[2] David Cressy, *Literacy and the Social Order* (Cambridge, 1980), p.136

[3] Spufford, 1974, pp. 210–211; and Spufford, 1981, p.48

[4] N.R. Evans, 'Testators, Literacy, Education and Religious Belief', *Local Population Studies*, 25 (1980), p.47

[5] D.A. Cressy, 'Education and Literacy in London and East Anglia, 1580–1700', (unpublished University of Cambridge PH.D. thesis, 1972), and *Literacy and the Social Order* (Cambridge, 1980), p.75

VIII

Weavers enjoyed a reputation for radicalism in politics and religion. In Leicestershire many early framework knitters were Nonconformists as an expression of their independence of the power of squire and parson,[1] and the same motive probably influenced weavers. Evidence of the political views of East Anglian linen-weavers does not exist, but it is possible to find some indications of their feelings about religion. Was Silas Marner typical of late eighteenth-century members of his trade, or was his type of religious affiliation a peculiarity of urban craftsmen? Unfortunately there is little evidence about nonconformity among linen-weavers after 1730, although there is a reasonable amount from the preceding 70 years.

Only a dozen or so linen weavers are known to have had definite links with nonconformity, but Baptists, Presbyterians, Congregationalists and Quakers all flourished in the Waveney and Little Ouse valleys and the surrounding region. This connection goes back as far as the early fifteenth century when the Beccles area was a centre of Lollardy.[2] After the Declaration of Indulgence was issued in 1672, many licences were granted to preachers and meeting houses in north Suffolk and south Norfolk. Information also comes from the episcopal returns for the 1669 enquiry into conventicles, although the survival of these for the diocese of Norwich is very patchy. The places mentioned in these two sources include Bungay, Syleham, Dickleburgh, Winfarthing, Pulham, Hepworth, Denton and Rickinghall and many others known to be the homes of linen weavers in the seventeenth and eighteenth centuries.[3] At both Beccles and Diss four meeting places were licensed in 1672, and there were two in many of the villages.

Independents, as congregationalists were then known, predominated over other denominations in this region, but Presbyterians were found at Lopham and Quakers at Hempnall and Wymondham for instance. Besse mentions several linen-weavers, including Daniel Gridley of Haverhill from whom fustians worth £27 were seized on a distress warrant.[4] In 1664 Thomas Woods, a linen-weaver of Badwell Ash, was committed to the county gaol at Ipswich together with five other Quakers.[5] Many members of this sect were imprisoned for

[1] Mills, 192

[2] *Heresy Trials in the Diocese of Norwich, 1428–31*, edited by Norman Tanner, Camden Fourth Series, 20 (London, 1977)

[3] G. Lyon Turner, *Original Records of Early Nonconformity under Persecution and Indulgence* (London and Leipzig, 1911), 2 vols, I, pp. 101–4, 417, 524; II, pp. 888–9, 902–3, 913–4, henceforth Lyon Turner

[4] J. Besse, *Sufferings of the People called Quakers* (1753), I, p.678

[5] ibid, I, p.673

attending meetings or refusing to take oaths, and the goods of those who would not pay tithes were seized. In 1670 a Quaker meeting was held in Hoxne at the house of John Ameson, possibly the whitester of this name who died in 1713. John Edwards of Wingfield, who with his wife was also fined for attending this meeting, may well have been the linen weaver of the same name and parish.[1] The will of neither man gives any indication of adherence to Quaker tenets.

The Quaker connection at Wingfield continued into the next century. Henry Clough, a wealthy but childless linen weaver of this parish, made his will in late 1718 asking to be buried in Diss or Tivetshall 'Burying Place'. A Society of Friends meeting house and burial ground still existed at the latter place in 1845.[2] Clough appointed four trustees, presumably fellow Quakers, to manage land in Wingfield and a house, one of three owned by him. The rents and profits from this property were to be used for the benefit 'of the poorer sort of people of my persuasion called Quakers for ever', and the trustees were to choose tenants who would allow the dwelling to be used as a meeting house 'for those people called Quakers as for some years past it have been'.[3] One of the original four trustees was another linen-weaver, James Murton of Tivetshall. A third Quaker member of the trade was Edward Vynor of South Lopham, who in 1703 bequeathed 'unto my poor Friends of my profession commonly called Quakers the sume of five pounds.'[4] He too was a wealthy property-owning weaver.

Amongst the places mentioned as centres of nonconformity was Wattisfield, where the 1669 returns describe 30 independents gathering at the house of Samuel Baker esquire, and a Presbyterian meeting place was licensed in 1672.[5] A chapel was built in Wattisfield in 1678 by an independent congregation first formed at Market Weston in 1654. The registers and minute books of this chapel have survived and like many others of its kind it drew its congregation from a wide area.[6] Many of the surnames in its records are those of linen-weaving families, but it has been possible to make firm links for only half a dozen individuals, all of whom left surviving wills. Only one of these dates from the seventeenth century and is that of Richard Ruddock of Hinderclay, who the chapel register tells us was aged 50 when he died in 1679. He lived in a three hearth house, which he had himself bought, and which

[1] ibid, I, p.675
[2] White's Norfolk, p.721
[3] NRO NCC Bigot 178
[4] NRO NCC Piddocke 113
[5] Lyon Turner, I, pp. 101–4, II, p.903
[6] SROB Microfilm J526. Congregational Church Minute Book 1654–1928, includes register of baptisms, admissions and deaths 1654, 1679–1904.

he bequeathed to his son together with some land and a barn.[1] One of these noncomformist weavers was described in the Wattisfield chapel register as 'Mr Thomas Prentice' when his death was recorded in 1723; he lived at Palgrave. His will shows him to have been a substantial landowner, and that he left an annual rent charge of £6 for 40 years to the minister of the dissenting congregation assembling at Palgrave meeting house.[2] John Day of Redgrave, whose will bequeathed a house and land to his wife,[3] was included in the list of brethren drawn up in October 1735, two and a half years before his death was entered in the register. On 9 March 1714 Elizabeth, wife of Ebenezer Shelver, was admitted as a member of the Wattisfield congregation and so continued until she died on 1 February 1746. Her husband probably died about the time she joined the chapel as his will was written in March 1714. When Joseph Hart of Thelnetham made his will in 1746 he left 50s. to be distributed amongst the poor members of the dissenting congregation of Wattisfield, and one of his executors was a gentleman of that village, Denny Crabb, whose name appeared in the chapel register when his son was baptised there in 1750. By 1779 he, or possibly his son, was a deacon of this chapel, to the minister of which a Hinderclay whitester left an annuity of £2 in that year.[4] Joseph Hart was unmarried, but a man of property owning land and two houses in Thelnetham in addition to the building he lived in.[5] Lastly, Thomas Pett of Wattisfield made his will in 1717 leaving 5s. a quarter to Mr Wix 'so long as he preach the Gospell in Wattisfield'.[6]

In addition to the Quakers and the group who worshipped at Wattisfield chapel, seven other linen-weavers made bequests indicating their membership of nonconformist congregations. In 1775 John Wink of Bungay left gifts of £5 each to the Reverend Robert Shovel Bottom, minister to the congregation of dissenters at Bungay, and to the poor who attended the dissenting meeting house in the town during the twelve months preceding his death.[7] In nearby Beccles two eigtheenth-century linen-weavers were members of the congregation of independents. William Mattchett of Pulham Market, whose will was written in 1699, left £5, 'to the poor of the Church of Pulham that I am Sosiety with',[8] and John Pitts of the same place gave the identical sum to the poor 'that belong to the Meeting of Tivetshall'.[9] The only recorded

[1] SROB IC500/1/133/1
[2] NRO NCC Megoe 153
[3] NRO NCC Brereton 52
[4] SROB Dalton VII, f.90. Will of Thomas Flatman
[5] SROB Claggett VII, f.426
[6] NRO NCC Palmer 84
[7] NRO NCC Yallop 334
[8] NRO NCC Allexander 94
[9] NRO NCC Famm 485

Baptist linen weaver, William Swatman of Great Ellingham, died in 1742 leaving 20s. to the poor of the 'Particular Baptist Church of Christ meeting at Great Ellingham', and another pound to its minister to preach a funeral sermon.[1] The Quaker Henry Clough was not the only weaver to own a nonconformist place of worship, for in 1727 Abraham Bilny of Fersfield near Diss left to two trustees a messuage and yard in Winfarthing 'commonly called the Meeting House'. In addition he made a bequest of 20s. to Mr John Miller 'now preacher to the Congregation of the Meeting house in Winfarthing', and a further legacy of £100 to him and his successors to be used to repair the meeting house. The payment of the income from this gift was contingent on the congregation maintaining 'a preacher to preach a sermon once a fortnight as is the usual custom', and keeping the building in good repair. No pews or seats belonging to the Winfarthing meeting house were to be removed except those belonging to Mr Thomas Catermole.[2] Bilny had been admitted to membership of the Wattisfield chapel in 1706. The distance from Fersfield to Wattisfield is over 12 miles and Bilny may have found it more convenient to establish a meeting house nearer his own village.

The general impression given by the wills of these dissenting linen-weavers is that they were men of property living in comfortable circumstances, and not at all like Silas Marner except in their religious beliefs. All owned some land and at least one house, more often two or three, and several left substantial cash legacies. Six, including the two chapel-owners, were childless. The numbers are too few to draw any firm conclusions about the relationship between nonconformity and linen-weaving, particularly as none of the men considered here were poor; however, in a region noted for the strength of nonconformity it would not be surprising if many more linen-weavers were dissenters, particularly in the eighteenth century.

Adding data from other sources to that from probate records can do much to illuminate a linen-weaver's career. One of the handful for whom this has proved possible was Thomas Munns of Beccles. A rental of c.1661 shows that he held land in Beccles and Barsham at an annual rent of £18,[3] and when he died in 1680 he was leasing land from the town's Fen Corporation.[4] Other documents show that, in addition to being a member of the Corporation, he was also a feoffee of the Holy Ghost lands (town lands) as early 1659, and held the office of collector of their rents and profits in 1674/5.[5] Some members of the town's

[1] NRO NCC Woodrofe 116
[2] NRO NCC Thacker 139
[3] Beccles Town Hall, Rix Collection Division IV, Vol. I, p.105
[4] SROI ICAA1/110/205
[5] Beccles Town Hall, Rix Collection Division VI, Vol. IV, p.7

corporation belonged to the local Independent congregation and resigned after the Declaration of Indulgence was withdrawn, but Thomas Munns as an Anglican was not among their number. The hearth tax return of 1674 tells us that he lived in a four-hearth house. He was clearly an important citizen of Beccles.

The bachelor Francis Maiden of Old Buckenham was very particular about his funeral arrangements. His executor was to provide half a barrel of beer and 'ten duzen' bread, as well as gloves for himself and the four bearers.[1] In 1731 John Rix of Redgrave made an unusual, and indeed illegal, request when he desired his wife and sole executrix to 'Bury my Body in Linnen Cloth the product and growth of Great Britain.'[2] A Long Stratton linen-weaver, Robert Chittleburgh, followed an unusual second occupation for a weaver; he left his son Thomas all his looms and weaving tackle and 'all my barbering tools'.[3]

Finally an example, found by chance, of one of the many who were engaged in the linen trade, either as weavers or in other ways, but did not reveal this involvement in the occupational descriptions given in their probate documents: this is Abraham Haws of Horham, Suffolk, who was described by the writer of his inventory, made in December 1677, as a yeoman. His crops, livestock, butter and cheese amounted to about a quarter of the total value of £211, but in his hall chamber were stored two stones each of flax and 'hemping tow', a stone of hemp, two spinning wheels, eight clues of linen yarn and forty yards of new linen cloth. No looms are listed, but there was a bunching block in the shop.[4] If Haws was not a farmer-weaver, he was at least closely involved with linen manufacturing.

IX

Useful as probate records are for studying the wealth and activities of linen-weavers, they are little help as a guide to other aspects of the industry such as sources of raw material or the marketing of cloth. Unfortunately these aspects of East Anglian linen manufacture are poorly documented, and it is probably for this reason that a recent writer claimed that this industry declined in Suffolk in the seventeenth century, although admitting that its history is 'still uncharted territory'.[5] This argument for decline is based on negative evidence: the

---

[1] NRO NCC Famm 152 (1709)
[2] NRO NCC Smith 118. There is nothing in the parish register to indicate that he was not buried in woollen.
[3] NRO NCC Widdoson 2 (1730)
[4] NRO NCC INV60/52
[5] Michell, p.309

virtual ending of the import of raw flax through Yarmouth after 1661, and the very considerable increase in imports of hollands and osnabrigs between 1600 and 1714, over forty-fold in the case of the former.[1] What Michell ignores is that hemp, not flax, was the main raw material of East Anglian linen and that the native product was on the whole not of high quality and thus not in competition with high-class imported cloth.

The seventeenth century saw a steep rise in imports of hemp and high quality linen cloth at the same time as a decrease in those of flax. This surely indicates that English linen production was concentrating on the cheap end of the market, and thus making itself vulnerable to competition from a cheaper alternative when one appeared in the form of cotton in the late eighteenth century. Fedorowicz's figures for hemp imports from the Baltic, principally from Prussia, show that they rose from 2890 lasts (a last of hemp = 2 (2000 lb) tons) in the first to 44,563 lasts in the final decade of the seventeenth century.[2] In the second half of this century 'demand for hemp grew astonishingly' and was linked to naval expansion,[3] but hemp was presumably required for cloth as well as cordage in a period when the standard of living was increasing and the use of linen was growing. The English linen cloth industry was 'built largely on imports of foreign yarn', which combined quality with cheapness. 'English flax and hemp made perfectly acceptable coarse cloth' as well as thread, rope, fishing nets and so on, but could not compete with the overseas product.[4]

There is no lack of information about the quantities of hemp imported into England, and there is ample evidence to show that much of it was consumed by the Navy. Indeed most authors appear to assume that all imported hemp was used for cordage or sails, although flax was generally preferred for the latter. By comparison there is a dearth of evidence both about the sources of raw material used by East Anglian linen-weavers and about the destination of the flax and hemp imported through East coast ports. However, it is certain that an inevitable result of the importing of hemp, or for that matter of any other produce, was to depress its growth or manufacture in the port's hinderland.

The Baltic region was the principal source of imported flax and hemp, the bulk of which arrived at the ports of London, Hull and Newcastle.[4] Much of the flax was turned into cloth, but hemp was a

[1] ibid, p. 310 His figures for imports of linen into Yarmouth are drawn from PRO E 190.
[2] J.K. Federowicz, *England's Baltic Trade in the Early Seventeenth Century* (Cambridge, 1980), pp. 109–110, henceforth Federowicz
[3] ibid., p.108
[4] Thirsk, 1978, p.73
[5] Sven-Erik Aström, *From Cloth to Iron, the Anglo-Baltic Trade in the late Seventeenth Century*, (Helsingfors, 1963), pp. 55, 203, henceforth Åström

vital naval store and during the seventeenth century was the most important requirement of the Navy.[1] Not surprisingly the price of hemp rose in time of war and fell when peace returned. This can easily be illustrated in relation to the three Dutch wars in the middle of the century. From 1637 to 1651 the price of Russian hemp remained around 24s. per hundredweight, but rose steeply in 1652 on the outbreak of the first Dutch war and continued to rise until the end of the second Dutch war in 1667 when it suddenly fell to its pre-1652 level. During the third Dutch war (1672–4) hemp prices again increased, but came down immediately afterwards and decreased to a very low level in the 1680s.[2]

Unfortunately there is pracically no evidence to show what effect, if any, these fluctuations in price had on domestic hemp cultivation and prices. Beveridge's figures are all drawn from the purchase of naval stores, although he does say 'In the middle of the seventeenth century prices of English hemp are well below those' of the imported product.[3] The great increase in English shipbuilding in the second half of the seventeenth century may have stimulated the cultivation of hemp, but there is no way of assessing the truth of this hypothesis. Pepys experimented with English hemp but did not find it a satisfactory substitute either for the best kind from Riga or the cheaper Muscovy variety.[4] At the same time Pool says that the Navy Board attempted to encourage domestic hemp production because of the expense and complications of importing supplies. In February 1666 a Mr Fincham offered to supply Norfolk hemp at £46 a ton delivered to King's Lynn, but his price was too high as the best Flanders hemp could be bought for £50 including free delivery to the dockyards.[5] In 1694 the Navy Board purchased 1250 tons of hemp from Riga, 250 tons from Konisberg and a mere 150 tons in the United Kingdom.[6] This was in wartime, so it seems that despite all efforts to increase domestic hemp cultivation the Navy was still as heavily dependent on imports at the end of the seventeenth century as it had been at the beginning.

As the Navy purchased hemp almost exclusively for cordage, it is quite possible that its demands had no effect on East Anglian growers if their market was linen-weavers not rope-makers. On the other hand Suffolk was one of four counties described as the main sources of supply

[1] R.W.K. Hinton, *The Eastland Trade and the Common Weal in the Seventeenth Century* (Cambridge, 1959), pp. 47, 97, henceforth Hinton
[2] Hinton, pp. 110–111, and William Beveridge, *Prices and Wages in England from the Twelfth to the Nineteenth Century* (1939), p. 670
[3] Beveridge, op. cit., p.636
[4] Hinton, p.97
[5] Bernard Pool, *Navy Board Contracts, 1660–1832* (1966), p.30, henceforth Pool
[6] Pool, p.68

of domestic-produced canvas, and the demands of both a growing navy and merchant marine must have stimulated this industry. English sailcloth had been considered suitable only for lighter sails, but by 1700 there were indications that it was improving in quality.[1] In Suffolk, Ipswich and Bungay were known as centres of sailcloth manufacture, and reference to the former will be made in some account of this town's textile-producing history later in this chapter.

It is doubtful whether hemp-growers in East Anglia or elsewhere in England either could or would respond to the fluctuations in the Navy's demands. In the earlier part of the seventeenth century the building of large ships was concentrated on the Thames and East Anglian creeks, but later in the century the shipbuilding industry declined in these areas and the following century north-eastern ports, such as Whitby and Newcastle, supplanted Ipswich and its neighbours as shipbuilding centres.[2] This geographical shift in ship construction can have done nothing to stimulate the sailcloth industry or the gowing of hemp for cordage in Suffolk and Norfolk. As was shown in chapter 2, hemp was mainly grown in small fields and was a popular crop with cottagers and smallholders. These people would have been unable and unwilling to increase the quantity produced in response to demand from what to them would have appeared a distant and uncertain market.

If, as seems likely, East Anglian hemp and flax cultivation did not increase sufficiently to meet the demand from a growing local linen industry in the seventeenth century, from where did supplies of these raw materials come? A search of the port books of seven east coast ports for one year in the mid-1660s and for 1700–01 has not thrown much light on this problem.[3] The northernmost of these ports is Hull and here 558.3 tons of rough flax and 14.85 tons of rough hemp were imported during the year from Christmas 1665 to Christmas 1666. During the following twelve months the coastal port book records the shipping out from Hull of nine half lasts of flax, and over 30 tons of hemp. Almost all the flax went to Newcastle, but roughly equal quantities of hemp were sent to this port and to London and a lesser amount (4 tons, 7.5 cwt) to Great Yarmouth. It is impossible to be certain how much hemp was dispatched as much of it was described as bundles or dozens, so the figure of 30 tons is a minimum. However, almost all this hemp was described as English, so it appears that most of the foreign hemp and flax imported into Hull was destined for consumers in this port's hinterland; they may well have included the linen-weavers of Nidderdale.

Turning to the East Anglian ports there is no sign of really significant

[1] Pool, p.69
[2] Ralph Davies, *The Rise of the English Shipping Industry* (1962), pp. 55–56, 93
[3] Port books are not available for precisely the same year for all these ports.

quantities of hemp or flax arriving either from overseas or via the coastal trade. King's Lynn seems not to have imported these materials, although it had done so earlier in the seventeenth century when the two main sources of these imports were Scotland, and the Polish ports of Danzig (now Gdansk) and Elbing (today Elblag). Taking the year 1614, 293 ells of ticking, 2440 ells of Scotch linen cloth, 100 ells of hurden, and 22½ hundredweight of yarn came in from Scotland; and from the eastern Baltic was brought in 10 hundredweight each of rough or unwrought hemp and flax, 13 bolts of 'sprewce' (Prussian) canvas and 7 lasts of hempseed (a last in this case was proxably two tons of 4000 lbs). All this cloth imported from Scotland was of coarse varieties and thus in direct competition with East Anglian cloth, and most of the shipments from Prussia and Poland were either of untreated flax and hemp, or of seed.[1] Great Yarmouth was another port through which much hemp was imported up till 1640.

In 1661–62 King's Lynn received 6 tons of rough hemp from London and 13.25 tons of mainly English hemp from Boston, Spalding and Wisbech. A considerable quantity of hempseed also came from these Wash ports. Much of the hemp was presumably dispatched to inland Norfolk, but 12.5 hundredweight was sent to Southwold and 4.3 tons to London. In 1664–65 Great Yarmouth received 7 hundredweight of dressed flax and 10 hundredweight of rough hemp from abroad; in 1669–70 1.5 tons of English hemp came from King's Lynn.

In Suffolk only Ipswich and Woodbridge recorded any hemp or flax. During 1663–64 a total of 37.5 tons and 19 'hundred' of rough hemp came to the former from London, but its overseas trade was less important; in 1665–66 a mere 3 bundles of hemp and 63 hundredweight of undressed flax arrived from Holland. At the same time considerable quantities of linen cloth were arriving in Ipswich. No raw materials were received at Woodbridge in 1666–67, but 14.75 tons of hempseed and 7358 pieces of sackcloth and poldavis were dispatched to London.

By the end of the century even less hemp and flax was arriving in Ipswich. In 1700–01 none came from overseas, and just over 2 tons of hemp was received from London. At Woodbridge 5.5 tons, 20 hundred and 20 bundles of raw hemp arrived from London, and another 20 bundles from Newcastle.[2] At the same time there is a clear indication of a decline in the manufacture of sacking, for only 2342 pieces were dispatched to London, less than a third of the quantity sent 34 years

---

[1] G.A. Metters, 'The Rulers and Merchants of King's Lynn in the early seventeenth century', (unpublished University of East Anglia Ph.D. thesis, 1982). I am grateful to Dr Metters for allowing me to use data from his computer files based on the King's Lynn port books for the years 1604–14.

[2] The figures are drawn from Christmas 1700 to midsummer 1701, and if doubled give a minimum of 11 tons for the whole year.

earlier. The port book for 1700–01 ends at midsummer, but even if an equal amount of sacking had been sent in the second half of the year the total would still be nearly 3000 pieces fewer than in 1666–67. Ipswich played little part in the sacking trade, dispatching a mere 29 pieces in 1663–64 and none in 1700–01. What these figures seem to suggest is that Woodbridge had replaced Ipswich as the major Suffolk hemp port, but it could also be concluded that most of it was destined to be converted into sackcloth.

In 1700–01 Yarmouth imported no flax, little hemp (1 cwt) and 377 lbs of raw linen yarn. Through the coastal trade it sent 30.5 tons of foreign hemp to Chatham, presumably for the dockyards there, and received 4 bundles of hemp from London. There was just as little activity at King's Lynn where 100 stone of hemp arrived from Spalding and half a ton was sent to Boston. Only at Hull had flax and hemp not merely held their place, but in the case of hemp considerably increased it. A total of 351 tons of flax and 131.5 tons of hemp was imported in the year Christmas 1700 to Christmas 1701, in addition to a large amount of linen yarn. Most of the flax and hemp was described as undressed or rough. By contrast coastal trade from Hull included only 1 pack and 4 'matts' of English undressed flax sent to Newcastle. However, English linen, canvas and huckaback were dispatched to London.

Undoubtedly Hull was the principal east coast port for foreign flax and hemp, but little was being sent elsewhere. The active coastal trade of the 1660s was in English hemp, and this seems to have vanished by the end of the century. What is most surprising is that at the time of the East Anglian linen industry's fastest growth the amounts of hemp and flax arriving in the region's ports were declining sharply. The situation had been only marginally better in the early seventeenth century when the linen industry was beginning its development. In 1620–21 King's Lynn shipped just over 3 tons of hemp to Yarmouth and 1.25 tons to Southwold.[1]

Hemp and flax although light are bulky cargoes, and it seems reasonable to assume that they would not have been transported far over land. It must, therefore, be concluded either that the hypothesis that local production did not increase sufficiently to meet demand is incorrect, or the Norfolk and Suffolk linen-weavers were using yarn that had been processed elsewhere in England. It is known that in Pepys's day a 1000-ton warship required 10 tons of hemp for cordage and ground tackle,[2] but there are no figures to show how much hemp was required to make a yard of linen cloth. According to Yarranton an acre of land could produce three hundredweight of flax, which when dressed would

[1] T.S. Willan, *The English Coasting Trade 1600–1750* (Manchester, 1938), p.126
[2] Hinton, p.100

make 400 ells of cloth.[1] It is impossible to square this estimate with one given in a letter published in *The Gentleman's Magazine* in 1742. The writer, 'Samuel Homespun', estimated the average produce of an acre to be 50 stone 'Dutch weight' and that this would make from 2080 to 4419 yards of cloth depending on how finely the flax had been dressed.[2] A modern estimate is that in the eighteenth century one hundredweight of flax produced 50lbs of yarn, while Horner's view was that 3550 cwt of yarn was required to make a million yards of linen.[3] However, there is no similar estimate available for hemp. This lack of reliable statistical data makes it impossible even to hazard a guess at the quantities of raw materials required by the East Anglian linen industry.

Both the quantity of flax and hemp imports and contemporary exhortations to grow more and rely less on foreign sources point towards the conclusion that home grown supplies were inadequate. At times the flood of imports was actively damaging, as in the early 1620s when English flax and hemp dressers were thrown out of work because Dutch dressed hemp and flax were cheaper,[4] but by December 1630 the company of flax-dressers was complaining that the Eastland Company was not importing enough flax to keep its members employed.[5]

No evidence has been found for any sophisticated organisation for marketing linen cloth, nor for any equivalent of the clothiers who put out work and sold the finished product. There is no point looking for an elaborate organisation or for capital accumulation, neither of which existed in the case of many manufactures as Dr Thirsk has pointed out: 'The simplicity of the industrial structure supporting substantial rural industries requires emphasis.'[6] If the assumption that East Anglian weavers were producing cheap linens for a predominantly local market is correct, then there was no real need for entrepreneurs and middlemen. Most linen cloth produced in the region was not of sufficiently high quality to be exported nor could it compete with the fine quality materials produced on the continent and imported into England in increasingly large quantities. The linen-weavers of Suffolk and Norfolk were catering for a local demand for household linens, aprons, shirts, sacks and so forth, from customers who neither needed nor could afford expensivs foreign linens.

In the early modern period there were well over 700 places in

1 Andrew Yarranton, *England's Improvement by Sea and Land* (1677), p.51, henceforth Yarranton
2 Warden, pp. 374–5
3 Harte, pp. 104–5
4 PRO SP 16/250, no 123 printed in *Seventeenth-Century Economic Documents*, edited by Joan Thirsk and J.P. Cooper (Oxford, 1972), pp. 254–5, henceforth Thirsk and Cooper.
5 Federowicz, p.106 quoting APC 1630–1, p.149, no 406
6 Thirsk, 1978, p.111

England where weekly markets were held;[1] in East Anglia no one can have lived more than 10 miles from a market town and most people were within easy reach of two or more. Access to a market as an outlet for their cloth was thus no problem for linen-weavers, and, as we have already seen, many owned at least a horse on which to convey it thither. For those without transport, carrier services were developing in the seventeenth century and many linen-weavers lived near navigable waterways. By 1564 there was a regular carrier service between Ipswich and London via Stowmarket, so access to the capital was available by land as well as by sea.[2] It is known that most Norwich-made cloth was dispatched throughout England by pack horse, and if any East Anglian linens did reach a wider market they may well have travelled in this way.[3] The seventeenth century saw a growth in the public road-carrying industry and this had a significant effect in extending markets.[4]

The greatest market in Eastern England was Stourbridge Fair, held just outside Cambridge for two weeks in September. This was a fair of not merely national but of international importance. Elsewhere in the region there were many lesser fairs as well as weekly markets. Certain towns were renowned as linen markets. Writing about Diss Blomefield said 'The market is kept weekly on Friday, the chief of which consists in the linen-cloth manufacture, for which this market is famous, great quantities of it being sold here.'[5] The same author also gives the cost of stalls at Diss Fair: '2*d*. for every tilted stall, and 1*d*. for every one untilted'; market stall holders paid a weekly or annual rent, 'but all that stand under any houses, penthouses, etc pays the bailiff 4*d*. per annum'.[6] At Beccles in 1705 a linen-weaver was paying a quarterly rent of 1*s*. 6*d*. for a stall in the market place and 2*d*. extra at each of the three fairs. Writing in the eighteenth century, Cox mentions three other East Anglian linen markets: at East Harling where the weekly market was 'chiefly for Linnen Yarn and Linnen Cloth', at Woodbridge whose market he described as 'very considerable for most Necessaries of Life, but especially for Hemp, and Goods made of it'; and thirdly at Halesworth. Describing this last place he wrote: 'The Town is populous, and the Market good, occasion'd chiefly by its Plenty of Linen-Yarn, which the Women of this Country spin, partly for the use of Families, and

[1] John Goodacre, 'Lutterworth in the sixteenth and seventeenth centuries: a Market Town and its Area', (unpublished University of Leicester Ph.D. thesis, 1977), p.2
[2] John Patten, *English Towns 1500–1700*, (Folkestone, 1978), p.269
[3] N.J. Williams, 'The Maritime Trade of East Anglian Ports, 1550–1590', (unpublished University of Oxford D.Phil. thesis, 1952), p.207, henceforth Williams.
[4] J.A. Chartres, *Internal Trade in England 1500–1700* (1977), p.40
[5] Blomefield, I, p.38
[6] ibid, p.15

Partly for Sale; which being readily bought up here, is esteem'd a good Commodity for Trade.'¹

In 1635–6 Norfolk quarter sessions received a petition from William Johnsom, a linen-weaver, complaining of his treatment at Swaffham market. Johnsom claimed to be an inhabitant of King's Lynn where 'all my howshowld ar', but he himself 'keepe in' South Wootton, which is today almost a suburb of Lynn. His petition indicates where he sold this cloth: 'my trading doe ly in the Cuntry and most part of my dealings. I am a Lining weaver and I have as much Cloth to whit and a whitining as will serve me whilst the tym of our Linne Mart which is in Febrewary and shall not ned to fech one yard from Linne nor will not by the grase of God for to keep my Markett in Swaffom.' His complaint was that at Swaffham 'the last Market day the Cunstibl did tak away my stale and threw my ware on the grownd and did hinder my Market which is my living'.² Lynn Mart was a week-long fair in early Feburary.

Recent research into the commercial activities of petty chapmen has shown that nowhere in England was beyond the reach of these itinerant traders whose stock provided much of the material for the increase in domestic comfort amongst all social classes in the later seventeenth century.³ These men carried the linens from which bed hangings, window curtains and other soft furnishings, as well as simple items of clothing, were made. Dr Spufford points out that 'undoubtedly the most important wares carried by all the chapmen were textiles. Amongst them, linen cloths dominated quite outstandingly.'⁴ Many chapmen obtained their supplies of both English and imported linens from linen drapers, but there seems no reason why some should not have dealt directly with weavers, for whom they probably acted as yarn suppliers. The records of fairs held at Beccles between 1680 and 1705 show that yarnmen, sometimes as many as eight, were always among the stall-holders. It is impossible to distinguish between dealers in woollen and linen yarn, but linen-weavers also rented stalls at the fairs.⁵

It is impossible to estimate East Anglian linen production because no figures are available for inland trade, and it is probable that it was all destined for home consumption, much of it local. The data exist for quantifying exports and imports, but the extent of home-based industries remains a matter for speculation. Local linen weaving may not have achieved its full potential and, like home production of flax and

¹ Thomas Cox, *Magna Britannia et Hibernis*, 6 volumes (1720–31), III, p. 336, V, pp. 192, 225
² NRO C/S3 Box 30
³ Spufford, 1984. I am extremely grateful to Dr Spufford for allowing me to read the MS of this book before publication and to refer to it.
⁴ ibid, p.77
⁵ Beccles Town Hall, Rix collection Division IV, vol. 4

hemp, may have been inadequate to satisfy demand. In spite of a dense population in East Anglia, the demands for yarn from the fast-growing Norwich worsted industry meant that there were probably not enough local spinners to fulfil the requirements of all the different types of weavers in the region. Stocking knitting, which we have already seen to be widespread, drew away from spinning the labour of many women and children.

X

In the seventeenth century, just as in the sixteenth, writers on trade and commerce constantly harped on the necessity to decrease imports by encouraging home manfacturers. There were numerous proposals to increase the cultivation of flax and hemp, to employ the poor in their preparation, and to introduce the weaving of a variety of linen cloths. Most imported linens were of superior quality, while English-made cloth was usually coarser. As a result East Anglian and other home-produced linens were not competing for the same market and were thus little affected by imports. Henry Best in 1641 wrote 'Short Remembrances for Buying all sorts of Linen Cloths' in which he listed the prices of a wide variety. English linens, 'commonly called huswife cloth' varied in price from 14*d*. to 2*s*., but all the finer cloths listed here were foreign-made and much more expensive, ranging from the 'worst sort of Scotch cloth' at 18*d*. a yard to Cambric lawn costing 10*s*. a yard. Even the best Scotch cloth cost 6*d*. a yard more than the dearest English variety.[1] Earlier the epithet 'Scotch' had been synonymous with cheap and poor quality.

There exists in the Norfolk Record Office, amongst the Kirkpatrick manuscripts, a small account book dealing with cloth dispatched and received from Holland, chiefly in 1703–04.[2] The accounts deal mainly with linen cloth bought in Holland, usually at Haarlem but occasionally at Alkmaar or Amsterdam, for a Norwich merchant, Thomas Andrews, who imported a variety of linens: Osnabrucks, Borelaps, Tekelinburgs, Ravensberger as well as Hollands, all obviously of Dutch or German origin. Judging from the variety and quantities of foreign linen found in the probate inventories of late seventeenth and early eighteenth century drapers, there must have been many more importers like Thomas Andrews and some justification for the frequent complaints about imports.

---

[1] Henry Best, *Rural Economy in Yorkshire in 1641, being the Farming and Account Books of Henry Best of Elmeswell in the East Riding*, edited by C.B. Robinson, Surtees Society XXXIII (1857), pp. 105–6, reprinted in Thirsk and Cooper, pp. 252–3.

[2] NRO Shelf 21, Box 12/92

Nordern's *The Surveyor's Dialogue* of 1607 made various suggestions for the profitable use of all land such as sowing hemp on small areas of land left idle and overgrown with weeds which hemp would smother. 'The hemp is of great use in a farmer's house, as is found in Suffolk, Norfolk, Sussex, Dorset . . . not only for cordage for shipping, but also for linen, and other necessaries about a house.'[1]

After the Restoration the number of tracts on commerce increased, and many dealt with the linen industry. An Act of 1663 'for Encouraging the Manufactures of Making Linen Cloth and Tapestry' was intended to end the import of linen cloth and other goods manufactured from hemp and flax. To encourage home manufactures the Act permitted anyone, native or foreign, 'to set up and exercise the trade, occupation, or mystery of breaking, hickling, or dressing of hemp or flax as also for making and whitening of thread, as also of spinning, weaving, making, whitening or bleaching of any sort of cloth whatsoever made of hemp or flax only'.[2] How successful this Act was may be judged from Thomas Andrews's accounts, and from the 1697 report of the commissioners of trade and plantations on the state of trade: 'We don't find that the linen manufacture in this kingdom hath made any great progress of late.' Like so many before them they claimed that 'as good linen for all ordinary uses may be made in England as any that comes from abroad', and proposed retaining 'a considerable duty on all linens imported except from Ireland' in order to 'prevent the importation of great quantities of linen now imported on us from France and other foreign countries'.[3]

Sir Richard Haines in a tract explaining the causes of 'the Decay of Trade' written in 1674, wanted linen imports banned because this would be 'most advantageous to the general good . . . for it is most certain that our English ground will produce hemp and flax in such abundance, as may make linen cloth sufficient for all occasions'.[4] Haines was only one of an important group of late seventeenth-century writers who thought that the spread of linen manufacture would shift the balance of trade in England's favour and do much to solve the problem of poverty. Their aim was often to start a new industry in counties where none existed, as in Yarranton's proposal. He believed Leicestershire, Northamptonshire, Oxfordshire and Warwickshire to be the best for linen because their land was suitable for growing flax and there was no other local industry.[5] Yarranton had been apprenticed to a

---

[1] Thirsk and Cooper, p.109
[2] Thirsk and Cooper, pp. 738–9, printing 15Car. II, *c*.15
[3] Thirsk and Cooper, p.576
[4] Sir Richard Haines, *The Prevention of Poverty* (1674), p.5, henceforth Haines
[5] Yarranton, p.48

linen draper and so claimed to know 'something of Linen'.[1] He produced very ambitious plans for a 'New Brunswick' and a 'New
Haarlem' at Stratford-on-Avon,[2] but seemed to think little of the
chances of success of a similar scheme in Suffolk. 'About seven or eight
years since there was a Proposal of setting up the Linen Manufacture in
and near Ipswich', and Yarranton was invited to visit the town and give
his views. When he gave his opinion that the plan would not succeed,
mainly because of the competition for labour from the stuff and say
trades, the scheme was dropped.[3]

The wars of the latter part of Louis XIV's reign were partly responsible for the trade depressions of this period, but some English writers,
such as the anonymous and unduly pessimistic author of *Britannia
Languens, or a Discourse of Trade*,[4] found other reasons. He claimed that
English-grown hemp and flax could not compete with imports because
their price was raised by the payment of tithes on these crops, and that
the decay of the English cloth trade to the Baltic meant that hemp and
flax bought at Hamburg had to be paid for in cash instead of by
exchange. He also blamed the Navigation Acts for the high cost of raw
materials leading to the decay of the manufactures of linen, cables, sails
and fishing nets. A third reason advanced for the decline of English
linen production was 'the more general Use of Dear Fine Hollands, and
other fine Forreign Linnens of great Value; which till of later Years
were only worn by some People of Quality, and be them very
sparingly'. This view of the damage caused by the increased wearing of
foreign linens was echoed by Samuel Fortrey, who suggested that heavy
import duties on a range of luxury goods, among which was linen cloth,
would make them 'so dear to the people that it will much wean them
from so lavish an use of them'.[5] Although the writer of *Britannia
Languens* was undoubtedly protesting too much, there was some truth
in his claims.

Interestingly the author of *Britannia Languens* seems to imply that
women operated linen looms in 'Cheshire, Lancashire, and the Parts
adjacent' and 'did keep very many Thousands of Linnen Looms at
work in England, and did supply the greatest part of our National
occasion for Household and Coarse Linnens of all sorts'. He goes on to
make the rather improbable claim that 'the Huswifely Women of
England now employ themselves in making an ill sort of Lace . . . or are
idle, bringing a Scandal on themselves and their Families; so that there
is hardly a working Linnen Loom left in a County'. Does he perhaps

---

[1] Yarranton, p.55   [2] ibid, facing p.135   [3] ibid, p.49
[4] Reprinted in *Early English Tracts on Commerce*, edited by J.R. McCulloch (Cambridge,
1952)
[5] Samuel Fortrey, *England's Interest and Improvement* (Cambridge, 1663), pp. 28–29

mean not that the women used to operate looms, but that they used to spin yarn for weavers?

XI

Although linen-weaving in rural East Anglia appears to have flourished in the seventeenth century, the history of Ipswich in the same period illustrates its failure to become established in urban centres. Unlike Norwich, Ipswich had no dominant trade in this century, during which its cloth trade was declining. A modern study of the town shows how the canvas industry developed there in the last quarter of the sixteenth century[1] Reed writes: 'In Ipswich the linen and canvas sector of the textile industry was probably as important as the woollen.'[2] He thinks that the granting to the Collins brothers in 1574 of a 21-year monopoly in making mildernix and poldavis in Ipswich and Woodbridge was an attempt to establish a new industry in England. Williams pointed out that canvas was the major import from the French Channel Ports, and that most of it was made in or near Caen and Rouen. He places the beginning of English canvas manufacture as late as 1590.[3] In 1603 an Act was passed 'against the deceitful and false making of Mildernix and Powle Davies, whereof Sail-Cloths for the Navy and other Shipping are made.' Its aim was to regulate the manufacture of these two types of canvas, both of which originated in France and were extensively used for sail cloth. It complained that the cloth had been made too thin and in incorrect lengths and breadths, and decreed that in future they should be made only by those who had served a seven-year apprenticeship in their making. After 1 August 1603 no one was to make or weave these cloths 'of any other Stuff than of good and sufficient Hemp, nor of any less Length than Three and thirty Yards, nor of any less Breadth than Three Quarters of a Yard'. Before being sold 'the stuff was to be well beaten, scoured, bleached, and the Cloth well driven with a brazen or iron shuttle'.[4] Reed says that the industry became well established and there was a considerable demand for Ipswich canvas for the navy during much of the seventeenth century. Bungay was another Suffolk town where the sail cloth industry flourished. Bungay canvas is mentioned in the description of the fitting out of a herring buss in 1615; 96 yards were

---

[1] Michael Reed, 'Ipswich in the Seventeenth Century'; (unpublished University of Leicester Ph.D. thesis, 1973), henceforth Reed, 1973. Much of this section on Ipswich is based on this thesis.
[2] Reed, 1973, p.30
[3] Williams, p.132
[4] 1 James I cap. XXIV

required for the main topsail and 20 for the mizzen sail.[1] In Pepys's time five warships, each of 1000 tons, required 50 tons of hemp for cordage and ground tackle.[2] Thus it is not surprising that farmers were so frequently exhorted to grow hemp and that so much had to be imported.

As explained in chapter 3 all the twill and sack cloth weavers found in probate records lived near Woodbridge or Ipswich, and, with one exception, the same is true of poldavis weavers; the exception lived at Dennington near Framlingham. Apart from a Marlesford poldavis weaver who died in 1661, the nine known all died in the first half of the seventeenth century; five lived in Ipswich, one at Woodbridge and the last at Wickham Market. Two other poldavis weavers are known because they were named as executors of the wills of fellow craftsmen. All but the Ipswich poldavis weavers were part-time farmers or at least owned land; well over half the value of the inventory of Thomas Rindge of Woodbridge comprised his crops and livestock.[3] The Marlesford man was only a smallholder with one cow, but his yarn and cloth were worth nearly £50.[4] The two surviving inventories of Ipswich poldavis weavers have both been printed.[5] Thomas Hawkins died in 1610 leaving goods worth £40 16s. 9d., the most interesting of which are seven looms worth a pound each and 'ii bybeles being eould' valued at 5s.; he also had £17 in cash in his house. Five years later died Henry Piper, whom Reed describes as 'a master manufacturer'. His goods were worth £26 more than those of Thomas Hawkins, but he owned only one bible. There were three looms in one of his workshops and six in the other and five had partly-made lengths of cloth on them. In the yard outside some yarn was drying on poles well out of reach of his two pigs and poultry. He also owned a mare and colt, and some fodder for them. For a town house his was quite substantial and was approached through a two-storey gatehouse. His will shows that he owned not only the house he lived in, but two other tenements and some 'taynters' yards, all in the parish of St Nicholas.[6]

The Ipswich Cloth Hall rents show that later in the seventeenth century the textile trade declined, and after the Restoration several attempts were made to encourage new industries in the town.[7] Nothing came of proposals made in 1668–9 to settle Dutch immigrants here to

[1] E. Smith, *Britain's Buss* (1615) quoted in Ethel Mann, *Old Bungay* (1934), p.151, henceforth Mann
[2] Hinton, p.100
[3] NRO NCC INV18/251 (1602)
[4] NRO NCC INV49/D11
[5] Reed, pp. 74, 82
[6] NRO NCC Angell 226
[7] Reed, 1973, p.65

make linen, even though they were offered a bleaching place. This is presumably the proposal referred to by Yarranton. In the 1680s considerable efforts were made to establish Huguenot refugee linen-weavers in Ipswich. In 1681 they were offered a church and sufficient stock to set up some 20 to 30 linen looms.[1] A London merchant named Thomas Papillon, who must surely have himself been a Huguenot, was treasurer of a fund to buy yarn for the French refugees at Ipswich.[2] In March 1683 £612 worth of manufactured linen, some holland and some coarse, was in hand. The French weavers were reported as being numerous and peacable, but very poor; the accounts of the fund show that clothes were 'furnished in necessity' for some and hearth tax was also paid on their behalf. They had their own minister, M. Caesar Beaulieu, who was paid a salary of £52 a year. Due to a shortage of spinners the town had to buy foreign yarn to keep the French weavers at work. In spite of all these efforts this attempt to establish linen weaving in Ipswich did not succeed; the reasons for this failure are not clear. A letter written in the spring of 1686 to the Bishop of Norwich asked him to request the Bishop of London to assign some of the money granted by the Crown to French Protestants to maintain the 'French linen manufacture now in Ipswich'. The writer, Mr Gardeman of Ipswich, added that £2000 or £3000 would 'settle the manufacture for ever and employ not only the French that are now in Ipswich but many others alsoe, who will come to work in the same manufacture'. If no help was forthcoming the French would 'want work' before the end of the summer and leave the town.[3] It seems likely that this plea was not granted. Ipswich Corporation gave the French weavers £100 in March 1686, and in November of the same year granted them leave to convert six linen looms 'to the use of the Woollen trade'. In the following February the Ipswich Assembly book records 'the Frenchmen shall have liberty to make Hatts & open shopp & sell them in this Towne'. In December 1690 the Corporation was making yet another attempt to establish linen manufacturing in the town. On this occasion a company or 'Corporation' was set up, and offered a 'Convenient Workhouse' and a warehouse rent free, as well as a bleaching ground ('Blechery') at a low rent. In March 1691 the committee appointed by the Corporation to superintend the setting-up of a linen manufactury was expecting the visit of a gentleman from London 'about the Lynnen Manufactory'. After this entry in the Assembly book no more is heard of the committee or of the linen manufacturing. However, in 1693 there were

[1] Reed, 1973, p.71
[2] The accounts of this fund presented to a General Meeting held on 25 March 1683 have been printed in *East Anglian Notes and Queries*, New Series, II (1887–8), pp. 375–7
[3] Bodleian Library, Tanner MS 92, f. 124

still 50 French Huguenot families living in Ipswich and engaged in making lutestring, a silk cloth.[1] As Reed points out, this French community failed to maintain itself and contributed little to the 'faltering economy of Ipswich'.[2] A plausible reason for their failure is that the fine linens they produced suffered from the competition of imported cloth. This seems more probable than the rivalry of rural East Anglian linen-weavers, who concentrated on the cheap end of the market.

Apart from the dornix weavers already mentioned, the registers of Norwich freemen list 20 linen-weavers between 1548 and 1713; 14 date from the sixteenth century and the other 6 between 1600 and 1640. Linen-weaving thus seems to have been declining rather than growing in importance in Norwich as at Ipswich in the seventeenth century.

XII

Many contemporary writers advocated the development of the linen industry as a means of solving the problem of poverty, and it may be this that has led modern authors to view it, in the words of one, as 'essentially a pauper industry'.[3] However, this approach to English linen-weaving ignores the fact that in the seventeenth century at least it made a considerable contribution to the economies of several regions. In East Anglia there were a number of prosperous linen-weavers catering, as elsewhere in England, for a largely local market. Lack of evidence about the industry explains both why it has been largely ignored by historians, and why it has been assumed to have been the province of the poor. It would be idle to deny that hemp preparation and spinning were amongst the principal occupations of paupers for well over two centuries or that many weavers were poor, yet it is equally misleading to ignore the prosperous side of the linen-weaving industry.

Sir Richard Haines's proposals, published in 1674, are typical of those stressing the benefits of increasing the manufacture of linen yarn and cloth. He claimed that there were some 580,000 members of pauper families who had little employment except in harvest time, and that they and wandering beggars could be employed in making linen. 'Thirdly, by this means every parish, which by reason of poverty is not

---

[1] *East Anglian Notes and Queries*, New Series, II (1887–8), pp. 398–400

[2] Reed, 1973, p.72. More recent work by Reed on the overseas and coastal Port Books has shown that the town's economic situation was less gloomy than he earlier thought. Although Ipswich's overseas trade declined, its coastal trade continued to prosper. Michael Reed, 'Economic Structure and change in seventeenth-century Ipswich', in *Country towns in pre-industrial England*, edited by Peter Clark (Leicester, 1981)

[3] Dorothy Marshall, *The English Poor in the eighteenth century* (1926, second edition 1969), p.40, henceforth Marshall.

able to set up a manufactory for the employment of their poor, in making of woollen cloth, according to the statute in that case made and provided, may easily provide employment for them in making of linen, whereby many thousands that now wholy rely on the parish wherein they live for maintenance might very well support themselves.'[1] Writers like Haines seem not to have considered whether their proposals might undercut and throw out of work those already engaged in the linen trade, nor whether a market existed for the yarn and cloth they envisaged being produced by the poor.

Recent work on 2500 Suffolk probate inventories, dating from 1560–1700, has revealed that a high percentage of poor people owned spinning wheels.[2] They were also common amongst the possessions of the better-off, and were doubtless used by female servants if not by members of the family. In the Forest of Arden the percentage of households of below average wealth in which carding and spinning equipment were found increased from 33 per cent in 1530–69 to 60 per cent in 1570–1609. Here, as in other weaving districts, 'the effect which weaving had on the employment situation in the area must have been even greater than these figures' – the increase in the number of weavers – suggest. For this craft did more than provide work and earnings for the full-time weavers themselves. Since it took a quite disproportionate amount of labour to keep one weaver supplied with yarn, it also generated what was easily the area's most important domestic by-employment.'[3] In East Anglia too the preparation and spinning of hemp and flax, like stocking knitting, was mainly carried out by the wives and children of husbandmen and cottagers, and as Skipp says, the preparation of yarn for weavers was an 'absolutely vital cottage industry'.[4]

Winding yarn onto the spools to be inserted into shuttles was an occupation for children and could be started at a very early age. As Ariès has told us, a child entered the adult world 'Once he had passed the age of five or seven . . . this concept of a brief childhood lasted for a long time in the lower classes.'[5] This is borne out by the evidence of mid-nineteenth-century census returns in which it is not unusual to find boys of 8 or younger described as farm labourers. The linen industry was frequently advocated as suitable for the employment of those who were too old or weak or unskilled to find other work. Alice

[1] Haines, p.5
[2] Rachel Garrard, 'Domestic Interiors 1560–1700', paper read to the Centre of East Anglian Studies research seminar, 16 March, 1979
[3] Skipp, p.57
[4] ibid, p.57
[5] Philippe Ariès, *Centuries of Childhood* (1962, 1973 edition), p. 316

Clark has shown how low were the wages paid to spinners of flax and hemp, so low that women who depended on their earnings were condemned to pauperism. For spinning the finest wool the rate of pay was sixpence a pound, but for linen thread only one penny per skein.[1]

In Elizabethan Ipswich the wardens of the Tooley Foundation and the Governors of Christ's Hospital bought tow cards to employ the poor, and made frequent purchases of canvas, hempen cloth and other kinds of cheap linens to make clothes and sheets for the poor in their care. On more than one occasion canvas to make shirts, smocks and sheets for inmates of Christ's Hospital was bought in London; this suggests that in the 1580s insufficient quantities were being produced locally to meet demand.[2] The register of the poor for 1569–83 records at Michaelmas 1579 the apprenticing of Nathaniell Wylson, aged 9, who was 'delyveryd and put to service with Robert Patten, lynnen wever' for nine years; this boy and his widowed mother had been admitted to Christ's Hospital three years earlier.[6] A census of the poor of Ipswich was made in 1597, and survives for nine of the twelve parishes then existing. This document lists ages, work and wages of adults and children, any relief being received and their wants. It includes four women spinning flax, one dressing hemp and five picking oakum; there were also a male oakum picker, a poldavis weaver and a twill weaver. Many of these people, including the poldavis weaver were out of work, but Barnard Knatt the twill-weaver, was earning 3s. a week, and his wife who 'helpeth him in his work', 1s. This couple were aged 40 and 26, and the eldest of their four children, who was only 6, 'windeth quiles' (spools) for 2d. a week. The Knatt family were in need of firing and 'Stock at xxs to set himselfe a-worke'. Oakum-pickers' earnings varied from 4d. to 1s., and most spinners in work earned 6d. a week. The majority of the women listed in the census spun, or knitted or made lace when employment was available.[4] Celia Fiennes's comments on knitting and spinning have already been quoted, but she also wrote that some used 'the rock and fusoe' or spindle, 'others at their wheeles out in the streete and lanes as one passes'.[5] The evidence of Elizabethan Ipswich records suggests that spinning was as common amongst the poor in large towns as in the countryside.

Overseers' accounts dating from the seventeenth century are not common, and even rarer is any reference in them to the provision of work for able-bodied paupers. The accounts for two Bedfordshire

[1] Clark, pp. 129–30
[2] *Poor Relief in Elizabethan Ipswich*, edited by John Webb, Suffolk Record Society, IX (1966), *passim*, henceforth Webb
[3] ibid, p.82
[4] SROI EE2/I/I Eye Assembly Book 1649–69
[5] Webb, pp. 122–140

Figure 4.1   A flax spinning wheel from Charles Tomlinson, *The Useful Arts and Manufactures of Great Britain* (1854). Due to the length of the fibres, wheels used for flax and hemp are much taller than wool wheels.

parishes provide evidence of the employment of their poor.[1] At Kempton in 1631 flax and hemp were purchased by the overseers and spun and woven by the parish poor; the cloth was sold at a loss of approximately 11*s*. Detailed accounts exist for cloth-making at Goldington between 1649 and 1654, and show that a profit was never made. As this parish had no workhouse the work must have been carried out in the paupers' own houses. Flax and hemp were purchased for 6*d* or 7*d*. a pound; 4*d*. a pound was paid for spinning hemp; in 1651–3 whiting and winding 68 pounds of yarn cost 9*s*. 3*d*. and weaving

---

[1] Fiennes, p.146

2*d*. the ell. The finished cloth was sold at prices varying from 9*d*. to 12¾*d*. per ell. Presumably the constant losses were the reason for the end of this experiment, and may explain why so few parishes implemented the clause of the 1601 Act concerning pauper employment. At Eye, in the Suffolk hemp district, in 1649 the burgesses ordered the purchase of a stock of hemp to set the 'poore on Worke'. The sum of 18*s*. was spent on hemp, which was to be sold to the poor at a reasonable rate, and another £10 on purchasing a stock for use in the workhouse. The borough minutes contain no further references, so presumably this scheme too proved a failure.[1]

There undoubtedly existed poor linen-weavers in the seventeenth century, but they have left practically no evidence; the situation was different in the two following centuries. Dorothy Marshall pointed out that the attraction of the linen trade to those who sought to employ the poor was the small outlay required on tools and materials, and that it required neither great skill nor strength. As was shown in chapter 2, this latter statement, if it applies to weaving, is open to considerable dispute. She quotes from a seventeenth-century writer: 'This manu-factory was an employment for the weakest people; not capable of stronger work, being widows and children and decrepit and aged people, now the most chargeable, as likewise for Beggars and Vagrants, who live idly and by the sweat of other Men's labours.'[2]

It is to be doubted whether many paupers, either in workhouses or living at home, were employed in weaving; hemp and flax dressing, and spinning were far more usual occupations for these people. Clearly there existed a polarisation within the linen trade between the poor spinners on the one hand and the very rich weavers on the other; between them lay a large number of weavers of varying wealth, as well as ancillary workers, many of whom were only partly dependent on their earnings from spinning or other tasks connected with the prepara-tion of yarn. As Dr Thirsk has pointed out, by-employments were not subsidiary to farming but were an integral part of the way of life in pastoral regions.[3]

XIII

'It seems reasonable to suggest that the pasture-farming regions of the kingdom in the seventeenth century presented a picture of greater

[1] David H. Kennett, 'A Pauper Cloth-making account of the seventeenth century', *Textile History*, 4 (1973), 125–129

[2] Marshall, p.40, quoting Sir Richard Haines, *Proposals for a Working Hospital, etc* (1678), p.4

[3] Thirsk, 1970, p.172

economic prosperity for larger numbers of people than the arable regions.'[1] Dr Thirsk's conclusions about the economic circumstances of areas such as wood-pasture East Anglia are borne out by the history of Norfolk and Suffolk in this century, when the close integration of rural industry and farming protected peasant workers from the worst effects of both agrarian and trade depressions. An industry whose products were sold almost entirely in the domestic market, and most of whose workers were part-time, has left few traces of its existence in government records and no contemporary statistical accounts.

A recent inventory-based study of the dual economy in south Staffordshire has shown a decline in the proportion of families engaged in livestock farming during the seventeenth century, and that this decline was particularly marked amongst metal workers. This suggests that 'agricultural and industrial occupations were becoming increasingly divorced from each other' with an increased dependence on cash income from the produce of manufacturing. In the long term this led to the decline of Staffordshire metal-workers from a position of relative security in the sixteenth century to the depths of poverty in the early nineteenth century.[2] It is certainly true that the majority of East Anglian linen-weavers, in common with many other craftsmen, followed the same path, but there is no indication in their inventories of a decline in livestock ownership during the seventeenth and early eighteenth centuries. It seems that here the decay of the dual economy – a destruction brought about by its very success – occurred in the later eighteenth century. Dr Thirsk has shown how the rise in the wages of textile workers in the period 1700–50 reflected the rapidly rising demand for their goods. The inability of farmer-craftsmen to satisfy this demand led to pressure on them to give up their land and become full-time industrial workers. This change seems to have occurred earlier in the pastoral regions of the north and midlands than in the southern half of the country. Technical innovation and the appearance of large numbers of full-time factory and out-workers were the response to increased demand in the areas to be most directly affected by the industrial revolution.[3]

Linen-weaving made a major contribution to the economy of East Anglia in the seventeenth century, but during the next century the balance between agriculture and industry tipped towards the latter. As a result rural craftsmen everywhere suffered impoverishment, but more acutely so in regions where technical innovations were not

[1] ibid, p.175
[2] Pauline Frost, 'Yeomen and Metalsmiths: Livestock in the Dual Economy in South Staffordshire 1560–1720', *Agricultural History Review*, 29 (1981), 40–41
[3] Thirsk, 1970, p.176

adopted. Here in the later eighteenth century competition from new industries in the north combined with changes in agriculture to pauperise peasant workers.

5   The Eighteenth Century

'Linen is a Thing universally worn and wanted'
                    Daniel Defoe, *A Plan of the English Commerce.*

I

Defoe, writing in the 1720s, described the heyday of dual occupations which already lay in the past, albeit the recent past. This system ran into trouble during the eighteenth century when hand craftsmen came into competition with factories and their economic position grew insecure. What in the seventeenth century had been merely an additional source of income had by the end of the eighteenth century often become for many families their sole support. The bad reputation of the domestic system of industry comes from its dying days when workers laboured excessively long hours for a mere pittance. In the period when the balance of the economy was favourable to cottage industry and multiple occupations, the system had provided an adequate, and in many cases a comfortable living for large numbers of country dwellers. By the end of the eighteenth century the disastrous economic and social effects of the decay and collapse of the domestic system were apparent.

Although little is known of English linen manufacture in the eighteenth century and no effective legislative measures were taken to encourage it before a bounty on exports was introduced in 1743, it grew to be an important industry during this century. The bounty lapsed in 1753, but was renewed from time to time until its final abandonment in 1830. Native sailcloth-makers had received some assistance a few years earlier, in 1736, when an Act of Parliament obliged every ship built in England to have one suit of sails made of English cloth.[1] The active encouragement of the industry led to 40 or so years of expansion, followed by a decline during the final decade of the century. A steep rise in exports in the third quarter reached a peak of 9,555,000 yards in 1760; in 1700 the figure had been a mere 181,000 yards; although there were some fluctuations, exports remained at much the same level until 1790 when they were 9,223,000 yards.[2] Even before the introduction of the bounty, one contemporary writer believed that between 1728 and

[1] Geo. II, cap. 37
[2] Harte, p.108

1734 English linen production considerably exceeded that of either Scotland or Ireland,[1] and a modern writer considers that for most of the eighteenth and early nineteenth centuries enough linen was produced for it 'to rank as a major textile industry in England'.[2]

During the first half of the century imports remained high enough to impress Defoe, although they had ceased their earlier speedy growth. 'The quantity of linen imported yearly into England is so prodigious great . . . that no estimate can be made of it. The least that I have heard it valued at, has been a million sterling per annum.'[3] Thus Defoe wrote in 1726, and modern figures show his estimate to have been not far out. At the beginning of the eighteenth century the value of imported linens was just under a million pounds and by the middle of the century not very much more. During the same period flax and hemp imports had more than doubled and re-exports of linen, chiefly to the colonies, had increased nearly as much.[4] Defoe was much concerned by England's reliance on imported linens, and seems not to have realised how much the introduction of heavy duties after 1690 had discouraged imports and encouraged the growth of the home industry, particularly in Ireland and Scotland. These customs duties were not protective, but purely fiscal in purpose and were leived to raise money for William III's and Queen Anne's wars with France.[5] Although not intended to be protective, these duties bore especially heavily on French products and were thus more than merely fiscal in their effects. This led to pressure from interest groups to continue protection of English manufactures.[6] The small increase in the value of linen imports between 1700 and 1750 indicates the success of this unintentional protection of the home industry.

Writing in 1728, Defoe referred to imports of 'great Quantities of Linen-Yarn, for our own people to manufacture'. Most of this yarn came from Holland, Hamburg and Russia, and in Defoe's opinion was used mainly by linen-weavers in the northern English countries and by manufacturers of linsey-woolsey in and around Manchester and Kidderminster.[7] His view confirms the findings from the seventeenth-century port books noted in chapter 4. According to Defoe 'the Consumption of Wine and Linen in England is prodigious', and more

---

[1] Horner, pp. 223–7

[2] Harte, p.103

[3] Daniel Defoe, *The Complete English Tradesman*, 2 volumes (1841), 2, p.16, henceforth Defoe, 1841

[4] B.A. Holderness, *Pre-Industrial England: Economy and Society, 1500–1750* (1976), p.130

[5] Harte, p.97

[6] D.C. Coleman, *The Economy of England, 1450–1750* (Oxford, 1977), p.188

[7] Daniel Defoe, *A Plan of the English Commerce* (Oxford, 1927), p.160

was imported than by any other country.[1] He was, however, aware that recent Acts prohibiting the wearing or use of imported calicoes had led to an increase in home linen manufacture and to a rise in imports from Scotland and Ireland,[2] and claimed that two million yards, chiefly of printed linen, were annually imported from the latter country.[3]

Apart from the years 1782–5, for which statistics concerning the bounty paid on home-grown flax and hemp are available,[4] it is impossible to know how much the industry relied on native or imported raw materials. Horner gives the value of flax and hemp grown in 1773 in four counties, one of which was Norfolk. This county's hemp production was worth £19,000, considerably less than that of Lincolnshire, and its flax crop at a mere £1000 was nothing compared to the £70,000's worth grown in Yorkshire.[5] The bounty seems to have achieved little. Writing in 1805, Oddy said : 'The bounty given some years ago, by government, on hemp and flax, produced no visible effect in increasing the growth.', and added that many growers never claimed the bounty because of the difficulties attendant upon obtaining it.'[6]

In 1788 an order was given at the quarter sessions held at Beccles for the publication in two local newspapers, the *Ipswich Journal* and the *Bury and Norwich Post*, of a list of Suffolk growers who claimed the bounty on hemp and flax. There were only two claimants in 1788, one living at Bungay and the other at Beccles; the latter's claim was in respect of hemp grown during the four years 1784–7 on land in and around his home town. The following year there were 15 claimants growing hemp in 20 different parishes, mostly in the Eye and Hoxne district with the Rickinghall and Stowmarket areas next in importance. All except the last-named lie in the traditional hemp-growing area of Suffolk. The farmer growing the largest amounts was James Read of Hoxne, who claimed for 149 stone produced from three acres in 1787 and for 174 stone grown on four acres in 1788. Arthur Young considered 40 stones an acre a reasonable yield for hemp.

Both rough hemp and rough flax were imported in growing quantities throughout the eighteenth century, but the former increased 9 times while the latter grew only 6.5 times between 1700 and 1799.[7] England was at war for 47 years during the period 1702–1802, but the relation-

---

[1] ibid., p. 59
[2] ibid., pp. 221–2
[3] ibid., p.156
[4] Harte, p.106, using PRO BT6/97, 28 and BT6/99, pp. 6, 14
[5] Horner, p.234
[6] Joshua Jepson Oddy, *European Commerce* (1805), p.573, henceforth Oddy
[7] E.B. Schumpeter, *English Overseas Trade Statistics, 1697–1808* (Oxford, 1960), tables xiv and xvii

ship between hemp imports and international conflicts does not resemble that between hemp prices and the Anglo-Dutch wars of the preceding century. In 1799 imports of hemp were 752,547 hundredweight and of flax 418,737 hundredweight;[1] these figures provide justification for the complaints of Oddy and Arthur Young. (see p. 127)

The uncompetitive nature of English linens cannot too often be stressed. Most English linen was a very poor quality huckaback, 'which did not seriously compete with imported Holland and Silesia linens.[2] Dr Ormrod also points out that it is impossible to quantify English linen production.[3] The fall in linen imports after the mid-1730s cannot be taken as an indication of declining demand, for it was balanced by increased production in Scotland and Ireland and almost certainly in England as well. In the absence of statistics the evidence for the growth of English linen manufacture can only be circumstantial. Contemporary estimates suggest it rose from 21 million yards *c*.1730 to 26 million in 1754, and a modern view is that by 1770 'it seems likely that the output of the English industry was in the region of 33 million yards.[4] The likelihood is that the English linen industry grew in much the same way, although at a lower rate, as the Scottish, with growth starting around 1730, reaching a peak in 1763 and thereafter growing more slowly with output probably falling in the final quarter of the century.[5] The imports statistics for yarn and flax support the opinion that the fastest expansion of the English linen industry occurred between 1740 and 1770.[6] Contemporary opinion confirms the view that the English linen industry was in decline in the late eighteenth century.

Although there is little reliable information about English linen output, there are various pointers to its growth. The home market for linen was expanding throughout most of the eighteenth century. Between roughly 1680 and 1750 low food prices and slow population growth combined to increase the real value of wages, and so created a rise in demand for manufactured goods in general. The rise in expectations resulting from the improvement in the real value of earnings surely increased demand for linens as well as for other consumer durables, and there is evidence to show that the consumption of personal and household linen rose during the seventeenth century. Mrs Garrard's very detailed study of Suffolk probate inventories provides

---

[1] ibid
[2] David John Ormrod, 'Anglo-Dutch Commerce, 1700–1760', (unpublished University of Cambridge Ph.D. thesis, 1973), p. 55, henceforth Ormrod
[3] Harte (1973, pp. 105–7) makes the best attempt to estimate this.
[4] Phyllis Deane and W.A. Cole, *British Economic Growth, 1688–1959* (Cambridge, 1964), p.53
[5] ibid, p.53
[6] ibid, p.53 footnote

the data to support this view. A comparison between testators with personal estate worth £12 and under in 1570–99 and those with goods worth £25 or less in 1680–1700 reveals an increase of 85 per cent in median wealth, and one of 271 per cent in the value of linen of all kinds.[1] This dramatic increase in the value of linens found in the inventories of the poorest group to have left probate records is very significant, and there is no reason why it should not be extrapolated into the eighteenth century. It was just these people who were most likely to have been the customers of East Anglian linen-weavers. Not only in linens did a wider range of qualities and prices appear in the later seventeenth century to meet the demand for consumer goods from a new class of purchasers.[2]

Dr Ormrod suggests that from 1706 the duties on imported linens probably discouraged the import of the cheaper and coarser linens from Holland.[3] This development must have given encouragement to the native industry, which had always concentrated on just these types of linen. In 1731 stealing linen from bleaching grounds was declared a felony.[4] If this Act indicates an increase in bleaching in England, it could also be taken as a sign of rising linen production.

Unfortunately both contemporary and modern writers ignore the linen industry of East Anglia. The report made by the House of Commons committee set up to consider the petitions from the dealers in and manufacturers of linen in Great Britain and Ireland noted an increase in the manufacture of coarse linen in many English counties, mainly in the north and south-west, but made no mention of Norfolk or Suffolk.[5] Deane's and Cole's estimates of linen production refer mainly to north-west England and are largley based on imports of flax. In East Anglia hemp was widely used by linen-weavers, and there is some evidence that not all the locally produced cloth was of the coarse variety.

During the eighteenth century, just as in the seventeenth, East Anglian linens continued to be produced chiefly for the local mass market. Luxury stuffs, many of mixed fibres, were manufactured in Norwich, but broadly speaking in this region, as elsewhere in England, the cloth produced in the countryside was of cheaper quality. Dr Thirsk thinks that this difference between urban and rural industries

---

[1] I am extremely grateful to Mrs Garrard for allowing me to see her data, and to Dr M Spufford for letting me use her analysis of this data. The size of the sample for 1570–99 is 349, and for 1680–1700 is 397.
[2] Spufford, 1984, *passim*.
[3] Ormrod, p.79
[4] 4 Geo. II, cap. 16
[5] *Reports from Committees of the House of Commons*, II (1737–65), pp. 65–72

was true of all 'wares'.[1] Sixty years earlier Horner made much the same point: that the English eighteenth-century linen industry is little known because its products were chiefly sold in villages and towns near the place of manufacture.[2] Owen's *Book of Fairs*, published in 1756, lists 54 dealing in linen and flax, and by 1783 *Owen's New Book of Fairs* listed 72 fairs specialising in these goods, but none were in East Anglia.

II

Although the history of English linens has been neglected, this is no longer true of the Scottish linen industry in the eighteenth century, which saw its growth 'from a small, backward and unimportant . . . craft to . . . a major British industry'.[3] In Scotland, as elsewhere, linen-weaving had originated in the early Middle Ages as a part-time rural occupation. Around 1700 a few Glasgow merchants 'were the suppliers of linen for the chapmen and peddlars to take south each year',[4] but in fact 'Scotch cloth' is found in East Anglian drapers' inventories long before this. The inventory of a Great Yarmouth linen draper, made in 1614, lists Scotch cloth as does that of a St Albans dyer, drawn up in 1674.[5] Many chapmen were Scots and it is natural to find them carrying the products of their country. At Bury Sessions in July 1676 the justices blamed the increase in robberies on 'idle, loose and unbeknowne persons' (such as 'Pedlers petty chapmen jugglers & fortune Tellers') amongst whom 'are a great number of Scotchmen wnadering about as Pedlers petty Chapmen which lately have & still do daily increase'.[6]

At the time of the Union in 1707 Scotland was an extremely poor country, and this poverty hindered the development of its linen or any other industry because there was little demand and what did exist was for cheap, poor quality goods. The revolution in the Scottish linen industry was brought about by the injection of capital, by its promotion by merchants and landowners and by the imposition of standards by the British Linen Company. In 1727 an Act was passed 'for the Better Regulation of Linen and Hempen Manufactures in Scotland', and henceforth linen that reached the required standards of quality, length and breadth was stamped. Efforts to improve and encourage the growing of flax were less successful than those made to raise the quality of linen. The greatest expansion in the Scottish linen industry occurred

[1] Thirsk, 1978, p.109
[2] Horner, pp. 223–7
[3] Durie, p.1
[4] Durie, p.12
[5] NRO NCC INV26/252 and Herts CRO A25/3944
[6] SROI 105/2/10; Quarter Sessions Order Book 1676–83

after 1740 with the increase in urban production and in the number of factories. Earlier in the century it had still been a predominantly rural industry with weavers working at home. The success of Scottish linens was short-lived: in the 1770s it was the most important industry in the country, but by the end of the century it had lost this position to cotton in spite of the introduction of scutching and flax-spinning mills. Nevertheless, annual linen output in Scotland had risen from just over 2 million yards in 1728 to 36 million in 1815. No comparable information is available for England or Ireland, but the latter country certainly produced more than Scotland as English imports of Irish linen always exceeded total Scottish production throughout the eighteenth century.[1]

The history of the Scottish linen industry in the eighteenth century suggests why the East Anglian failed to develop in the same way. In 1700 the region was still rich, supporting a variety of manufactures as well as a flourishing agriculture, and Norwich, the largest provincial city, 'was at its apogee'.[2] Its economy did not appear to need revitalising by the introduction of new industries or the development of old. In Norfolk and Suffolk linen-weaving remained a largely rural industry, which failed to attract capital investment. Towards the end of the century small-scale factories began to be established and the number of linen manufacturers, as opposed to independent weavers, increased, but there was no equivalent of the British Linen Company. This failure to adapt to changing circumstances proved disastrous, but even had the East Anglian industry followed the same path as the Scottish it would have in the end met the same fate: destruction by the cotton industry. A more forward-looking policy in the eighteenth century would have only briefly postponed the inevitable collapse.

III

As explained in chapter 2 the mechanisation of spinning and weaving was largely ignored in East Anglia until after the virtual extinction of the local linen industry. Even in the industrial North hand-loom weaving of both linen and cotton continued well into the nineteenth century. The number of cotton hand-loom weavers probably reached a peak in the 1820s, but by this date linen manufacturers were reducing the rates paid to their weavers in order to compete with cotton.[3] Power-loom weaving produced material suitable for sheets and shirts, but high quality linen was still hand-woven.[4] The decline of hand-loom weaving

[1] This paragraph is based on Durie *passim*
[2] P.J. Corfield, *Towns, Trade, Religion and Radicalism: the Norwich Perspective on English History* (Norwich, 1980), p.15, henceforth Corfield
[3] Bythell, p.54
[4] Jennings, p.254

was only one example of the displacement of workers by machinery during the Industrial Revolution; more important was the disappearance of by-occupations, such as spinning and knitting, which had enabled women and children to supplement family incomes.[1] The loss of this type of work was disastrous for rural industrial communities.

Precisely when did spinning cease to be a widespread by-employment in East Anglia? Throughout most of the eighteenth century demand for both woollen and linen yarn did not slacken. Norwich was still a major textile town and, although its high quality stuffs were woven in the City, the worsted and silk yarns they required were spun in the countryside.[2] In order to keep the Norwich weavers at work yarn-makers employed spinners all over Norfolk and Suffolk, and the strong competition for their services kept up their wages. The demand for linen yarn further increased the work opportunities for women, five of whom were required to spin sufficient yarn for one linen-weaver.[3]

The activities of James Oakes of Bury St Edmunds, the leading yarn-maker in Suffolk, indicate how far afield it was necessary to go to find sufficient spinners. In the early 1790s when he was running down his yarn business, Oakes employed at least 50 woolcombers and on his own calculations he must have needed 1500 spinners. His spinning network stretched from the coast near Woodbridge to Burwell in Cambridgeshire and from the Essex borders to High Suffolk. Earlier in his career he employed more combers and thus a larger number of spinners. There were probably only three other yarn firms of comparable size in the county, all in Bury St Edmunds, but there were many other woolcombers in both Norfolk and Suffolk. According to the evidence that Oakes gave to Arthur Young, about 17.5 per cent of the population of the latter county were employed in the wool yarn industry, that is in combing and spinning.[4] This figure is similar to an estimate of the number of English labouring households supplementing their income by knitting for the home and export markets as a by-employment in the 1690s – at least 15.3 per cent and possibly as many as 25 per cent.[5] Describing Norwich in the first part of the century, Defoe wrote that wool for its weavers was sent as far north as Westmorland to be spun so great were the quantities of yarn required.[6] Oakes's estimates refer only to the woollen industry, so to them must be added the unknown number of persons engaged in all the stages of hemp preparation, including spinning.

[1] Bythell, p.65
[2] Corfield, p.23
[3] Durie, p.13
[4] Young, 1813, pp. 232–3
[5] Thirsk, 1978, p.168
[6] Defoe, 1841, II, p.189

Another man who travelled across Suffolk to obtain yarn was Thomas Watling, 'Hemp-Cloth Weaver' of Woodbridge. He placed an advertisement in the *Ipswich Journal* for 28 November 1767 announcing that he had taken over his deceased brother's business and 'will meet the spinners at Cockfield Swan in Suffolk as his late brother did'. Cockfield is in west Suffolk and some considerable distance from Woodbridge.

In the early 1780s the Melton House of Industry was spinning wool for Oakes, and during the same decade Mr Herring, a Norwich yarn merchant, suggested that the Wangford and Bulcamp Houses of Industry should use his spinning machine. Thomas Gilbert's report of 1776 to the Committee on Relief and Settlement of Poor shows that working hemp was found in workhouses all over England, and that beating it was one of the commonest occupations in houses of correction. Gilbert mentions the spinning of hemp in four Suffolk workhouses.[1] Thomas Ruggles noted that in all the Suffolk Houses of Industry in existence in 1793 the inmates were spinning wool and that in six cases out of nine the yarn was being spun for Norwich woollen manufacturers.[2] The advantage of workhouses was that costs were low and that, with a number of workers under one roof, they provided a kind of primitive factory.

Attempts to employ the poor gainfully seem to have met with as little success in the eighteenth as in the preceding century. Spinning wool was given up at Melton workhouse at midsummer 1783 and more than five years elapsed before the manufacture of hemp was adopted late in 1788. Both the wool and the hemp business were very badly managed, so much so that the authors of a report, presented in February 1791, on the affairs of the workhouse pointed out that it had totally failed to live up to its name House of Industry. A three-man committee which enquired into the running of the hemp manufactury reported in June 1791 that much of the hemp cloth in stock was unsaleable because it was ill-woven and had been made from unwhitened thread. As a result the work done by the paupers had been rendered worthless. The report recommended that the poor quality cloth should be kept for use in the House, that in future all yarn should be bleached before weaving as was the usual practice in workhouses, and that the existing considerable stock of yarn should be whited by bleachers 'as the Process is attended with difficulty and cannot so well be effected in the House.'[3] The very damning report of the inquiry into the running of Melton House of Industry led to a new Act of Incorporation.

---

[1] *Sessional Papers 1774–1802*, IX, p. 255
[2] Thomas Ruggles, *The History of the Poor* (1793)
[3] SROI ADA11/AB1/2; Quarterly meetings minute book 1784–91

The employment of workhouse inmates in spinning, and to a lesser extent in weaving was detrimental to the livelihoods of other workers as it depressed wages and flooded the market with cheap, and often poor quality, yarn and cloth. Indeed it was probably a factor contributing to the increase in pauperism in the decades around 1800. The association, made from the sixteenth century onwards, of hemp and flax preparation and linen-weaving with employment for the poor may well have served to discourage potential investors in the industry.

Oakes, like other yarn makers and dealers, faced problems in the control of his spinners and the quality of the yarn they produced. On occasion the law was invoked to punish dishonest spinners. In July 1770 the *Bury and Norwich Post* reported that a woman from Dickleburgh in south Norfolk was committed to Wymondham Bridewell for reeling false and short yarn, and in the same year several Bungay woman were sent to the Bridewell for exchanging yarn as well as for reeling false or short yarn.

The Norwich stuffs industry began to stagnate in the 1780s, and 'slid into serious crisis in the 1790s' when war with France cut off its European markets.[1] One consequence of this crisis was that Oakes ran down his yarn business and concentrated on banking; he had opened a bank in Bury in 1794. At least one Bury yarn manufacturer had run into serious difficulties a dozen years earlier: on 26 December 1782 the *Bury and Norwich Post* reported the bankruptcy of Samuel Golding, yarnmaker, dealer and chapman. The outbreak of war on 1 February 1793 had an immediate effect on Norwich: by March trade was very distressed and the wages of spinners had been cut twice.

Oakes found he could sell no yarn in the City and, although trade improved slightly in the following year, he lost altogether between £1600 and £1700 in these two years. His empty combing sheds were sold in 1799, and other Bury yarn manufacturers followed suit; for the next half century brewing was the sole industry in the town.[2]

Evidence of the decline of linen manufacturing comes from the autobiography (*A Brief Memoir*), written in 1833, of James Aldred of Long Stratton, Norfolk.[3] Aldred was born at Alburgh in the Waveney valley in 1775 of respectable parents 'somewhere about the middle sphere of life'. When he was 10 his family moved to Morningthorpe near Long Stratton and, after attending a school where he received 'a common education', young James Aldred 'attended to the Farming

---

[1] Corfield, p.33

[2] I am very grateful to Mrs Jane Fiske for allowing me to refer to her unpublished research presented to the Centre of East Anglian Studies research seminar on 5 March 1982. James Oakes's diaries are at Bury St Edmunds SROB HA521/1-14

[3] NRO R125C Acc. March 1968 (photocopy of ms). I should like to thank Mr Robin Lucas of the University of East Anglia for drawing my attention to this manuscript.

business' and 'to the Hemp Cloth Manufactory & the Bleaching business my Father being in the Hemp Cloth trade he having been brought up to it'. In due course Aldred established himself in the bleaching trade, and moved to Norwich where for 10 years he made hemp cloth in the parish of St Michael at Thorn. He owned a 'shop' or small factory 'in the weaving line' in which he employed 18 persons, and during his first eight or nine years in the City established a large trade. During this time he bought a farm at Long Stratton so that he had somewhere to bleach his cloth. Hitherto he had been paying over £200 a year to have his bleaching done 'at a great distance', and he could now bleach other manufacturers' cloth in addition to his own.

Aldred goes on to say that, after laying out considerable sums of money on his weaving and bleaching business, his prospects were blighted when 'a sudden storm arose Cotton goods became so cheap & so generally used that they were nearly in all cases substituted for hemp Cloth as they were sold for not more than a fourth of the price that hemp Cloth was and my Trade in both respects (i.e. weaving and bleaching) became entirely ruined and I was obliged to give it all up'. He added that all 18 of the 'shops' weaving linen in Norwich closed down. Aldred is not very precise about dates, but it seems probable that 1806 was the date of the collapse of hemp-weaving described by him.

After leaving Norwich Aldred tried milling, malting and farming and failed in all three. He blamed his ill-luck on a variety of misfortunes, but the reader is left with the impression that he was a poor businessman. Nevertheless, there seems no reason to doubt the truth of what he had to say about the ending of linen-weaving in Norwich. Confirmation that hemp cloth was still being produced in the City in the first few years of the nineteenth century comes from the following report published in the *Bury and Norwich Post* in February 1801: 'It is much regretted that although many large manufactories of Hempen Cloth are established in the City of Norwich all the spinning of the hemp is done in Suffolk & a sufficient quantity is without difficulty obtained from thence. Might not a spinning school under the patronage of some active & benevolent ladies be attended with most beneficial affects to the poor children of this city.' It is interesting to find this attack on rural spinners, as Norwich weavers blamed the city's decline as a textile centre on the competition of unskilled rural handloom-weavers producing cheap cloth and not on that of Yorkshire factory-made cloth.[1]

The answer to the question proposed above about the decline of spinning in East Anglia seems to be that it occured after 1790 and was closely linked to the decay of the weaving industry. It appears likely that hemp-spinners were affected later than those producing wool yarn.

[1] Corfield, p.23

By the end of the eighteenth century the Suffolk wool-combing and spinning industry had dwindled to almost nothing because of the competition of cheap Irish yarn imported through Yarmouth and of machine-spun yarn from Yorkshire.[1] The mechanical spinning of flax did not start until some 20 years after that of wool, and in any case East Anglian linen-weavers mainly used hemp. The main reason for the decline of hemp spinning was not so much mechanisation, but the competiton of cotton, which was a much cheaper cloth and an adequate substitute for the coarse linens produced in East Anglia. The collapse of demand for spinning coincided with a steep rise in poor rates in the region and was one of the factors contributing to this increase. A contemporary of Arthur Young's held views akin to his on the benefits to be derived from the cultivation of hemp and flax, and also extolled their growth and preparation as the best means of employing the poor and reducing the poor rates.[2]

During the same period that spinning and weaving were declining for the reasons given above, changes in agriculture caused a great decrease in the quantities of hemp grown in East Anglia. Arthur Young explains why this occurred: 'this culture has greatly declined; there is scarely one-tenth grown of what there was some years past: this is chiefly attributed to the high price of wheat.[3] One of Young's informants, himself a linen-weaver, blamed the cessation of hemp-growing not only on the price of grain but also on 'the high price of turnip seed; for the cottagers, etc. sow turnips on their hemp grounds, and if seed be high, they let them stand for a crop instead of sowing hemp every year in the common manner'. The necessity for annual manuring of hemplands was given as another reason against growing it.[4]

The cultivation of hemp and flax was one of Young's hobby-horses, but he was correct in blaming agricultural changes for the decrease in these two crops. Between 1780 and the end of the Napoleonic wars East Anglia changed from one of the most prosperous to one of the most poverty-stricken regions in England. The origins of this transformation can be found earlier, but in the final decades of the eighteenth century a number of factors combined to accelerate the decay of the once wealthy counties of Norfolk and Suffolk: changes in farming and industry combined with war-induced inflation, a rising population and unemployment to create great misery.[5]

[1] Mrs Jane Fiske, personal communication
[2] Oddy, pp. 592–5
[3] Young, 1804, p.326
[4] Young, 1804, p.330
[5] Nora E. Coleman and others, *People, Poverty and Protest in Hoxne Hundred 1780–1880* (1982) is a recent local study of conditions during this period, henceforth Coleman et al.

Table 5.1   **Expenditure on the poor in four parishes**[a]

	Raised by rates 1775/76 (£)	Spent on poor 1775/76 (£)	Raised by rates 1812/13 (£)	Spent on poor 1812/13 (£)
Great Ellingham	264	248	750	640
Palgrave	208	87	885	832
Thelnetham	141	137	742	690
Wortham	245	245	1609	1505

[a]Sessional Papers 1774–1802, IX and *Parliamentary Papers 1818*, XIX

Table 5.1 sets out the sums raised by rates and spent on the poor in the years ended Easter 1776 and 1813 in the four parishes whose social and economic conditions were analysed in chapter 4. The figures speak for themselves and indicate only too clearly the disastrous state of the local economy in the early decades of the nineteenth century.

IV

The eighteenth century saw a geographical shift of the main linen-weaving area. During the preceding century the most important rural centres of linen-weaving had been a group of nine Suffolk parishes in or near the Little Ouse valley, and another formed by three villages further to the east: Fressingfield, Hoxne and Stradbroke. The major towns, Bury St Edmunds, Ipswich and Norwich, were then also the home of far more linen-weavers than they were to be later; indeed the numbers found in the two Suffolk towns after 1700 are insignificant, and only two linen-weavers are recorded among the freemen of Norwich in the first half of the eighteenth century.[1] Linen-weaving was not completely dead in Bury for in February 1699 Robert Tipple, a linen-weaver resident in the town, was admitted as a freeman of the borough.[2] Over half a century later, in 1762, the will of Thomas Syer was proved and shows that he lived in Whiting Street, but gives no information about his activities as a linen-weaver.[3] Possibly he was the man referred to in an advisertisement in the *Ipswich Journal* for 26 July 1744 offering to let a dwelling house in Rickinghall Superior 'now in the occupation of Mr Thomas Syer.'

After 1700 Beccles and Bungay continued to flourish as linen-

[1] Percy Millican, *The Freemen of Norwich 1714–52*, Norfolk Record Society, 23 (1952), p.41
[2] SROB D4/1/3 Corporation minutes 1693–1767
[3] SROB Dalton III, f.60

weaving towns, although this craft was far from being the chief industry in either place. Meanwhile in and around Diss, a major linen market, there was a remarkable growth in linen-weaving in the eighteenth century. In Diss itself the number of linen-weavers increased from 3 in the 1600s to 23 in the following century, and the south Norfolk parishes to its north and west also showed an upsurge in numbers. A smaller cluster of parishes on the Norfolk side of the Waveney valley, between Harleston and Bungay, shared in this growth.[1] The three Suffolk villages of Hoxne, Palgrave and Wortham continued to be important linen-weaving centres in the eighteenth century, but this may be partly attributed to their proximity to Diss. It is also significant that out of 16 parishes with not more than 1 linen-weaver recorded before 1690, but with totals of 5 or more, 13 were in south Norfolk. A further 7 villages with no evidence of linen-weaving before 1700, but with 2 or more weavers at a later date were all in the same area.

Diss lay at the centre of the main hemp-growing and cloth-producing area. It is a large parish,[2] including a considerable rural area, and its commons were still extensive in the eighteenth century; these features may explain its attraction for linen-weavers, who seem not to have congregated in other towns noted as linen markets. Hemp cultivation was certainly not new to Diss. In 1594 complaints about tithes made against the rector of the town show that, in the words of a deponent, 'he hath knowne that tythe Hemp was brought & left for the Parson in the Church porch every tenthe sheffe retted in the dry shofe'.[3] One of the articles to be enquired of by the homage of a court of survey held for Diss manor on 13 September 1636 concerned the right of tenants to make hemp pits on Diss Moor and Cockstreet Green for the retting of hemp. The homage asserted that this right had existed 'time out of mind'.[4] The latter common lay in a built-up area and for many centuries was the site of the annual fair.

Even if a quirk of the sources has exaggerated the movement of the main linen-weaving centre from Suffolk to Norfolk, it seems clear that in the eighteenth century the industry was tending to concentrate around Diss, and to a lesser extent in and near Bungay and Beccles. At the same time the more remote rural parishes of the upper Ouse valley were declining as industrial centres. In its dying days in the early

[1] This apparent relative decrease in the numbers of linen weavers in north Suffolk parishes may well be an illusion as more of the villages on the Norfolk side of the river have good collections of poor law papers, in which the names of many linen weavers have been found.
[2] 3382 acres, of which 243 were enclosed in 1814
[3] NRO 17566 38D.2
[4] ibid.

nineteenth century linen-weaving became more of an urban industry than at any other period.

After 1730 the value of probate records as a source declines sharply, but this is to a certain extent compensated for by the appearance in the eighteenth century of three new sources: newspapers, apprenticeship registers and poor law records. The first are particularly valuable for the light they shed on aspects of the industry not covered by other classes of records. The use of poor law papers, chiefly settlement certificates and examinations, removal and bastardy orders, explains the shift in emphasis in research from the wealthy to the poor weavers. Settlement examinations are the most valuable of these records as they generally give a brief biography of the person being questioned. Marriage licences and parish registers have also proved more useful than in earlier centuries.

Table 1.1 showed that the number of linen-weavers found in each decade of the eighteenth century fluctuated, but, apart from the 1760s, the general trend prolongs the decline which appears to have started in the 1690s. This table also shows the sharp decrease in the number of probate records and the increased usefulness of other documentary sources. The peak of 107 linen-weavers in the 1760s coincides with the high point in English linen production reached in the same decade (see p. 119), and this is reflected in the national apprenticeship registers.[1] Even though the East Anglian industry contributed little to linen exports, it clearly benefited from the rise in demand described earlier in this chapter. Apprenticeship registrations by Suffolk and Norfolk linen-weavers averaged 14 per decade from 1710 to 1759, but rose to 55 in the 1760s. There were 35 in the following 10 years, but numbers then fell off sharply to 10 in the 1780s and a mere 6 in the last decade of the century. This response to a growing market was as short-lived as the boom itself, and the apprentices of the years of expansion doubtless swelled the ranks of pauper journeymen at the end of the century.

John Todd is the only registered apprentice who later appears in poor law records, and the link is not a firm one, mainly because Todd is a common name. In September 1763 his apprenticeship to John Boost of Beccles for a seven year term was registered, and a premium of £12 was paid. Less than ten years later, in March 1773, the parish of Mendham issued a settlement certificate to Dickleburgh for John Todd, a linen-weaver, with his wife and two children.[2] It is evident from poor law records that many apprenticeship arrangements were informal, and that it was not unusual for no premium to be paid. Some linen-weavers learnt their trade from their fathers, like Richard Page who was

---

[1] PRO IR1
[2] Records retained in the parish

examined in 1802, or from some other relation. John Aggas of Earsham registered an apprentice officially in 1754, but the 1766 settlement examination of his bastard grandson, another John Aggas, reveals that he had learnt 'the business of a linen weaver' from his grandfather.[1] Thomas Sone was bound apprentice by indenture in January 1785 to Joseph Green of Bromeswell near Ipswich, but no premium was paid. When Sone was examined as to his settlement on 11 October 1798 he was living in south Norfolk at Redenhall with Harleston, and said that he had parted with his master by agreement after serving four years of his seven-year term.[2]

Some masters did not record all their apprentices. Mark Butcher, an Earsham heckler, registered an apprentice in 1763 and another two years later, but in the same decade he took on two unregistered apprentices, who later in life underwent settlement examinations. Pauper apprenticeships were not registered or taxed, and John Smith of Bungay provides an example of this. In May 1765 he registered the apprenticeship of William Archer for two-and-a-half years, and in 1769 the parish of Hoxne bound John George, a poor boy, to him.[3] Some apprenticeships were doubtless not officially registered in order to evade the payment of the tax on premiums, and others were informal arrangements.

It is clearly impossible to use the national apprenticeship registers as an accurate guide to the number of linen-weavers taking apprentices in the eighteenth century, or as a comprehensive record of those bound to masters engaged in the linen industry. Over three-quarters of the 176 linen-weavers found in the registers appear once only; another 14 per cent registered two apprentices each and barely 8 per cent are known to have taken three or more apprentices. Over a period of twelve years William Colman of Attleborough took six boys into his service, but, assuming they all served their full terms, there were never more than three working for him at any one time.

Little is known of the linen-weavers whose names are recorded in the national apprenticeship registers; only 25 of them left surviving wills. The level of premiums paid by apprentices gives some indication of the status of different trades. The highest sums were commanded by attorneys and surgeons; apothecaries, drapers and grocers were amongst those who could demand a substantial premium; but linen-weaving was a comparatively lowly craft, ranking with cordwainers, tailors and carpenters. The average of the 262 premiums paid to East Anglian linen-weavers was £6 10s. 0d., but this mean is distorted by a

[1] NRO PD 205/50
[2] NRO PD 295/111
[3] Records retained in parish

few large sums and £5, which is both the median and the mode, gives a more realistic mean premium.

Less than 10 per cent of the premiums paid to linen-weavers were over £10 and only nine were above £20. The two largest were paid to a tradesman resident in the small Norfolk port of Wells, and described as grocer, woollen and linen-weaver, and to a linen-weaver living in Bury St. Edmunds. By and large the level of premiuns is not related to the length of the term to be served, and weavers registering more than one apprentice did not always charge the same fee. In 1765 Joshua Wool-nough of Stradbroke registered an apprentice who paid £20, and two years later took on another with a premium of one guinea; both were to serve a seven-year term. Such variations are not uncommon, and perhaps the premuim asked was related as much to the ability of the apprentice or his parents to pay as to the figure which the master felt he could demand.

V

Another new feature of the linen-weaving industry in the eighteenth century is the development of ancillary trades as separate, full-time occupations. Bleaching was less often carried out by individual weavers than in earlier centuries, but the most noticeable increase occurred amongst hecklers or hicklers, as the word was more often spelt. In eighteenth-century Scotland too heckling became a full-time occupation, and according to Durie was well-paid.[1] Many of the East Anglian hecklers were found in poor law documents, so it seems less likely that it was a profitable trade in this region.

Bleaching was a lengthy process which tied up capital for months at a time. Poor weavers probably could not afford to bleach their own yarn and cloth, and some capitalists owning a number of looms may have found it more convenient to put out bleaching to specialists. However, the story of James Aldred shows that not all master-weavers followed this course in the eighteenth century. Any increase in the production of linen cloth was inevitably accompanied by a greater demand for the services of spinners and hecklers. A rise in the numbers of the latter may be an indication that larger quantities of hemp and flax were being grown in East Anglia. Hemp and flax although light are bulky, and it is likely that most imports had already undergone the earlier stages of preparation for the loom.

In Yorkshire heckling hemp, together with spinning and bleaching linen yarn were generally controlled by the same people, while weaving and finishing were in the hands of another group. This arrangement

[1] Durie, p.3

Figure 5.1   The preparation of hemp; retting, breaking and scutching from Charles Tomlinson, *The Useful Arts and Manufactures of Great Britain* (1854)

differed from the organisation of the woollen industry where it was usual for clothiers to deal with all the processes of manufacture by putting-out to specialised workers.[1] By the late eighteenth century, if not earlier, many East Anglian master-weavers, like James Aldred, were bleaching their cloth, but buying yarn from its manufacturers.

The names of a number of hecklers have been found in the post-1750 registers and poor law records of 10 Waveney valley parishes. Heckling existed as a separate trade before this date, but the sources used do not exist prior to 1750. Similar caution must be exercised in considering the geographical distribution of hecklers. A search of the records of all Norfolk and Suffolk parishes would have been impossibly lengthy, so attention has been concentrated on the area known as the centre of hemp-growing. As with linen-weavers, poor law records revealed more hecklers in Norfolk than in Suffolk.

The decrease in the acreage of hemp grown in the Waveney valley and the simultaneous rise in imports of flax and hemp, so much lamented by Arthur Young, explains the poverty of many hecklers in the decades around 1800. As linen-weaving declined in East Anglia, so

[1] Jennings, p.176

did its ancillary occupations. Something of the career of a few hecklers can be learnt from their settlement examinations. Two men, both named Frewer and probably brothers, were bound apprentice to Mark Butcher, a heckler of Earsham, where they were born. Richard, the elder of the two Frewers, began his term of three-and-a-half years *c.*1763 when he was aged 18, while John Frewer, although only 13 at the time of his apprenticeship in 1768, served the same period. Both men subsequently worked as journeymen hecklers.[1] In the 1830s a Richard Frewer, described in the baptism register as a 'hatchelor', was living in Needham, and may well have been the son of one of the above two men, both of whom were dwelling in this parish at the time of their examinations.

Most of the hecklers who appear in poor law records had moved from place to place, presumably in search of work, but the Mathews family of Needham was an exception. In 1763 a 16-year-old boy was apprenticed to William Mathews 'hitchelor', and nearly 70 years later, in 1829, a child of James Mathews 'hatchelor' or 'tow comber' was baptised in the parish church. William Mathews's apprentice was Thomas Evens, who was born *c.*1747 at Syleham as 'he has heard and believes', and, with the consent of his widowed mother, was bound for five years; no 'consideration money' was paid to Mathews, so Evens may have been a pauper apprentice.[2] The long connection of this family of hecklers with Needham suggests that they were reasonably successful.

None of the hecklers whose settlement examinations have survived were apprenticed much later than 1790, by which time the linen industry was in decline and was soon to be in serious difficulties, and hemp cultivation in East Anglia was rapidly decreasing. Even in the years when the linen industry flourished, heckling was not a wealthy trade and this may explain why many apprenticed to it were pauper children. An example is Thomas Holmes, 'a poor child', whom the parish of Dickleburgh apprenticed for seven years from October 1771 to Robert Wilson of Shelfhanger in the trade of a hemp dresser 'which he now useth'. Holmes was to be taught and instructed in this trade.[3]

Most of the hecklers who are known from settlement examinations fell on hard times at the end of the eighteenth century, and James Emms is no exception. He was living at Needham when he was examined in June 1814, and stated that he had been born about 1778 a few miles away in Rushall, where he believed his parents had a legal settlement. When James was about 15 years old he was apprenticed by his father for five years to David Emms, a 'hackler' of Wingfield. No

[1] NRO PD205/50 and 52
[2] NRO PD205/52
[3] Dickleburgh records have been retained in the parish

indenture was drawn up, and, after living with David Emms for four years, James left him and then worked for himself as a journeyman.[1] Needham seems to have accepted James Emms as a resident, for ten years after the date of his settlement examination a child of his was baptised there. Just as with weaving, it is not unusual to find several members of a family following the trade of heckling. Three members of the Emms family were hecklers; two lived at Needham and another at Wingfield on the Suffolk side of the Waveney. In the present century the drabbett factory at Syleham belonged to a family of the same name. Stephen Fisher is an example of a son following his father's occupation, and apparently equally unsuccessfully. He was the son of a Hoxne heckler, was born about 1751 and lived there learning the trade from his father until the age of 17. After that time he worked as a journeyman heckler in various places, but never acquired a settlement in any of them. At the time of his examination in January 1800 his father, who must have started work as a heckler well before 1750, was still living in Hoxne.[2]

In July 1790 Robert Sparrow, with his wife and son, were removed to Weybread from Needham. Sparrow, a heckler born at the former place in 1740, had followed a more adventurous career than most of his fellow craftsmen, as he had spent some time at sea.[3] References to periods of time passed at sea or in the army are quite common in settlement examinations around this date, not surprisingly as England was at war for 36 years between 1750 and 1815. John Chaney was in difficulties rather earlier than most hecklers, at a time when English linen production was reaching its peak. His career suggests that personal circumstances may have been responsible. He was living in Starston when he was examined in March 1762. He had been born about 22 years earlier in Bressingham, and at the age of 10 was bound as a parish apprentice to Thomas Ellener, a linen-weaver of the same place. Chaney's term was 14 years, but after serving only six months he was 'assigned over' to John Syder, a Diss heckler, who three months later failed in business. Young John then went to Thomas Syder of Kenninghall, presumably a relative of his previous master, and remained with him for eight years learning the 'art of a hickler'. At the end of this time he left without his master's knowledge or consent, and up till the time of his examination worked as a journeyman for Mr Thomas Walne of Starston.[4] Fourteen years seems a remarkably long time to learn the trade of heckling, but doubtless Bressingham was anxious to make sure that its parish apprentices acquired a settlement elsewhere.

[1] NRO PD205/52
[2] NRO PD205/52
[3] NRO PD205/51
[4] NRO PD119/116

The brief accounts of their lives given by hecklers in settlement examinations suggest that work became increasingly difficult to find as the eighteenth century neared its end, causing them to lead a wandering existence and eventually to become paupers dependent on parish relief.

The bleaching of yarn and cloth was an important stage in the production of linen. Some eighteenth-century weavers still carried out this process themselves. One example is James Richards of Hempnall in south Norfolk, who in 1804 took a lease of a messuage with bleaching and other offices.[1] Nor was it unknown for men described as whitesters to be engaged in weaving, as for instance was Cornelius Reeve, a Weybread bleacher, whose bequests included three looms and his weaving tackling.[2] All of the seven known whitesters' wills were made by men of substance, such as Thomas Flatman of Hinderclay, one of the men who worshipped at Wattisfield congregational chapel. He owned a house, whiting office and shop in Hinderclay as well as two messuages in Redgrave. One of the latter was called the Fox, and this public house, together with the brewing utensils there, was to be sold in order to pay the testator's debts and cash legacies. Flatman's will refers to whiting and farming stock, so he was a man of two occupations; the Fox was let, so he was not actively engaged in brewing or beer retailing.[3]

Stealing from bleach gounds was clearly a common crime in the years between 1767 and 1815, but it is likely that unattended yarn and cloth had always been a temptation to thieves, particularly at night. On 30 May 1767 eight weavers, all but one living in south Norfolk, placed an advertisement in the *Ipswich Journal* stating that 'divers evil disposed Persons have of late made it their bussiness to steal large quantities of Hemp-Cloth and Hemp-Yarn, out of the Houses, Yards, Shops and Stalls of several weavers and whitesters in the Counties of Norfolk and Suffolk'. These eight men announced that they had entered into an agreement to help each other prosecute anyone stealing hemp cloth or yarn from any of their number. Forty years later an item in the *Bury and Norwich Post* for 25 March 1807 announced the sentencing at Bury Assizes to 14 years transportation of John Turner alias Webster, who had been convicted of stealing 20 yards of hempen cloth from a bleaching ground in Hinderclay. The owner of the cloth, Thomas Sturgeon, had recently died, and a week later the same paper carried a notice of the auction of his goods, which included a large stock of white and grey (bleached and unbleached) hempen cloth.

During the 70 or so years preceding the establishment of county

[1] NRO NCC Gooch 241 (1759)
[2] NRO Irby collection R158A, Box 5
[3] SROB Dalton VII/90 (1780)

Figure 5.2 'Linnen-Clothes': bleaching, sewing and washing linen from John Amos Comenius, *Orbis Pictus* (1659)

police forces many people resorted to self-help as a protection against crime, much of which, such as cattle-maiming and rick-burning, was an expression of agrarian discontent. Numerous associations for prosecuting felons were formed and during the 1820s (their peak period) there were about 40 such societies in Norfolk and roughly as many again in Suffolk. The survival rate of their records is poor, but the minute book of the Harleston Crown Association for the years 1773–1815 is in existence and records thefts from bleach grounds on several occasions.[1]

One of the original subscribers to this association was John Booty, a whitester from nearby Alburgh. He seems never to have called on the help of the society, but four other whitesters enlisted its aid in pursuing thieves. On four occasions between 1789 and 1800 John Burgess suffered considerable losses from his 'bleaching' at Alburgh. He never lost less than 40 yards of hempen cloth, and on one occasion as much as three pieces each 48 yards long. Twice Burgess was able to name the thief, as in the case of Joseph Whittum who was committed to Wymondham Bridewell in July 1789 on suspicion of robbing him of 40 clues of hempen yarn. Two other bleachers lived at Weybread on the

[1] NRO SO/6/1 Box 444x

Suffolk side of the Waveney valley, but the theft from Robert Leftley[1] occurred at the Red Lion public house in Harleston one January evening in 1792 when he lost 34 yards of bleached cloth worth 1s. 8d. a yard and packed up in a new 'double quilled' sack. John Matthews, the other Weybread bleacher, was robbed of 8 pieces of hempen cloth totalling 246 yards and of a piece of huckaback 20 yards in length. Both Robert Leftley and Mr James Hardingham, whose place of residence is not given, had marked their cloth with initials and numbers. The latter suffered two thefts from his bleaching ground in January 1796 and the stolen cloth was valued at from 2s. 3d. to 3s. a yard.

There seems no reason to think that the robberies from the bleach grounds of members of the Harleston Crown Association were in any way exceptional. No indication is given of what steps, if any, these men took to protect their property, but in the early nineteenth century at least one whitester used dogs for this purpose. A Miss Girling, who spent her childhood at Spexhall near Halesworth and celebrated her centenary in 1929, recounted her memories of the bleaching ground at Wissett where ferocious dogs were tethered near the lengths of linen to ward off thieves.[2] Pursehouse mentions that thefts of linen were frequently recorded in local newspapers, and these included stealing hempen cloth from waggons conveying it to Norwich as well as from workshops and bleach meadows.[3] The frequency of crimes connected with linen confirms the importance of this local industry.

VI

The anonymous complaint (quoted on p.xxx) about the concentration of hemp spinning in the hands of Suffolk workers proposed the establishment of a spinning school in Norwich. The teaching of this craft had long formed part of the curriculum of some charity schools, although in 1681 Houghton had complained that spinning schools were no good because they did not have sufficient teachers.[4] Efforts to educate poor children for useful employment have a long and interesting history, but only spinning need concern us here. In 1677 Yarranton wrote about the spinning schools for girls in north Germany. He described one where 200 little girls aged between 6 and 9 were taught to spin flax on distaffs; discipline was strict. Attached to this school was another where girls were instructed in making bone lace, and two more for teaching boys to

---

[1] This man was described as a linen weaver when he registered an apprentice in April 1779.

[2] *East Anglian Miscellany* column in *East Anglian Daily Times*, July 1929

[3] Pursehouse, pp. 179–80

[4] John Houghton, *A Collection of Letters for the Improvement of Husbandry and Trade* (1681), p.111

make and paint toys. Like many other early writers on economics Yarranton clearly had a poor opinion of the female sex. He complained that young women in England talked too much and that girls were idle, spending their time 'tearing Hedges, or robbing Orchards, and worse'.[1] Neither of these sound like full time occupations, and what did he mean by 'worse'?

After the passing in 1723 of the General Act authorising the building of workhouses,[2] the obvious advantages of making charity schools self-supporting led to many working schools being set up to teach children spinning, lace-making, stocking-knitting and other crafts. It was held that spinning was a skill that fitted children for many other tasks requiring manual dexterity, such as weaving and pin-making. In practice except in a few exceptional cases, attempts to make charity schools self-supporting were a failure. Just as with adult paupers, there were difficulties in obtaining cheap raw materials and adequate instruction, as well as in selling the work, often defective, turned out by children. Furthermore, charity schools were criticised for enabling their pupils to enter into unfair competition for jobs with their betters, the children of the self-supporting poor. This criticism could not be levelled at the Diss school to be described later, which catered precisely for poor children who were not paupers.[3]

At the end of the eighteenth century a second attempt to set up working schools also met with failure after temporary success in a few instances. Again spinning was one of the commonest skills taught to children of both sexes. Eden considered the economic value of spinning schools to be negligible and wrote: 'The experience of eight years has proved that although schools of industry may flourish for a while under the active zeal of the first promoters, yet, when after a few years' trial they are left to the superintendence of less interested administrators, they dwindle into the ordinary state of the parish poor house.'[4]

Two examples of spinning schools have been found in south Norfolk, and there were probably others elsewhere in East Anglia. The 1724 account of charity schools lists four such establishments in north Suffolk: those at Halesworth and Stradbroke each had 20 pupils, while there were 10 at Syleham and 34 at Wingfield.[5] It is surprising to find twice as many pupils in the small village of Wingfield as in the towns of Diss and Halesworth. The records of the Diss school do not continue

---

[1] Yarranton, pp. 45–47. I am grateful to Professor D.C. Coleman for drawing my attention to the description of this school.
[2] 9 Geo. I, cap. 7
[3] This paragraph and the beginning of the next is based on M.G. Jones, *The Charity School Movement* (Cambridge, 1938), pp. 87–89, 93, 155–157, henceforth Jones
[4] F.M. Eden, *The State of the Poor* (1797), 2 vols, II, pp. 400–401
[5] Jones, p.370

Figure 5.3   Guildhall Grammar School, Diss. The grammar school was held on the upper floor, while the lower was used for the charity school described on p. 140.

for long after 1720, so this school may well have been one of the many which failed to achieve its purpose. The Bressingham school described may have been more successful, and certainly lasted longer.

Early in the eighteenth century a school for poor boys was founded at Palgrave, but in 1714 transferred to Diss where it occupied the lower floor of the former guildhall; the upper rooms were used by the town's grammar school. In 1714 the trustees of this charity school proposed that it should be partly financed by purchasing 'a stock to putt such of the Ladds as are fitt & capable to the spining or the woolling Manufacture'. Seven years later the school rules laid down that its purpose was to teach 30 poor boys to read, to instruct them in the Christian religion as taught by the Church of England, and 'for learning them such other things as are suitable to their condition & capacity'. A woman was employed to teach the boys to spin and received 2*d*. a week for each pupil. One school rule read that '16 scholars be set to work to spinn or as many of the school as are able & have been learnt'.[1] This school had only 20 pupils in 1724.[2]

The Diss school had several interesting features, including the age of

[1] NRO PD100/311
[2] Jones, p.368

its pupils. Boys were not to enter the school under 10 years and had to leave at 14, when they were apprenticed. The late age at which pupils were accepted, combined with the absence of any mention of instruction in writing, is surprising. Recent research has suggested that if poor children were to receive any education it was likely to be at an early age.[1] Once a child reached 8 or 9 it was unlikely that his parents could spare him from gainful work. Reading was normally taught before writing, and the latter skill was considered less essential, but it is still surprising to find boys in the 10–14 age group receiving no instruction in this subject. Although the pupils of the Diss charity school were clearly drawn from poor families (clothing was provided once a year for those in need), they did not come from the very lowest stratum of society, thus maintaining the distinction between the poor who were on the parish and those who were in the parish but managed to maintain themselves without recourse to parish relief. Children in the parish workhouse and those whose parents received 'collection', or regular outdoor poor relief, were not admitted to the school.

Bressingham, a short distance to the west of Diss, is a village in which a number of linen-weavers lived in the eighteenth century, and here too there existed a school in which spinning was taught. In 1728 Mrs Barker, the widow of a clergyman, left a house and land to provide a school to teach poor children from the parish the catechism, reading, writing and spinning. The rector was to choose children aged over 8 and under 10 years. As at Diss the starting age seems a little high, but on the other hand these children were taught to write. The school continued for well over a century, and in 1845 eight pupils were receiving instruction in the catechism, reading and writing; the girls were also taught sewing and knitting. Its property consisted of a house for the master, a schoolroom and nearly six acres of land, worth about £15 a year in 1845.[2]

VII

Although very few linen-weavers are known to have lived in Bury St. Edmunds during the eighteenth century, the town was an important centre for marketing their products. Together with weavers of woollen cloth, they sold their goods in the Wool Hall, which stood in Woolhall Street near the market place. The corporation minutes for 8 March 1733 record the payment to Mrs Bean, a former tenant of the Wool Hall, of £4 2s. 6d. for certain items she had left there: 'the Bings (bins) being twenty nine in Number and the shew boards before Linnen

---

[1] Spufford, 1981, chapter 2
[2] White's Norfolk, p.711

weavers Stalls & other boards which were sett up and placed by her in the Wooll Hall whilst she was Tenant thereto she having left the same for the use of this Corporation',[1] Were the 'shew boards' used to display the weavers' names, or as extensions to the stalls to allow the laying out of more cloth?

A severe epidemic of smallpox broke out in Bury in 1744 and had a detrimental effect on the town's trade. On 17 March John Mallows and Joseph Hart placed an advertisement in the *Ipswich Journal* on behalf of 'several of the Linen Weavers who constantly kept the Weavers-Hall in Bury St. Edmunds with Hempen Cloths'. Due to the smallpox outbreak they wished 'to acquaint the Dealers in Hempen Cloths' that they would 'give our constant attendance weekly every WEDNESDAY, at Ten o'clock in the Forenoon, at the RED HOUSE of HORNING-SHEATH where our constant Chapmen, as well as others who will be pleased to deal with us, shall be well and kindly served'. In the eighteenth century, as today, Wednesdays and Saturdays were market-days in Bury, and The Red House at Horningsheath or Horringer, under two miles from the town, was a public house where a small market was held. It had a reputation as a house of ill-fame.[2] In the next issue of this paper there appeared another advertisement inserted by three other linen-weavers: Thomas Syer, William Bacon and John Constable. These men protested that removing the linen market from Bury was prejudicial to the town and announced their intention 'to keep the Market at Bury at the Hall as usual'. Apparently none of the five linen-weavers who were signatories to the two advertisements lived in the town, although Thomas Syer had moved there by the time he died in 1762.

Both the phrasing of the two advertisements and of the wills of the signatories suggests that these men were not single-loom weavers, but masters employing others and putting out work. John Constable, for instance, bequeathed trading stock and a fair amount of real estate including a weaving shop.[3] A man working on his own would have been unable to weave sufficient cloth to sell each week on the scale indicated in the newspaper announcements. Another weaver who probably operated on a similar scale was Robert Clamp of Ipswich, who, on 25 February 1769, advertised in the *Ipswich Journal* for two or three journeymen for whom he could provide regular employment. He made and sold 'all sorts of true English Hempen-Cloth, wholesale or retail, at his house in St Nicholas Parish, adjoining to the sign of the Falcon'. In addition he sold the same goods every Saturday from his stall in the

---

[1] SROB D4/1/3, p.461
[2] Mrs Margaret Statham, personal communication
[3] SROB Claggett VI, f. 258; will made May 1746

Buttermarket. Obviously by the middle of the eighteenth century the description weaver covered a very wide social and economic range. The accounts and other papers of John Woodrow, a Norwich worsted weaver, show that he was a considerable landowner, whose style of living was that of a gentleman.[1] Other weavers were involved in more than one stage of linen manufacture. One such man was James Godbold of Mendham, a linen-weaver and dealer in hemp, whose widow placed an advertisement in the local press asking his creditors to send in their accounts.[2] He may well have conducted a business similar to that of a master woolcomber, putting out work to hecklers and spinners.

Little is known about the customers of linen-weavers such as the men who sold their cloth in Bury, but many of them were presumably drapers like Thomas Jolley, a Palgrave linen draper, whose inventory was drawn up in February 1723.[3] He was a wealthy man, whose possessions were valued at nearly £500. The goods in his shop and warehouse were worth £373 and this sum included £40 for 'Several goods at Harleston, Buckenham & Botesdale'. Palgrave has never been more than a village, whose inhabitants could easily shop only a mile away in the market town of Diss, so it is a little surprising to find a linen draper there. However, the quotation from his inventory suggests as a probable explanation that he was an itinerant draper who rented stalls at several markets and stored goods in local inns or houses. From the latter part of the seventeenth century it became increasingly common for traders to use inns as places to conduct business, keep goods and so forth. The contents of Jolley's Palgrave shop included counters and drawers, so he was clearly trading there as well as at the three market towns where he had goods stored. Most of his stock was a range of varieties of linens, but he also sold some woollens as well as tapes, thread, shoes and clothes.

Occupational descriptions of shopkeepers and craftsmen often conceal the full range of their commercial activities. One example is John Dresser, a Laxfield grocer, whose 1729 inventory shows that he ran a village store, which, with its wide variety of goods, was very similar to many still existing in the mid-twentieth century.[4] Indeed, apart from the absence of perishable foodstuffs, its stock is similar to that carried by the largest shop in the same village today. Whether described as grocer, draper, apothecary or mercer many shopkeepers stocked the same range of goods. In Dresser's case the value of his drapery was nearly twice that of his groceries. Another example of the inexactitude

[1] NRO MC37/156–162
[2] *Ipswich Journal* 27 May 1769
[3] NRO NCC INV75A/65
[4] NRO NCC INV78A/118

of occupational labels is a St. Albans dyer, who died in 1674. His inventory makes no mention of equipment for his trade, but his shop contained a large quantity of cloth, mostly varieties of linen, valued at £89.[1]

The geographical pattern of Thomas Jolley's trading is not unusual. Accounts kept in 1765 by the widow of Jonas Cunningham, a Norwich linen draper, show that his commercial activities extended well over 20 miles to Eye in Suffolk.[2] His stock in trade, worth £65 18s. 0d., was sold partly in this town and partly in Norwich, and expenses included the cost of carrying goods to Eye for sale there and the payment of a debt owed to Mr Cunningham of the same place; presumably he was a relation. Twelve years earlier an account of the debts due to James Longridge, an Eye linen draper, lists bad debts for goods from his shop totalling £136 4s. 7d.[3] Most of these debts had been run up in the 1730s and 1740s, but a few went back as far as 1728. Longridge's debtors lived in 31 different places, mostly within 10 miles of Eye, but one as far off as Norwich. The majority of those who owed money to this draper lived in Diss, and Eye was the next most frequently named place. There were certainly linen drapers in Diss in the eighteenth century and it is curious that inhabitants of the town found it necessary to shop in Eye and Palgrave. Longridge may have rented a shop or market stall in Diss, but there is no indication of this in the accounts kept by his widow as executrix of his will. These show that his funeral expenses and the apothecary's bill came to £14 2s. 0d., and that most of the remainder of the sum of nearly £300 laid out went on paying bills, some to men living in London. Although only their names appear in this account, it seems likely that the persons to whom Longridge owed money had supplied him with goods for his shop in his lifetime.

Walter Colquhoun of Binham in north Norfolk described himself as a travelling linen-draper when he drew up his will in 1782. If he, and others like him, bought as well as sold cloth, this would have been a convenience for weavers living in remote places. There can have been little difference between the wares carried by a chapman and a travelling draper.

Newspaper advertisements also throw some light on the marketing of hempen cloth in the eighteenth century. On 19 June 1727 the *Suffolk Mercury* carried the following announcement: 'At Mr Brownings in Thetford, in Norfolk, are to be sold by Wholesale, all sorts of home made Hempen Cloath'[and] 'all sorts of Dowlas and Garlick Holland', [all in various widths as well as] 'Huckaback for Table Cloaths and

---

[1] Hertfordshire County Record Office A25/3944
[2] NRO NCC INV83/15
[3] NRO NCC INV82D/17

Napkins, likewise Hair Cloath for Maltsters, and Watermen, all to be sold off at very reasonable Rates.' Over half a century later, in September 1783, an advertisement in the *Bury and Norwich Post* announced a forthcoming auction at Aldeburgh of sheeting, diaper and drill from Russia and Prussia. Sales of this kind, whether of imported or home-produced cloth, were probably not particularly frequent. November 1767 Thomas Watling, a hemp-cloth weaver, begged 'leave to acquaint the public' through the pages of the *Ipswich Journal* 'that he has taken the entire stock of his late deceased brother Simon Watling & carries on the business in all its branches, wholesale & retail, at Woodbridge and Ipswich'. The next month a second advertisement announced the opening, by Watling and a partner, of a warehouse in the Buttermarket at Ipswich where customers might depend on having 'right true made English hemp, both whited and unwhited'. The following January Thomas Watling's widowed sister-in-law, Sarah, set up a rival establishment when she 'begs leave to acquaint customers etc. she has taken a shop in the Thoroughfare in Woodbridge, where she sells all sorts of English hempen cloth'.[1] Home-made and Suffolk are epithets often used (in advertisements) to describe hempen-cloth and were clearly intended as a guarantee of quality.

Watling called himself a hemp-cloth weaver, but the scale of his operations suggests that like Frederick Norman of Stowmarket, 'manufacturer of hempen cloth' would have been a more accurate description. Norman placed an advertisement in the *Bury and Norwich Post* on 11 September 1783 to thank customers who had bought his cloth and to assure them that he would continue to make the best quality. He wanted 'a twine spinner, who is a good hand', and offered to supply tow to anyone wishing to spin it either for their own use or for him. In December 1769 Nathaniel Rye of Botesdale used the columns of the *Ipswich Journal* to announce that he had taken over Mr Rudduck's shop and stock, and that he made and sold ticks, twills, drills and all widths and prices of hemp cloth from 10*d.* to 5*s.* a yard. The considerable range of Rye's prices may indicate that in response to growing demand East Anglian weavers were producing a wider variety of hemp cloth than in earlier centuries, and that some of it was of high quality.

None of these advertisements mention fustian, but this cheap cloth of Mediterranean origin and made from a linen warp and cotton weft, had been made in Haverhill for some time. This town is near the broadcloth region of south-west Suffolk, but seems to have branched out into fustian manufacturing in the seventeenth century. Fustians were being made in Norwich in the 1590s, and probably much earlier,

[1] *Ipswich Journal*, 16 January 1768

and by 1600 were also a booming industry in Lancashire. Of the handful of Suffolk fustian-weavers found in probate records and the index to marriage licences, all but one lived at Haverhill; the exception was an inhabitant of Ipswich when he appraised goods for an inventory in 1606. Although four are known from the seventeenth century, rather more is known about Haverhill fustian-weavers in the next century. Edward Scandrett died in 1764, and his will shows that he owned considerable property in the town.[1] His residence, together with a whiteing yard and orchard, were left to his eldest son, Thomas, who also received his father's coppers, tubs, 'Callender' and all other 'Utensills' used in 'the Trade of a Weaver and Dyer'. The younger son was bequeathed a messuage occupied by four tenants in Beggars Row, Haverhill, and his two sisters were left a similar tenement in the same lane. In 1753 Scandrett had leased for one year a cottage containing rooms on each of two floors;[2] his tenant was a fellow fustian-maker, William Ward. Was this perhaps one of the Beggars Lane houses? Scandrett had lived a long time in Haverhill as his signature appears on a deed made 30 years before he died. Ward borrowed £14 from his new landlord in 1753, so it seems possible that he was employed by Scandrett.

Although the evidence is scanty, it seems likely that fustian making expanded in Haverhill during the eighteenth century, at the end of which the most important Suffolk firm to be engaged in manufacturing first this cloth, and later drabbetts, was founded (see p. 159).

VIII

Far fewer linen-weavers appear to have made wills after 1730 than before, only 82 compared with 599.[3] Both the percentage of wills including bequests of houses and land and that of weavers able to leave property to more than one heir were considerably higher than in the period 1601–1730 when the figures were 70 per cent and 17 per cent. What is more significant as an indication of the economic fortunes of linen-weavers is that the number of later eighteenth-century wills is less than a seventh of the total known for the preceding period. It is extremely doubtful that a search of all the archdeaconry registers would even double this figure.[4] A significantly higher proportion of testators

[1] SROB Dalton III/194
[2] Lease in the possession of Messrs Gurteen of Haverhill, as are the other documents referred to in this paragraph.
[3] The 82 include 17 wills proved between 1800 and 1814. As these testators lived most of their lives in the eighteenth century, it seems reasonable to include their wills in this chapter.
[4] The sampling of these registers, described on p.4, found only three linen-weavers, all dating from before 1730.

Table 5.2 Wills 1731–1814

	No.	As % of 82 wills[a]
Bequests of real estate	68	83
Bequests of real estate to more than one legatee	23	28
Large cash bequests (totalling over £100)	18	22
Looms mentioned	15	18
Cloth/yarn mentioned[b]	2	2

[a] Many wills appear in more than one category.

[b] Many other wills refer to stock in trade.

gave really substantial cash legacies, and this too reflects the high economic status of a small number of weavers. Amongst this group it is not unusual to find their children receiving portions of £100, or even more in some cases. The cash legacies Jacob Gowing of Haddiscoe gave to his grandchildren and dependants in 1777 totalled £490,[1] and in the following century Daniel Filby, who lived at Thrandeston, left his three daughters £200 each.[2] Several of the men who made large cash bequests to female heirs had also provided a son with a house and land.

Clearly farming, or at least the ownership of land, continued to be common amongst will-making linen-weavers, but it seems likely that there were far more landless weavers, who did not leave wills, than in earlier centuries. The very steep fall in the number of wills may reflect a change in the pattern of will-making, but, even if this true, it must also reflect a change in the circumstances of linen-weavers. Unfortunately the evidence is negative, but it does seem to suggest that as the eighteenth century proceeded the proportion of landless weavers, who did not leave wills, increased. This change in their fortunes is not peculiar to weavers; practitioners of other crafts suffered a similar deterioration of their economic circumstances during this century.

The wills left by post-1730 linen-weavers suggest that they were likely to employ journeymen, were engaged in other branches of the industry in addition to weaving, and were in general widening their business interests.

There is some diversification in the kind of property owned by these men. Five possessed public houses, one of which was the important Three Tuns in the centre of Bungay,[3] and George Burlingham owned a windmill in his own parish of Shropham as well as the Red Lion at

[1] NRO NCC Yallop 400
[2] NRO NCC Goodrun 259 (1813)
[3] NRO NCC Butter 286 (Henry Mickleburgh of Kirby Cane, 1719)

nearby Kenninghall.[1] Benjamin Harper of Hoxne owned houses and land in four parishes including Brockdish, where he had a malthouse,[2] and John Betts of Tibbenham had converted a former malthouse into weaving shops.[3] When Joseph Last, a wealthy Debenham weaver, made his will in 1796 he owned four messuages in this little town, one of which stood in Gracechurch Street. There were workshops adjacent to the house he himself lived in, and the shop in which he kept his cloth for sale formed part of another; his whiting yard also lay next to this building.[4] Another urban linen-weaver, Benjamin Primrose of Beccles, owned a bleaching ground as well as vats, coppers and other utensils for whiteing, and instructed his executors to 'carry on the several trades and businesses which I now use'.[5] A third man with much property was Thomas Deale, who called himself a linen-weaver and shopkeeper when he made his will in 1755 leaving everything to a bastard nephew, who inherited eight cottages in Brockdish, and a shop with its stock, counters and drawers. Thomas and his nephew lived in one of the cottages and the others were let; and tenants included a butcher, a wheelwright, a carpenter, a cordwainer and a tailor.[6]

Three testators specified that their wives should carry on their trade in order to support themselves and their children, and each was left looms and stock in trade to enable them to do this.[7] Such arrangements may well have been quite common when widows were left with young children.

Francis Roper of Rickinghall Superior was childless when he died in 1811, and his chief legatees were three nephews, one of whom was described as a linen-weaver 'now living under my roof'. Bequests to this nephew included reeds, slays and other utensils belonging to the weaving trade, a cart usually used for carrying cloth and £200's worth of stock in trade; this was comprised of hemp, tow, yarn and hemp-cloth, all to be valued at wholesale not retail prices. This testator employed at least two journeymen, each of whom was left a 'weaving frame or loom'.[8]

A few wills exist for various ancillary trades, such as hemp-dressers, linen-drapers and whitesters; the wills of the last have already been

[1] NRO NCC Franklin 176 (1801)
[2] NRO NCC Woodrofe 163 (1743)
[3] NRO NCC West 192 (1805)
[4] NRO NCC Burrough 138
[5] SROI ICAA1/163/46 (1734)
[6] NRO NCC Roper 185
[7] SROI ICAA1/166/11 (Robert Dawson of Beccles, 1737); NRO NCC Overton 197
[8] NRO NCC Mullenger 183

discussed. John Theodorick, who died in 1742, was a hemp-buyer and owned two houses in 'Outwell in the Isle' as well as land there and at Walsoken.[1] At this date hemp may still have been a popular crop in the fens. The known dressers of flax, hemp and tow were all three men of property, and only John Page of South Elmham St Nicholas who described himself as a labourer and hemp dresser seems to have owned no land. The 20 linen-drapers, whose wills were read, were almost to a man at least comfortably off and the 9 from Norwich can all be classed as wealthy; the two richest made cash legacies respectively totalling £1490 and £1700.[2] Not surprisingly almost all the linen-drapers lived in towns. Their wills throw no light on the local linen trade, but that of Thomas Jolley of Palgrave, whose inventory was referred to on page 143, has some interest.[3] It shows that, in addition to two houses in his own village, he owned property in two other parishes and a house with yards in the neighbouring market town of Diss. Thomas Jolley was sufficiently rich to leave portions of £200 to his only son, and £100 each to his four daughters, all to be paid when these children attained their majority; all five were also left some real estate.

IX

There are a number of surnames that crop up several times amongst seventeenth and eighteenth century linen-weavers, and it is not unusual for the same name to occur three or four times in one parish or in neighbouring villages. Attempts to trace dynasties of linen-weavers have had little success, and only in the case of the Negus family, who lived in three of the Little Ouse valley weaving parishes, has it been possible to establish links covering three generations. Wills are the most reliable source for relating individuals, but their coverage has proved too patchy to do more than match fathers and sons in all but the instance mentioned above. Even though the gaps between wills may be too long to provide definite links, the persistence of a name in the same place over a century or more suggests the likelihood of a relationship, particularly when the individuals all followed the same trade.

Five members of the Burlingham family lived in Hepworth, Ricking-hall and Wattisfield over a period of 123 years, but a firm link can be established between only two. There are several instances of wills surviving for a father and two of his sons, such as the rich Morphews of Hoxne; Gideon died in 1633 and the wills of two of his sons were proved during the reign of Charles II. When Robert Weeting of Redgrave

---

[1] NRO NCC Woodrofe 142

[2] NRO NCC Gardiner 100 (William Hill, 1771); NRO NCC Curtis 197 (John Nicholls, 1768)

[3] NRO NCC Frances 94

made his will in 1661 he bequeathed a capital messuage which had belonged to his father, who had died 30 years earlier, and to his grandfather. Robert's brother Jonathan was also a linen-weaver and lived in Thetford. Four members of the Prentice family of Palgrave were linen-weavers and three left wills, but it has proved difficult to work out the relationships. William died in 1660, but there is a gap of more than 60 years before the other two wills – too long for a single generation. Samuel and Thomas died in 1722 and 1723, but it is not clear whether they were brothers or cousins; both made bequests to their cousin Samuel Algar, another Palgrave linen-weaver. Thomas was by far the richer of the two and gave legacies to several Prentice kinsmen, including his brother John, a Palgrave gentleman, an attorney living at Rickinghall and a Bungay grocer. The Prentices are an example of the wide social and economic range often found within a family, whose prosperous and poor members kept in touch despite these differences.[1]

The decline of linen-weaving in the late eighteenth century compelled not only hecklers to move from village to village in search of work. The history of Roger Brock and his father illustrates the change, and a change for the worse, in the circumstances of rural craftsmen from part-time farmers to journymen workers. The son was living at Needham when examined in 1758 and was then 39 years of age. Born at Alburgh, he had subsequently moved with his parents to Denton and then to South Elmham St Cross, at both of which places his father had rented a small farm as well as carrying on the business of a linen-weaver. While living with his father he had 'learned of him the Busyness of a linnen weaver' and since then 'has wrought of his Busyness as a Journeyman' for nine years.[2] Several other linen-weavers who underwent settlement examinations had learnt their trade from their fathers, and all had worked as journeymen in a number of places and had failed to gain a settlement at any of them. In earlier centuries few weavers were really rich, but many had some small stake in the land which helped to keep them in one place and gave then a secure economic base.

Little direct evidence has been found for the continued existence of independent weavers working their own loom, or perhaps assisted by weaver sons. Nevertheless, it cannot be assumed that this class, so common in the seventeenth century, had completely vanished or that all linen-weavers were employed in their trade full-time. Bythell's comment that 'many hand loom weavers would have found the concept of following one occupation full-time an alien one' is probably as true for eighteenth-century East Anglia as for northern England.[3] The diary

---

[1] Spufford, 1974, pp. 108–11 gives a good example of this type of family.
[2] NRO PD205/50
[3] Bythell, p.58

of a Yorkshire farmer-weaver, Cornelius Ashworth of Halifax, illustrates the varied activities of a rural craftsman: weaving, carrying his cloth to market, fetching wood, tending his calving cow, harvesting, ditching and jobbing with a horse and cart are but some of Ashworth's multifarious tasks.[1] Thompson also comments on the work pattern of alternate bouts of intense labour and idleness which was typical of men who were independent and thus controlled their own working lives.[2] The Rossendale area of Lancashire was another district where farming and manufacture continued to be combined for much of the eighteenth century, although here the latter half of the century saw a rise in the numbers of cottager-weavers who were 'almost wholly, if not completely divorced from agricultural employment'.[3] As recently as the 1920s the publican, postman, blacksmith and other inhabitants of at least one Suffolk village each 'practised farming as well as his usual trade'. The only exception was the shopkeeper.[4]

In East Anglia the eighteenth century was the watershed between the flourishing dual economy of the seventeenth and the grinding poverty of the early nineteenth century. The changes undergone by the linen industry during this hundred years were typical of most rural manufactures, and its decline was inseparably linked to that of small part-time farms. The two counties of Norfolk and Suffolk described by Arthur Young and Eden around 1800 were very different from those visited by Daniel Defoe some 80 years earlier.[5] The decay of the East Anglian linen trade was only part of the general decline of the region from the position of economic pre-eminence which it had occupied for so many centuries.

[1] E.P. Thompson, 'Time, Work-Discipline, and Industrial Capitalism', *Past and Present*, 38 (1967), 71–2
[2] ibid, p.73
[3] G.H. Tupling, *The Economic History of Rossendale*, Chetham Society, new series 86 (1927), pp. 178–9, 189
[4] Adrian Bell, *Corduroy*, 3rd edition (Oxford, 1982), p.54
[5] F.M .Eden, *State of the Poor* (1797)

6 Decline and Decay

I

The early decades of the nineteenth century were not a happy period for East Anglia: unemployment and underemployment were acute problems; discontent was expressed in sporadic outbreaks of violence; poor rates were high; wages were lower than average; agriculture was depressed; old industries were failing and new ones had not yet developed to replace them. Linen-weaving was in serious trouble by 1800, largely because of the competition of cheap cotton goods, and the collapse of this local manufacture was just one of the factors contributing to the general economic and social malaise.

In 1834 a House of Commons Committee reported that since 1815 the cost of the 'necessaries of life' had fallen by 30 per cent while handloom weavers' wages had declined by 60 per cent.[1] This report refers only to Ireland, Scotland and the counties of Lancashire and Warwickshire, but there is no reason to suppose that the situation differed much elsewhere. A year later, a return of the numbers of power looms showed that there were none in Suffolk, and 300 weaving silk in Norfolk; all these belonged to one firm, Grout Bayliss and Company.[2] No mills of any kind, not even for flax, were found in either county.[3] Clearly the East Anglian linen industry had remained unmechanised, and this is confirmed by the report of the Commission on Hand-Loom Weavers presented to Parliament in 1840.[4]

The Commissioners visited several places in Norfolk, three of which lay in the Waveney valley, but Haverhill was the only Suffolk town on their itinerary. Their report depicts a decaying, or rather dying, industry, apart from 'one green oasis in the vast desert of discontent'. This cheerful spot was North Lopham near Diss, which together with its sister village had long been a centre of linen-weaving and was to be the only place where the manufacture of hand-woven hempen-linen survived into the twentieth century. A recent history of the Lophams has done justice to their local industry, which is also described by

[1] *Parliamentary Papers*, 1834, XIII, p.13; Report from Select Committee on Hand-Loom Weavers' Petitions
[2] D.C. Coleman, *Courtaulds, an economic and social history* (Oxford, 1969), 3 vols, I, p.63
[3] *Parliamentary Papers*, 1836, XLV
[4] *Parliamentary Papers*, 1840, XIII

Pursehouse.[1] Elsewhere there was nothing to report but distress, with low wages and irregular work.

At Harleston, according to the 1840 Report, the chief product of the looms was bombazine woven for the Norwich manufacturers. Although earlier made with a linen warp, by the early nineteenth century this cloth was a cotton and worsted mixture. Some of the weaving at Harleston was carried out in a 'large shop or factory', but work was also distributed to cottages in neighbouring villages. This pattern of a workforce divided between a small factory and outworkers also existed at Diss, and was probably typical of many enterprises of a similar size in East Anglian towns. Eight linen-weavers are known to have lived in the parish of Harleston with Redenhall and, as at Wymondham, linen may have preceded bombazine-weaving. In 1789 there were 6 weavers (undifferentiated by their thread) and 26 spinners living in Harleston, which seemed at that date to have no other industry.[2]

Norwich manufacturers also provided work for a third of the 300 looms at Wymondham, where one weaver told the Commissioners that after weaving a variety of linen fabrics for 15 years, he turned to bombazine because of the decline of linen-weaving in Norfolk. Four years after the Commission on Hand-Loom Weavers made its report, *The Times* of 16 July 1844 carried a report from its own correspondent concerning the extreme poverty of the Wymondham and Hethersett districts of Norfolk. At the former place he was told that two-thirds of the population of about 5000 were either paupers or close to pauperism. He reported that the chief manufacturer of bombazine had recently failed 'throwing some 300 or 400 men out of work.', and that many of the weavers had 'gone to seek work at Norwich'. He wrote that to earn 7s. a week a man must work 14 hours a day, and that 'many, to do their best, cannot earn more than 6s. a week'. 'The wages are so low, that neither weavers nor labourers can lay by anything; and they get into debt and distress, if out of work but for a few days. Their extra earnings at harvest time all go to meet their rent, and to pay off their debts. The parish clerk told me the weavers get about 1s. a day, and are "just alive".' In this district the workhouse was greatly disliked, and many labourers had left to work as excavators on the railroad. In 1845 White's *Directory of Norfolk* said that the 600 looms working at Wymondham ten years previously had been reduced to about 60. By 1844 linen-weaving had already gone the way of bombazine-making, and it is not hard to see why it had ceased to be a viable occupation.

[1] Michael Friend Serpell, *A History of the Lophams* (1980), *passim*, but particularly chapters 12, 15 and 21; and Pursehouse
[2] Young, 1804, p.112

In earlier times hemp had been much used for sacks, but the growth of a prosperous jute industry at Dundee in the 1820s and 1830s had caused the collapse of this East Anglian trade too. A notice in the *Ipswich Journal* for 11 November 1820 advertised that a sack and cord manufactory in St Mary Elms parish in the town was available for leasing, and that the business had been established for over one hundred years. This may be an indication of the decay of sack-making in Suffolk. The 1840 Report described sacking-weaving in Norwich as 'merely the expiring embers of a trade about to be extinguished', an apt description of the once flourishing East Anglian linen industry. A few sacking-weavers survived at Diss and were described as old men able to earn only about 7s. a week.

Diss is only short distance from the Lophams, and here in 1838 there was still one manufacturer, Henry Warne, who employed 40 men, 20 boys and 3 women in the making of drabbetts, huckabacks, sheeting and shirting. Some of the men worked in a factory in Mere Street in the town centre, but others in their own homes, and Mrs Warne told the Commissioners that the latter earned more because they had less temptation to spend money. Warne explained that the fly-shuttle running on wheels was employed in drabbett making, and that all the fabrics he produced could be made on power looms but that 'they have not as yet been made to such an extent by power as materially to effect the market'. His employees laboured long hours, some as many as 15 to 16, to earn up to 16s. a week but 12s. was the average earnings from which had to be deducted 6d. each for starch (to dress the warp) and candles, and 1s. paid to the child who wound the weaver's quills or spools. Even so these men were receiving a shilling or two a week more than agricultural labourers in this district. In addition to the above expenses, weavers were expected to provide their own looms and harness, which cost around four guineas. A loom would last a lifetime and more, but the cords of the harness needed constant mending and renewing and this expense amounted to some 8s. a year.

During the early decades of the nineteenth century spinning hemp and sack-making were still regarded as occupations for paupers. In April 1807 Barton Mills advertised in the *Bury and Norwich Post* for a man to instruct the poor of the parish 'in the spinning of Hemp and manufactory of sacks'. At Wortham in December 1823 a 'committee for managing affairs of the poor' of the parish put a number of questions concerning sack-making to a Mr Tyson. His answers gave the sums that could be earned by spinners and sack-weavers, and indicated how much yarn and sackcloth they ought to produce. The working hours proposed for both spinners and weavers were 8.0 a.m. to 8.0 p.m. with two hours off for meals. Women spinners could earn 4s. a week clear, after paying a child 1s. a week for turning the wheel. This sounds as though the English great wheel, which did not have a foot treadle, was still in use. Many spinners were children and Tyson said, 'A brisk Girl 13 or 14 yrs of age can with ease earn 6*d*. a day clear.' A child of 7 could earn 7*d*. a week winding yarn onto quills, and a 10 year-old could keep two looms supplied with yarn for which the weaver would pay him 1*s*. 4*d*. a week. Weavers also had to find their own candles, which cost them 3*d*. each week during the winter half of the year. Sacking-weavers were paid by the piece, 46 to 47 yards in length, and Tyson calculated that a good workman could weave five pieces with ease in a fortnight, thus earning 10*s*. 4*d*. a week clear after paying his expenses. These wages are almost identical to those earned by Warne's employees at Diss. An inferior workman should make four pieces in two weeks and 'he must be very slow or lazy to do less'. After the sackcloth had been woven it was cut up and women and children sewed up the sides and hemmed the ends of the sacks; this work was paid at 10*d*. per score of sacks.[1] The Wortham parish records do not indicate whether Mr Tyson's suggestions were adopted, but even had such a manufactory been set up it could not have succeeded for long as sack-making in East Anglia was already feeling the effect of the competition of Dundee jute factories and was virtually to disappear by 1840.

II

Shortly after the Report on Hand-Loom Weavers was presented, Warne closed his Diss factory and moved first to Hoxne and then to Syleham. The 1851 census for Diss lists only one person connected with the linen trade; this was James Cooke, a 67-year-old linen manufacturer, who may well have been retired. In his 1845 *Directory of Norfolk* White states that 'Diss was formerly noted for the manufacture of Suffolk hempen cloth, worsted yarn and knit hosiery . . . the business is now wholly discontinued . . . Weavers' Hall, at the Saracen's Head, was formly the great mart, for the hempen linen manufacture in the town and the surrounding villages.'[2] From the 1851 census it is clear that brush-making had become the town's main industry; there were also a number of straw hat and basket makers.

White's *Directory of Suffolk*, published in 1844, mentions under Hoxne 'a large old corn mill on the Waveney, which has recently been converted into a flax and linen manufactory' and was then in the possession of Thomas Coleby, linen manufacturer and spinner. The 1841 census had listed two flax dressers and two spinners at Hoxne. Some of the workers at the Hoxne mill were very young: a report in the

---

[1] SROI FB13/G21/10. This paragraph is mainly based on this document.
[2] White's Norfolk, p.714

Suffolk Chronicle for 1 Feburary 1840 is concerned with the drowning of two little factory girls, aged 9 and 11, in the River Waveney as they returned home from Hoxne water-mill where they were employed by Mr H. Warne. The 1851 census gives no indication of linen manufacturing in this parish, so it must be assumed that the Coleby business had closed before that year. Thomas Coleby had been a party to a deed as long before as 1799, so must have been an old man by 1844. It seems possible that he was in partnership with Henry Warne.

Warne cannot have stayed long at Hoxne for in 1844 he appears in the Directory as a cotton and linen manufacturer at Syleham mills, about a mile and a half downstream. These mills were described by White as 'an extensive water corn mill, the greater part of which was converted into a linen and cotton manufactory, about five years ago'.[1] According to the 1851 census Warne was a drabbett manufacturer employing 96 hands, of whom only six lived in Syleham, including the Staffordshire-born 'overlooker' who was Warne's brother-in-law; two elderly retired hand-loom hemp weavers also lived in the parish. The population of Syleham was small, only 399 in 1841, and much of Warne's workforce lived at Brockdish in Norfolk just across the Waveney. In 1851 the census enumerator found 32 weavers living there, in addition to a power-loom manager and four other workers connected with the industry. Only 4 of the weavers were over 30 and several were in their teens; 22 of their number were unmarried girls, most of whom were lodgers. Starting in 1838 Pursehouse found 85 weavers, of whom 53 were women, in the Brockdish baptism and marriage registers.[2] Workers at Syleham mills were concentrated in Brockdish on the Norfolk side of the river. At neighbouring Needham for instance there was a 76-year-old hickler and no weavers. On the Suffolk side of the Waveney there were no weavers in any of the parishes bounding Syleham, so the source of 53 of Warne's labour force remains unaccounted for.

The existence of Warne's factory at Syleham may have helped to relieve unemployment in an area where there was practically no alternative employment to farm work. Yet the drabbett industry arrived there about the same time that East Anglian farming entered its mid-century period of economic success. The employment opportunities offered by Warne might have been more welcome earlier in the century when so many persons emigrated from the borders of Norfolk and Suffolk.[3] Few people left for the New World from Hoxne, where Warne briefly established his business, but in 1836 a total of 236 migrants left this village for northern industrial towns and seem never

---

[1] White's Suffolk, p.472
[2] Pursehouse, p.185
[3] Coleman et al., p.31–33

to have returned.[1] Probably the numbers employed at Syleham were not sufficient to make any real impression on the problem of unemployment, particularly as so many of the weavers were women. The presence among them of a number of unmarried girls lodging with local families suggests that they may not have been of local origin.

It would be interesting to know why Warne moved from Diss where there can have been no shortage of labour. The move could well be connected with the mechanisation of spinning and weaving. At Diss Warne was clearly employing hand-loom weavers, and the river Waveney is probably too small there to turn a water mill of any size, but there were already water-powered mills at both Hoxne and Syleham to which places he in turn transferred his business. Steam-power had been adopted at the Syleham mill by 1872, but how long before this had occurred cannot be determined and it was used only as an auxiliary source of power.

The connection of Syleham with linen-weaving went back at least to the late seventeenth century and 10 weavers are known to have lived there between 1677 and 1782. It is also one of the two places in Suffolk to have a continuing link with the old linen industry. Today, on the same site as the old mill, there is still a factory making clothing. The following information about the recent history of Syleham mill comes from a previous owner.[2] The mill was put up for sale by auction in 1872, probably shortly after the death of Henry Warne, but remained unsold and was leased out by his executors until Mr Richard Emms purchased it from Charles Warne and two others in 1899. The auctioneers' particulars of 1872 are full of interesting details and describe the mill as a 'substantial structure with spacious floors, the greater part being occupied by Weaving looms'. The premises also included an engine and boiler house, a 16-foot in diameter wheel, counting house, warehouse, storage lofts, three pairs of stones for grinding corn and accommodation for dyeing and drying. The dyeing process was carried out in a building across the road from the mill; it was called a 'drying hovel' in 1872. The floors in this building were slatted and within living memory it contained tenters on which cloth was stretched to dry after being dyed. In this century there were three storeys in the mill itself with looms at ground level, spinning machines on the first and preparation on the top floor; the corn mill was at the west end of the building. All the machinery could be driven either by water or steam power, but the latter was used only when the water level was too low to turn the wheel

[1] ibid, p.13
[2] I am extremely grateful to Mr E.G. Emms of Pulham Market for giving up his time to tell me about Syleham mill during the time it belonged to his father and himself, and for showing me documents in his possession.

or high enough to create a backlash. The mechanisation of the weaving process meant that women could be employed, and each operator could work three looms as both the shuttles and slays were moved mechanically.

Syleham mill was destroyed on 24 May 1928 by a fire believed to have been started by an overheated bearing. In appearance it was typical of a large early nineteenth-century watermill, several of which still remain in the Waveney valley. Weaving had ceased there long before the fire and after 1914 only ready-made garments, mainly trousers, were produced. Up till the First World War drabbetts were woven, but demand was already falling before the war began and the skilled male weavers joined the forces; they could not be replaced and a large order for dungarees for the French army left no time for weaving. One of the last surviving weavers told Mr Emms that when she began work at the age of 13 as a winder, she started at 6.0 a.m., and that the weavers still had to buy their own candles. This woman worked at the mill until she was over 70.

Drabbett was a coarse cloth made with a linen warp and cotton weft. The linen warp used at Syleham early in this century was almost certainly made from flax as it came from Ulster ready beamed; no warping was done at Syleham. Cloth was made in diagonal or herringbone weave in 80-yard lengths and mostly sold to tailors in 20-yard 'ends', either dyed or undyed. The former was usually tan in colour and was popular for fishermen's clothing, while the natural coloured cloth was made into smocks for farmworkers. Garments had been made at Syleham before Mr Emms purchased the mill in 1899, and earlier in the nineteenth century canvas was also made there. The dyke to the west of the mill was at one time used for retting, as were the meadows below the Scole flax mill to be described later. The cessation of drabbett manufacture at Syleham in 1914 ended the long connection of the village with the linen industry.

When the Hand-Loom Commissioners visited Haverhill in the far south-west corner of Suffolk they found some 450 looms making drabbetts, using hemp warp from Leeds and cotton weft from Stockport; the material was made into smocks and pantaloons for labourers and servants. The necessity of obtaining hemp warp from Leeds shows that local supplies were not available because of the decline in hemp cultivation. Working the looms were 150 men and 100 each of women, girls and boys. As elsewhere wages were low, and the price for the cloth had fallen over the preceding 10 years from 11s. to 6s. a chain.[1] The Commissioners added that drabbetts had been produced there for some

---

[1] A chain of drabbett was about 40 yards in length

twenty-five years, and that previously fustians and blue and white checks had been made in Haverhill.

In chapter 5 it was shown that the connection of the town with cloth-manufacturing extended as far back as the seventeenth century, if not earlier, and has been continued almost to the present day. When Daniel Gurton (the spelling later changed to Gurteen) opened a bank account with £1000 on 28 September 1784 he founded a firm which is to celebrate its bicentenary in 1984. Fustian-weaving was already established in Haverhill, and in order to acquire capital of £1000 Gurton must previously have been trading in a considerable way.[1] However, nothing precise is known of his antecedents or of his activities before 1784. As the deeds concerning the cottage Scandrett let in 1753 (see p. 146) are in the possession of Messrs Gurteen it seems likely that this building stood on or near the site of their present factory in the centre of Haverhill. The factory is believed to have occupied the same position throughout its existence. The firm's earliest account book shows that in 1801 fustians, checks and drabbetts were being manufactured, and in 1807 there appears the first record of selling ready-made smocks. During the early nineteenth century Gurteens were providing cloth and garments for customers in London, Essex, Norfolk and Suffolk; L. Fincham of Diss, for example, purchased fustians in 1811 as well as 40 yards of hemp-cloth for two guineas. At this date a smock cost from 5s. 6d. to 8s. 9d. depending on its length; the higher price is roughly the same as a week's wages for a Suffolk farm labourer in the early nineteenth century. Supplies of yarn were purchased in London and Norwich, and from Marshalls of Leeds.

In their early days the Gurton family were not without rivals in Haverhill. Robson's Directory of 1839 lists five other manufacturers of drabbetts, a hemp and silk-manufacturer and a ropemaker. Five years later White's *Directory* gives much the same information, although one drabbett-maker has disappeared. Its description of the town states that 'it was formerly noted for checks, cottons and fustians, and has now a silk mill, employing about 70 hands, and several manufacturers of drabbetts'. About 330 weavers were employed making drabbetts, and many women made it up into smock frocks. A memoir of Daniel Gurteen (1809–94), grandson of the firm's founder, explained that when he was a child 'all the industry [of Haverhill was] carried on in the houses of the people, and in nearly every cottage might be heard the rattle of the loom',[2] and added that around 1830 his father was carrying on a thriving business in a small way in drabbett weaving.

---

[1] I should like to thank Messrs Gurteen for allowing me to see their records and I am particularly grateful to Mr C.W. Gurteen for showing me round their works and museum.

[2] Crampton's *House Almanack* for Haverhill for 1894

In the early 1850s there was still much poverty and unemployment in Haverhill, but this situation was revolutionised by a modernisation programme begun by Gurteens in 1856. In this year two beam engines were purchased and a new 'steam drabbett' factory was built. Twenty years later steam-power was applied to driving sewing machines and from this time on garments were made up in the factory instead of in the houses of outworkers. In 1879–80 the original steam engines were replaced by more powerful models, and one of the new engines, called Caroline after the Director's wife, has been retained as a showpiece. The firm continued to diversify by starting hair-weaving and mat-making in the 1880s.

The drabbett factories at Haverhill and Syleham have survived until the present day, although in a different guise, because their owners mechanised production, introduced new lines and dropped outmoded ones in response to changes in demand. The North Lopham firm of Buckenham owed its continuation until 1925 to quite different reasons. Up to the end all weaving was carried out by hand, and production only ceased because when the last member of the family died nobody wished to take on the business. The firm concentrated on producing very good quality household and table linen, including damasks, for a high-class clientele, amongst whom were the royal family and the Travellers' Club. According to an article in the *East Anglian Daily Times* in April 1936, the demand for the products of the Lopham weavers continued until the very end. Buckenhams was the sole survivor of 15 linen-manufacturers listed at the two Lophams in 1845 by White's *Directory of Norfolk*.

III

The first editions of White's Directories of Norfolk (1836) and Suffolk (1844) list a few linen-manufacturers, as does Robson's Directory of 1839. It is generally accepted that the early editions of White's Directories are reliable, but discrepancies between these and Robson suggests that the latter was already out of date when published and may have copied earlier descriptions. For instance, what Robson has to say about Diss disagrees with the quotations from White given on p. 155. The former wrote that the market was supplied with large quantities of linen cloth, and the 'greater part of the inhabitants are employed in the manufacture of hempen cloth and stockings'. Yet only Henry Warne is listed as a manufacturer and spinner of flax, hemp and tow. Robson's descriptions of industry at Diss and elsewhere are reminiscent of those of eighteenth-century writers, such as Cox. Needham, a village on the road from Diss to Harleston, had still been the home of linen-weavers and hecklers early in the nineteenth century, but the occupational description (in the baptism register for 1831) of George Reeve as formerly a weaver and now a husbandman is an indication of the decline in the trade. An auction notice, in the *Bury and Norwich Post* of 21 September 1836, concerning the sale of a house in Needham called the White Hart and standing near the road from Harleston to Scole, describes the village as a place 'where extensive trade in hemp cloth manufactory *had* been carried on' (emphasis added). Yet White's Directory of 1845 lists Jonathan Blackmore, linen-manufacturer, at Needham, so a vestige of the industry may have survived there. Was this man perhaps the same person as the 76-year-old hickler, Jonathan Blackman, recorded in the 1851 census?

'Here are manufactories for knit stockings and hempen cloth' wrote Robson of Bungay, but none such appear in his list of trades in the town, and White mentions only a silk and crape mill, which was sited in Ditchingham across the Waveney. Thirty linen-weavers are known to have lived in the town during earlier centuries, but the latest reference dates from 1826. However, a local author thought that hand-loom weaving continued in Bungay until 1855 and said that 'the last cloth made in Bungay was woven on the premises belonging to Mr John Henry Smith in St Mary's Streeet' where six looms were employed.[1] There is no mention of this Mr Smith in White, who merely says that Bungay was 'formerly noted for the manufacture of knitted worsted stockings and "Suffolk hempen cloth", but these trades are now obsolete'.

At Stowmarket Robson lists one hemp manufacturer, while White has two linen-manufacturers who also made sacks, as well as two rope and twine-makers and a third producer of sacks. In his description of this town White says it 'still gives employment to a number of persons in the manufacture of linen of "Suffolk hempen cloth", and in making sacking, rope, twine, etc.' One linen-weaver lived in this town when he made his will in 1606, but the next reference to the trade dates from 1783 (see p. 145). There was a general trend in the late eighteenth century for linen-weaving to be concentrated in towns as it came more and more into the hands of manufacturers, who found it more convenient to have their workers grouped together rather than scattered around the countryside.

In his general comments on the occupations of the inhabitants of Suffolk White wrote that the county's 'ancient staple manufacture of "Suffolk Hempen Cloth", is now nearly obsolete, except in the vale of the Waveney, on the borders of Norfolk and Suffolk, where there are a few flax mills, and a number of looms, etc., employed in producing this useful fabric for shirts, sheets, etc., at and near Hoxne, Syleham, Diss

[1] Mann, p.151

and Harleston'. He goes on to comment on the annihilation of the hand spinning industry in both Norfolk and Suffolk, which had formerly given 'employment to a large portion of the female population' of both counties.[1] This writer was clearly aware of the former importance of the East Anglian linen industry.

Several small-scale manufacturers of Suffolk hempen cloth survived into the early decades of the nineteenth century, but were it not for newspaper advertisements the very existence of some would be unknown. In 1807 a firm with premises on the corner of Abbeygate Streeet and the Butter Market in Bury St Edmunds advertised Suffolk hemps for sale,[2] and similar advertisements are not uncommon. This material seems to have been highly esteemed, particularly for its hard-wearing qualities, and was widely sold in the county, although it was probably virtually unknown outside East Anglia. With the exception of the Lopham firm of Buckenham, Norfolk and Suffolk linen-manufacturers appear never to have attempted to widen the market for their products. To the last the linen-weavers of the region produced their cloth solely for local consumers.

Most of these manufacturers were to be found in small market towns, such as Halesworth, and rather more is known about what was probably the last hemp-cloth firm here than about many others. Hemp manufacturing continued in Halesworth until at least 1830 when James Aldred placed the following advertisement in the *Ipswich Journal* in March of that year: 'Real Suffolk Hemp Cloth Manufactory By James Aldred, Halesworth. James Aldred Begs to introduce to the Public the above Article the quality of which is extensively approved by many highly respectable families, and the durablity of which far exceeds any other article made for family linens. James Aldred believes the only negative to its more extensive use has been its high price; but, in consequence of the great reduction of the Raw Material, as well as Labour, he is enabled to offer the above Article at a reduction of at least 25 per cent. James Aldred has witnessed with regret, that a consider-able part of the Cloth sold to the public for Suffolk Hemp, had been composed of Flax and not real Hemp; but, he trusts an established reputation of thirty years, will be a sufficient pledge for his supplying a Genuine Article.' To enable customers living at a distance from Halesworth to obtain his cloth, at the same prices as at his own factory, Aldred appointed agents to sell it in Ipswich, Norwich, Yarmouth, Lowestoft, Beccles, Benhall, Stradbroke and Peasenhall. Five of these persons are listed as drapers in White's 1844 Directory, and it may be assumed that all were engaged in the same trade.

---

[1] White's Suffolk, p.16
[2] *Bury and Norwich Post*, 8 April 1807

James Aldred was a member of a family living at Wissett, two miles west of Halesworth, and it was here that bleaching was carried out. One of the executors of the will of a Wissett farmer, dated 1788,[1] was John Aldred, linen-weaver of the same parish. This may have been the man of the same name, whose will was drawn up early in 1827, in which year he died aged 75[2] He then described himself as a farmer, but his will mentions his shop near Halesworth bridge and 'my farming and bleach-ing business'. His bleach ground was leased from the parish of Alburgh, which had purchased the land with money left for the pur-pose, in or before 1508, by one Richard Wright. John Aldred asked his executors to sell his business if his son Robert did not wish to continue it. The Wissett tithe map, dated 1839, shows that Robert Aldred was the owner-occupier of Whitehouse Farm and the tenant of Bleach Farm.[3] The tithe apportionment names three bleach meadows near Bleach Farm and one elsewhere in the parish, as well as ten hemplands and five parcels of land to which the name 'retting pit' was attached.[4]

Although the exact connection between John and James Aldred is not known, they were presumably related and the latter acted as an executor of the former's will. John Aldred's advertisement, quoted above, referred to 'an established reputation of thirty years', but the family's connection with the linen trade went back at least as far as the 1780s. It is not known for how long after 1830 James Aldred continued to manufacture hempen cloth.[5] Robert Aldred moved away from Wissett, where he had been a deacon of the congregational chapel, around 1846 and died at Norwich in 1865. After his departure the bleaching business was carried on for a time by the Lincoln family. James Aldred's factory is believed to have stood in Chediston Street, and a number of semi-derelict industrial buildings still stand behind the houses in this street.[6]

Hempen-linen manufacturing seems to have disappeared from Halesworth before the middle of the nineteenth century. By 1851 the only persons connected with the Suffolk hemp industry still to be found in the town were a blind pauper hemp-weaver and a heckler. In Wissett there were none. White says that 'great quantities of hemp were for-merly grown in the neighbourhood, and many of the inhabitants were employed in the manufacture of Suffolk hempen cloth, but the trade was discontinued many years ago'.[7] On the other hand Robson,

---

[1] SROI ICAA1/210/35; will of Robert Bartram, proved in 1790
[2] SROI ICAA1/118/172
[3] SROI FDA294/A1/1.b.
[4] SROI FDA294/A1/1.a.
[5] He is listed in Pigot's Directory for 1840, but not in White's of 1844
[6] I am indebted to Mr Peter Northeast for information about the Aldred family, and to Margaret Meek, 'The Hempen Cloth Industry in Suffolk', *Suffolk Review* II, 82–85
[7] White's Suffolk, p.372

probably again out of date, speaks of large amounts of hemp being grown in the district and of spinning yarn as the chief occupation of the town. In fact by 1839 the main industries were malting and the making of agricultural machinery at the iron foundry. In earlier times Halesworth had indeed been an important linen market, but there is little evidence of linen weavers living there at any date.

It is clear from his advertisement that Aldred used drapers' shops as his main retail outlet, and this was probably the case with most other local linen manufacturers, but not all did so. In April 1820 the *Ipswich Journal* reported a case heard by Quarter Sessions concerning the settlement of a pauper, in the course of which reference was made to George Thurlow, a Wortham linen-weaver, who 'travelled the country to sell cloth'. Travelling pedlars or chapmen were still fairly common in the nineteenth century, but after about 1840 neither they nor drapers can have had any East Anglian-made linens to sell.

IV

Little is known of the men who worked for Aldred and other employers like him, or as independent weavers. Amongst the records of the overseers of the poor for Metfield is a copy of the 1811 census return for the parish.[1] It lists five hecklers, a tow-comber and two weavers, so here at least the linen industry was still providing employment. In 1811 the census gives only the names and occupations of heads of households, so there may have been more weavers and ancillary workers living in this village. It is unfortunate that so few of the original returns for the censuses made between 1801 and 1831 have survived. By 1851 very few linen-weavers, or anyone alse connected with the industry, were to be found in Norfolk or Suffolk. A search of the returns for a number of parishes, formerly linen-weaving centres, in both counties has revealed no indication of the survival of the industry. This survey included the four parishes whose economies were analysed in chapter 4, and showed that linen-weaving had totally vanished from all four. A few weavers survived here and there, but not in any numbers apart from the places supplying the workforce for the mill at Syleham. Two handloom weavers of hemp, a father and son, were living in Old Newton not far from Stowmarket. The father, who was aged 60, had been born at Fersfield in the hemp district of south Norfolk and his weaver son was only 17-years-old. His wife was a grocer and his elder son a carpenter, so this family was not wholly dependent on weaving.

In 1841 two linen-weavers named Catchpole were living near each other, one in Laxfield and the other at Stradbroke. The latter, called

[1] SROI FC91/G7/1

James, is also listed in White's Directory as living at Barley Green, one of several hamlets in Stradbroke parish. Another Catchpole was amongst the five hecklers resident in Metfield in 1811. In 1801 Robert Balls of Fressingfield left £30 to Elizabeth, wife of Edward Catchpole, linen-weaver of Laxfield,[1] and in 1817 Robert Balls's niece, Lucy Wake, bequeathed £20 to Edward Catchpole.[2] It is possible that his wife was also a niece of Robert Balls. Edward was ill when he made his will in August 1837, but he did not die until March 1847.[3] He owned a row of three copyhold tenements, in one of which he lived and which the tithe map shows to have been in Market Street, a veritable rookery of sub-divided cottages.[4] This building together with his household furniture and effects and book debts was left to his son Righteous Wake Catchpole, a Laxfield schoolmaster. His other son, a London tailor, was left £8 and his father's clothes. 'A good decent suit of Mourning' was to be made at the testator's expense and presented to Sarah Rose 'for her kindness and attention to me, at and before the time of my decease'. Righteous Wake was to be the recipient of the sum due to his father from 'my Society Club' and was instructed to spend 5s. at each of the four public houses in Laxfield for those members of this club who attended his funeral.

Apart from Edward Catchpole practically nothing is known of the circumstances of linen-weavers in the nineteenth century, and even in his case there is no indication whether he worked on his own or employed other weavers. Early in the century a number of linen-weavers, hecklers and so on appear in poor law records and parish registers belonging to villages in the linen-weaving district, particularly around the Lophams. In 1861 a tow-comber aged 77 was a resident of the Hoxne Union workhouse, as was a young female drabbett-weaver. After 1800 only 74 linen-weavers are known, and 22 of these left wills which were analysed in chapter 5.

V

By the middle of the nineteenth century the East Anglian linen industry, with the exception of the Lopham firm of Buckenham, was virtually dead. Hemp-growing had almost certainly ceased, rather more than a hundred years before its cultivation was made illegal.[5] However, in the second half of the century there was an attempt, ultimately unsuccessful, to re-introduce flax as a crop. During the

1 SROI ICAA1/224/3
2 SROI ICAA1/251/3
3 SROI ICAA1/267/87
4 SROI FDA163/A1/1l. b. (1840)
5 Dangerous Drugs Act, 1965

1860s there were a number of reports in the *Ipswich Journal* concerning the growing and preparation of flax. In 1860 the Ipswich sanitary authorities had closed the Grey Friars Flax works and rettory on the marshes, but only two years later the Ipswich Farmers' Club received the report of a committee set up to examine the advisability of setting up a flax rettory. By 1864 the owner of a rettory at Henley, five miles north of Ipswich, was advertising first-class seed for sale. It was probably this establishment which was sold by auction in the autumn of the following year when it was said to be situated in a flax-growing district and was described as 'newly erected premises known as the "Flax Manufactory" ', which contained a horizontal 10 horsepower steam engine, a well 'with an inexhaustible supply of water' and 5 brick vats.[1]

Scole, near Diss, and Eye in north Suffolk were the main centres of the new flax industry. Pursehouse gives an account of the factory, built at the former place in 1854, and of its associated processing factory and rettory at Eye.[2] A return, of the number of flax, hemp and jute factories subject to the Factory Acts, presented to the House of Commons on 11 Feburary 1862 lists two flax factories in Norfolk employing 130 hands with 70 looms and 200 spindles. The motive power was steam. These were probably the factories at Scole and Eye.[3] The owner of the factory supplied seed to growers and also hired land on which to cultivate flax, the growing of which he encouraged by lectures, demonstrations and advice. At first this propaganda was successful: for example in 1863 250 acres in the parish of Debenham, not far from Eye, were planted with flax. Charles Costerson, the builder and owner of the Scole factory, saw his venture as a means of providing alternative employment to agriculture in an area where poverty was still acute. The products of the Scole works were twine, rope and sacking; for all of which there was a demand both from farmers and industrialists. Costerson's enterprise had a life of less than 30 years: a fire destroyed the Eye works in 1864 and they were never rebuilt; at Scole the factory survived five severe fires, but a decline in both demand for its products and local supplies of flax led to its closure in 1881.

There was an even more short-lived flax factory at Long Melford, which unlike Scole lies far from the traditional hemp-growing region. From *c*. 1830 horse hair and later coconut matting weaving had become the chief occupations in Long Melford and other nearby places, including Lavenham. Flax was a later arrival on the scene and its brief history in Long Melford can be traced through trade directories. In 1875 there was a flax merchant there, but no indication of a factory; ten years later

---

[1] *Ipswich Journal*
[2] Pursehouse, pp. 193–5
[3] Warden, p. 680

160 hands were employed in a flax works about a mile west of the village, but by 1892 the directory reported that these works 'formerly gave employment to about 160 hands, but is now practically closed, only a few persons being employed'.[1] The flax processed here was grown locally, but was sent to Belfast for spinning and weaving.[2] Almost the only relic remaining in Long Melford of this short-lived industry is a public house called the Scutchers' Arms.

Fifty years after flax processing had ceased at Scole, three acres of flax were planted on the Sandringham estate at the suggestion of the Linen Industry Research Association, and its produce was made into household linen for George V and Queen Mary. In 1934 a small flax factory was built at Sandringham and a large one at West Newton followed in 1939. During the Second World War it was impossible to import flax from the Baltic region, and this gave an impetus to cultivation of the crop in the United Kingdom, where a peak of 60,000 acres was reached in 1944; this included 5600 acres in Norfolk. In 1947 linen made from English flax was second only to whisky as a dollar-earning export, but by this date the area devoted to growing flax in Norfolk had already declined to 1100 acres.[3] The high price of linen compared with that of cotton, and later of synthetics, made this revival of flax growing in East Anglia of brief duration.

VI

If the independent craftsman-smallholder was the typical linen-weaver of 1650, by 1800 his place had been taken by the wage-earning out-worker forced to move from place to place in search of employment. Although, as we have seen, semi-industrial linen weaving did linger on in a few places until the 1830s, the industry was effectively dead in East Anglia by 1820. Hand-loom weaving was only one of the many skilled trades which were devalued by the industrial revolution. New skills replaced the old, but rarely were the same artisans transferred from one to another even in manufacturing districts. Rural workers in old industrial centres, such as East Anglia, had no opportunities for alternative employment and no escape from chronic under-employment and low agricultural wages.

James Aldred's advertisement, quoted on p.156 of this chapter, gives a great fall in the cost of labour as one of the two reasons which enabled him to offer a large reduction in the price of his hempen-cloth. This

[1] White's Suffolk, 1885, p.488 and 1892, p.549
[2] Mr David Dymond, personal communication
[3] R. Brett, 'Flax Growing in Suffolk', *East Anglian Magazine*, VII, no 5 (January, 1948), 265–7

probably means that he had reduced the wages paid to his weavers, something which was not peculiar to Suffolk. The depressing of hand-loom weavers' wages was almost universal,[1] but was made worse in East Anglia by the loss of by-employments such as spinning and knitting. For many families this meant a reduction in their incomes from several wages to one. There were no cotton mills to employ the women and children.

In its origins as a peasant manfacture for local markets, its subsequent development into a major regional industry playing an important part in the area's economy, and its decay at the time of the industrial revolution, East Anglian linen making typifies the history of many rural industries. It may have had unique features, but until more investigations have been made into the growth and decline of other manufactures both in East Anglia and in other regions it will not be possible to substantiate or refute this suggestion. Nevertheless, it seems likely that the economic and social conditions which in the seventeenth century fostered the growth of linen-weaving in the pastoral districts of Norfolk and Suffolk existed in other counties where rural industries flourished, and that similar factors lie behind the collapse of these manufactures in agricultural counties all over southern England.

It seems not unreasonable to claim that the history of linen-weaving in East Anglia has a more than local interest, and illustrates an important but somewhat neglected aspect of economic history. More attention has been paid to the development of new manufactures than to the decay of old; this book is an attempt to right the balance and to do justice to the importance of an industry which once played a major part in the economy of the old industrial heart of England.

[1] E.P. Thompson, *The Making of the English Working Class* (1963), chapter 9

Glossary

blades	Wheel onto which yarn was wound.
borelaps	Strong linen cloth much used for shirts and shifts.
canvas	Fine, unbleached cloth made of flax or hemp and used for sheets, clothing, etc.
clue	A clue or ball of hempen yarn was 4800 yards in length in eighteenth century Suffolk according to Arthur Young.
denim	Twilled cotton or linen material originating in Nimes.
dornix, dornick, darnick	Coarse linen damask much used for hangings and curtains. Originally made at Doornick (Tournai).
drabbett	Coarse cloth with linen warp and cotton weft.
fustian	Mixed fabric made from cotton and flax or from cotton only.
hambrow	Cloth from Hamburg.
heckle	Comb, with several rows of long teeth, through which bundles of hemp or flax were drawn in a process similar to the combing of wool.
holland	Fine linen of various qualities.
inckle	Linen tape made in varying widths and qualities. Used for girdles, garters, apron strings and the cheaper sort of trimmings.
linsey woolsey	Originally a wool and flax mixture, but later woven from coarse, inferior wool on a cotton warp, or made from poor quality wool alone.
mildernix	Sail-cloth originating in France.
oakum	Coarse part of flax or hemp separated in heckling.
osnaburg, osnabrigs, osnabrucks, ossenbrigs	Coarse linen or fustian made in Germany.
poldavis, powledaveis	Coarse sacking much used for sailcloth, and originally made at Poldavide in Brittany.
quills	Spools onto which yarn was wound ready for warping.
scutching	Bruising of stems of flax or hemp by hand or

	machine, and beating away of woody parts of the fibre.
slay or reed	A weaver's slay or reed consists of two parallel strips of wood about 5 inches apart; the space between them is filled with pieces of metal about a sixteenth of an inch wide and the thickness of a pen nib. Originally reed or cane was used instead of metal. The purpose of a slay is to keep the warp threads straight, to act as a guide for the shuttle and to push the woven weft close to the previous threads.
studdles	Archaic word for looms or weavers' implements.
tecklinburgs	Coarse, strong fabric similar to Osnaburg (q.v.), but broader and thicker.
temple	Contrivance for keeping cloth stretched to its proper width on the loom during the process of weaving.
tenter	Frame on which cloth is stretched after fulling or finishing.
tow	Short fibres of flax or hemp thrown off in heckling process.
twill	Coarse linen cloth woven with parallel diagonal ridges produced by causing the weft threads to pass over one and under two or more warp threads instead of over and under in regular succession as in plain weaving.
warping	Arranging yarn threads into a warp to be placed on a loom.

Index

Acle 34, 57, 87
agrarian discontent 137
Alburgh 125, 137, 150
Aldeburgh 145
Aldred family 162–3
Aldred, James, linen manufacturer 125–6, 132
Aldred, James, linen manufacturer of
   Halesworth 162–3, 164, 167
Alkmaar 103
Alva, Duke of 53
Ameson, John, whitester 91
Amsterdam 103
Antwerp 54
apprentices 46, 47, 48, 56, 87, 88, 130–2;
   bequests to 56–7, 88; linen weavers' sons
   as 88; numbers of 130; paupers as 48,
   106, 131
apprenticeship, length of 47, 48, 131;
   premiums for 131–2; registers of 73, 130–
   2
Arden, Forest of 63, 66, 72, 110
Armada, The 53
army 66
Ashill 40
Ashwellthorpe 40
Attleborough 70, 71, 131

Bacon, Nathaniel 9, 51
Badingham 81, 82
Badwell Ash 34, 90
Baltic 52, 53, 95, 98, 105
Baptists 90, 93
Barker, Thomas, dornix weaver 84
Barsham 93
Barton Mills 154
basket making 64, 155
Beccles 46, 48, 64, 84, 85, 92, 93, 94, 102, 118,
   128, 129, 130, 162
Bedfordshire 64, 111
Bedingfield 83, 88
Beeston 51
Benacre 41
Benhall 162
Binham 144
Blackbourne hundred 68, 69
Black Death, The 41, 44, 66
Blackmore, Jonathan, linen manufacturer 161
Blakenham, Little 17
blanket 84
bleachers, see whitesters
bleaching 28, 30, 31, 32, 126, 132, 136, 163;
   agents used in 30, 32; carried out by
   weavers 136; Dutch method of 32;
   equipment for 84; field names 32;
   improvements in 32; length of process 30–
   2

bleaching grounds 108, 126, 163; thefts
   from 115, 136–7
bobbins, see spools
Blythburgh 17
bombazine 153
books 77, 84, 89
Booty, John, whitester 137
borelaps 103, 169
Borough English 62–3
Boston 72, 99
Botesdale 68, 143, 145
Brampton 37, 85
Bressingham 135, 141
brewing 125
British Linen Company 121
broadcloth 1
Brockdish 148, 156
Bromeswell 131
brush making 155
Buckenham linen firm 160, 162, 165
Buckenham, New 143
Buckenham, Old 14, 94
bucking tubs 30–1, 77
Bulcamp House of Industry 25, 124
bunching 23; blocks 22, 23, 27, 94; mills 23–4,
   25, 53, 54
Bungay 32, 40, 41, 46, 50, 57, 79, 84, 85, 86, 90,
   92, 118, 128, 129, 147, 150, 161; sailcloth
   making at 93, 102
Burgess, John, whitester 137
Burghley, Lord 53, 54
Burgundy 23
burial in linen 94
Bury St Edmunds 121, 123, 125, 128, 132, 136,
   141–2, 143, 162; dornix weavers in 83;
   regulation of weaving in 46–7; restraints on
   weavers in 46–7
Butcher, Mark, heckler 131, 134
butter 62, 65, 78, 94
by-employments 64, 65, 113, 168; see also
   occupations

cables, see ropes
calico 118
Cambridge 101
Cambridgeshire 75
Canterbury 24
canvas, English 97, 99, 105; for sails 24, 53, 97,
   105; imports of 52, 53; made from
   hemp 18, 52, 105, 158, 169; to clothe
   poor 111
capital accumulation 100
carding, equipment 110
carrier services 101
Caston 79, 82
Cawston 82